U.S. Diplomacy in Israel-Palestine Conflict

U.S. Diplomacy in Israel-Palestine Conflict

By

Samuel Jacob Kuruvilla
Assistant Professor,
Department of Political Science,
University of Kerala, Trivandrum, Kerala

New Century Publications
New Delhi, India

NEW CENTURY PUBLICATIONS
4800/24, Bharat Ram Road,
Ansari Road, Daryaganj,
New Delhi - 110 002 (India)

Tel.: 011-2324 7798, 4358 7398, 6539 6605
Fax: 011-4101 7798
E-mail: indiatax@vsnl.com • info@newcenturypublications.com
www.newcenturypublications.com

Editorial office:
LG–7, Aakarshan Bhawan,
4754-57/23, Ansari Road, Daryaganj,
New Delhi – 110 002

Tel.: 011-4356 0919

First Published: **2015**

ISBN: **978-81-7708-397-2**

Published by New Century Publications and printed at Salasar Imaging Systems, New Delhi.

Designs: Patch Creative Unit, New Delhi.

PRINTED IN INDIA

Contents

Preface

West Asia has been a particularly tortured arena of human activity, throughout history and especially in the present age and time. The exigencies of Western involvement in the region, given the European geographic proximity, strategic interests and hydrocarbon resources that lurk beneath the surface of many of the nation-states in the area have seemingly condemned the region to being forever in the flashpoint of world affairs.

Western involvement in the area has a long history, stretching right back across millennia to the time of the Roman Empire and even before. It was the Romans who first realised the strategic potential of the area and particularly the region of the Fertile Crescent in the Mediterranean Levant. This area had long been a melting pot for various civilisations and conquerors that sought to dominate the region. The Romans built massive fortifications and harbours, not to mention whole cities in the Syria-Palestine region and contributed to the economic and military development of this area on a scale unprecedented in recorded history until then.

The rise of Christianity and the Jewish revolts contributed to further confusion in the region, with the iron hand of Rome being made more than apparent in the land on a number of occasions. The Jewish inhabitants of Palestine were scattered as a result of the brutal suppression of the Jewish revolts against Roman rule in the region. Christianity supplanted paganism and Emperor-worship as the official religion of the Roman Empire in the fourth century AD. Christian rule contributed to the further development of the area with many massive churches being built. A majority of the inhabitants also became Christian, albeit of the Byzantine Greek Orthodox persuasion. The split in the Roman Empire followed by the collapse of Rome and the weakening of Byzantium as well as Sassanian Persia paved the way for the rise of the Bedouin Arabs of the Peninsula under a new leader, the Prophet

Muhammad, espousing a new faith in the one and only God, Allah.

The early forces of Islam were victorious throughout the West Asia/North Africa region and conquered Palestine and Syria in the seventh century AD. Palestine henceforth was under Muslim rule almost continuously for the next millennia and a quarter until the end of the First World War. The British established their rule in Palestine at the end of the war. British rule contributed to the economic development of Palestine thereby attracting immigrants to Palestine from across the region and abroad. Predominantly, European Jewish immigrants were drawn to Palestine as conditions in Eastern and Central Europe and Russia worsened during the later part of the nineteenth century and the early twentieth century. The ideology of Zionism or the return to Zion (Jerusalem) played a major role in this process.

The British were forced to pander to the aspirations of a section of world Jewry for a state or territory of their own in what was seen as their ancestral patch of land from which Jews had been alienated for almost two thousand years. However, this process of allowing mainly East European Jews to settle in Palestine created tensions with the native Arabs of the area, particularly as a result of the land acquisition policies of the Zionist Executive in Palestine. Matters went from bad to worse and inter-communal relations in Palestine between British, Jews and native Palestinian Arabs suffered as a result.

On the eve of the British withdrawal from Palestine in 1948, as a part of their policy of withdrawing from all colonial territories east of the Suez Canal, Palestine was broadly divided into two opposing camps, the pre-State Jewish Yishuv as the Palestinian Jewish community was known as and the Arabs of Palestine. The unilateral withdrawal of the British on May 15, 1948 coincided with the declaration of Jewish independence by the Yishuv as the State of Israel. The Palestinians and other Arab states protested and fought, but to no avail as the better trained forces of the Yishuv won convincing victories both on the battlefields as well as in the diplomatic arenas like the then fledgling United Nations (UN). The new Jewish state also managed to get the recognition of the United States (US) within minutes of its declaration of independence due to astute diplomatic endeavours.

The story of Israel and the Palestinians has gone through many twists and turns since the early post-Second World War days and much water has flowed under the bridge. Today, a majority of the original Arab inhabitants of Palestine remain outside the state of Israel or the Palestinian Territories as refugees, either in the Gaza Strip or in neighbouring Lebanon and Jordan where their conditions are pitiable to say the least. Israel and the neighbouring Arab states have fought many wars since 1948 and Israel has emerged victorious in almost all these affairs. The question of Israeli withdrawal from the present internationally recognised Palestinian Territories such as the West Bank and the blockade of the Gaza strip has been continually debated and discussed for decades without any satisfactory resolution to this highly controversial issue in international conflict resolution.

The purpose of this book is to highlight one aspect of the Israel-Palestine conflict, namely the issue of United States involvement in conflict resolution in this area. The US has a long history of direct involvement and activism in the region starting in 1948 and going on through the Suez Crisis of 1956 and the 1967 war that set the modern borders and occupied Palestinian territories of the region. After the 1973 Ramadan/Yom Kippur war between Israel and the main Arab states led by Egypt and Syria, the US adopted and donned the role of a peacemaker, albeit a biased one, but a role that was focussed on bringing lasting peace between Israel and her Arab neighbours. This policy first bore fruit in the Camp David Accords between Israel and Egypt in 1978. Israel and Egypt have engaged in a cold peace that has stood the test of time until the present time.

However, the Americans were not successful in their other

endeavours to bring peace, particularly between Israel and Syria as well as between Israel and the Palestinians. The present work seeks to detail US efforts to bring about peace between Israel and her Arab neighbours primarily Egypt and the Palestinians since 1967. The book has been arranged into nine chapters that are all consecutively connected to each other and seek to provide detailed analysis as regards the US role in the region from 1967 until date. The first chapter seeks to be an introduction to the conflict as well as a snapshot of early US involvement in the Israel-Palestine conflict. The chapter ends in the period just before the Camp David Accords of 1978. The second chapter deals with the Camp David Accords between Egypt and Israel. It seeks to critically analyse the role of the main players in that period such as American President Jimmy Carter, Egyptian President Anwar Sadat and Israeli Premier Menachem Begin. The third chapter looks at the Reagan interlude through the prism of Israeli-Palestinian affairs and its impact on US foreign policy towards the Middle East during that period. Reference is also made to the US Presidency of Bill Clinton and the main Israel-Palestine agreement known as the Oslo Accords that was crafted during that period.

The fourth chapter seeks to trace the rise of Ehud Barak as prime minister of Israel and his attempt along with President Clinton to iron out an agreement with the Palestinians, again in the sanguine settings of the Camp David presidential retreat in Maryland. The fifth chapter attempts a detailed analysis of the so-called Camp David-II peace process and tries to flesh out the reasons for the failure of what was generally accepted to be one of the best opportunities to date in resolving the Palestinian-Israeli conflict. The sixth chapter seeks to provide much needed analysis of contemporary Palestinian political movements particularly those on the religious right and tries to bring to light their attitude towards the peace process and the state of Israel in general. The seventh chapter focuses on detailing the peacemaking efforts following the Clinton presidency, the arrival of George W. Bush in the US and the former Israel army general and right wing hawk Ariel Sharon as premier of Israel. The 'Road Map to Peace' as the Bush doctrine for the Israel-Palestine issue was known as is sought to be described in some detail.

The eighth chapter highlights the attempts at peacemaking that followed the incapacitation of Ariel Sharon and the arrival of his deputy Ehud Olmert as premier of Israel. The attempt to revive the Road Map is described followed by the victory of Binyamin Netanyahu in the Israeli elections and then the arrival of Barack Obama as President of the United States. The latest attempts as peacemaking in the region are sought to be discussed. The ninth and final chapter is the conclusion that provides a brief summary of various American presidential efforts at peace in the region and ends with a discussion of the Obama presidency's potential to bring the two disputing parties to a lasting agreement in the near and not so distant future.

The book would be extremely useful to students of politics and international relations, both at the undergraduate, post-graduate and research level. Students of West Asian politics will find the book invaluable in understanding the Israel-Palestine conflict and particularly the United States role in both solving as well as prolonging the conflict. This book is strongly recommended for university and college libraries throughout India and abroad. West Asia specialists will find this volume useful as a reference resource. Professors and teachers would be interested in recommending this book to their students as a good introductory and descriptive study of the issue at hand. Other non-academic casual readers will also be attracted by this work which seeks to explain the nuances of the main Arab-Israeli conflict in simple terms understandable to any person conversant in the English language.

I am indebted to many people for the help and support extended to me in the production of this work. In particular, I would like to express my profound gratitude to Professor K.M.

Seethi, Director, School of International Relations and Politics (SIRP), Mahatma Gandhi University (MGU), Kottayam for his guidance and encouragement.

I would also like to express my gratitude to Professor Raju K. Thadikkaran, Professor A.M. Thomas, Professor Mathew Kurian, Professor K.D. Kapur, Dr. A.K. Ramakrishnan, Professor K.M. Sajad Ibrahim, Professor G. Gopakumar, Ms. Annu Unny and Professor A.K. Ampotti.

Finally, I must express my profound gratitude and appreciation to my beloved family—father, mother, wife and two sisters—who supported me wholeheartedly and provided moral and spiritual support at all stages of the completion of this work.

October 2014 **Samuel Jacob Kuruvilla**
Trivandrum

Abbreviations/Acronyms

JPS	Journal of Palestine Studies
RIIA	Royal Institute of International Affairs (London)
US-DOS	United States Department of State
MFA	Ministry of Foreign Affairs (State of Israel)
ISA	Israel State Archives (Tel Aviv, Israel)
PLO-NAD	Palestine Liberation Organisation-Negotiations Affairs Department (Ramallah, Palestine)
CNN	Cable News Network (US)
PASSIA	Palestinian Academic Society for the Study of International Affairs (East Jerusalem)
PMC	Palestine Media Centre (Ramallah, Palestine)
BBC	British Broadcasting Corporation (London)
NYT	New York Times
IHT	International Herald Tribune
OCHA	United Nations Office for the Coordination of Humanitarian Affairs
CSM	Christian Science Monitor (Boston)
UNNC	United Nations News Centre (UN, New York)
AFP	Agence France-Presse (Paris)

1

Early American Involvement in Arab-Israeli Conflict

American efforts at mediating an end to the Arab-Israeli conflict have been in active gear since the early 1950s. In 1952, the celebrated Afro-American diplomat Mr. Ralphe Bunche managed to secure armistice agreements between Israel and various neighbouring Arab states (Quarles 2012). [1] Henry Kissinger's emergence as US Secretary of State in the early 1970s cátapulted American conflict mediatory efforts in the Middle East onto the world stage. Kissinger established the American foreign policy doctrine that Arab-Israeli conflict management as well any future peace settlement should be concluded through the prism of US mediation alone. American-led peace efforts again gathered momentum after the 1991 Gulf War.

The first ever multilateral Arab-Israeli Peace Conference was convened in Madrid, Spain (*JPS* 1992: 117-149). This acted as a precursor to the now defunct Oslo process. [2] This chapter will seek to cover in some detail early attempts at mediating the Palestinian-Israeli conflict, particularly Kissinger's efforts during the 1970s.

Diplomacy and Negotiation Defined

Negotiation is the central function of diplomacy, and diplomacy the carrying out of foreign policy. Diplomacy and Negotiation are thus interrelated terms that describe one of the primary functions of the nation-state; namely to carry out the business of state in international relations. Again, negotiation is specifically the bargaining process used in adjusting differences within international relations, and so it is the most important task of diplomacy. A couple of interesting definitions of the terms diplomacy and negotiation are given below:

Diplomacy is the management of international relations by negotiations; the method by which these relations are adjusted and managed by ambassadors and envoys; the business or art of the diplomatist (Nicolson 1939). Negotiation may be called the process of combining divergent viewpoints to reach a common agreement (Zartman 1974). Negotiation is a cunning endeavour to obtain by peaceful manoeuvre and the chicanery of cabinets those advantages which a nation would otherwise have wrested by force of arms, in the same manner as a conscientious highwayman reforms and becomes a quiet and praiseworthy citizen, contenting himself with cheating his neighbour out of that property he would have formerly seized with open violence (Steibel 1972, in Whelan 1983: 4).

Washington Irving, noted early American writer and diplomat declared that: Negotiation is an enduring art form. Its essence is artifice, the creation of expedients through the application of human ingenuity. The synonyms of the word "art" are qualities we have long since come to admire in the ablest of negotiators: skill, cunning and craft. We expect negotiators to be accomplished manipulators of other people, and we applaud this aspect of their art when we observe it in uncommon degree. Negotiation is considered to be the management of people through guile, and we recognize guile as the trademark of the profession (Irving in Winham 1977: 87). Diplomacy is usually defined as the practice of carrying out of a nation's foreign policy by negotiation with other nations. This definition correctly stresses that diplomacy is an instrument and not policy itself; the procedures of foreign policy and not the substance (Duchacek 1939, in Whelan 1883: 4).

To quote Zartman again, Negotiation may be called the process of combining divergent viewpoints to reach a common agreement (Zartman in Whelan 1983: 5). Negotiation is a process in which explicit proposals are put forward ostensibly for the purpose of reaching agreement on exchange or in the realization of a common interest where conflicting interests are present (Ikle 1964: 3-4).

Another American authority on international politics, Charles Burton Marshall, stressed the importance of 'terms' in negotiation. Thus, for him 'negotiation is the process of talking about terms, the achievement of terms, and the terms.' (Marshall, in Whelan 1983: 5). In the end, diplomacy can be defined as the management of international relations by negotiation. Negotiation is diplomacy's principle instrument, a continuing bargaining process for adjusting conflicting interests in order to reach a common agreement. The aim of both is to seek solutions, adjust differences, and establish a harmony of interests among conflicting parties, in short, to create international stability. This would, by and large, define the American perception of negotiation.

Palestine Issue and United Nations

When the Second World War ended, Palestine was a territory administered by the United Kingdom under a mandate from the League of Nations. Faced with escalating violence resulting from increasing Jewish immigration to Palestine and strong Arab opposition to such immigration, the United Kingdom brought the matter before the UN in 1947. The General Assembly then established a committee of 11 states to investigate all matters relating to the question of Palestine and to recommend solutions. The majority in the committee recommended that Palestine be partitioned into an Arab state and a Jewish state, with a special international status for Jerusalem. A minority of three favoured a federated state comprising Arab and Jewish components, with Jerusalem as its capital. After intense debate, the Palestine Partition plan as given by UNGA resolution 181 (II) was approved on 29 November 1947 with 33 votes in favour, 13 votes against and 10 abstentions. [3]

Significantly both the USA and the USSR supported the

partition resolution while the mandatory power UK abstained from voting. The Jewish leadership accepted the Assembly's resolution while the Arabs rejected it, stating their opposition to any scheme which would dissect segregate or partition their land and give preferential treatment to a minority. Fighting intensified between Arab and Jewish communities in Palestine (UN 1997: 7).

In May 1948, the UK gave up its mandate over Palestine and the Jews promptly proclaimed their state of Israel in the territory identified under the partition plan as belonging to them. The Arabs contested this and full scale fighting broke out as neighbouring Arab states sent their armies into Palestine. Fighting continued despite the efforts of a UN mediator. By the time a truce called for by the Security Council come into force in July 1948, Israel controlled much of the territory allotted to the proposed Arab state. Jordan and Egypt respectively administered the remaining portions of the West Bank and Gaza strip. In December 1948, the Assembly declared that refugees must be permitted to return to their homes and live in peace with their neighbours, and that those choosing not to return should be compensated. Under resolution 194 (III), the Assembly also called for the demilitarization and internationalization of Jerusalem. [4] The resolution was never implemented, but its provisions on the special status of Jerusalem and the rights of Palestinian refugees to return have been reasserted by the Assembly almost every year since 1948.

Israel was admitted into the United Nations in May 1949 (UN 1990). [5] Between February and July of that year, under the auspices of the UN, armistice agreements were signed between Israel and Egypt, Jordan, Lebanon and Syria. Notably the agreements accepted establishment of the armistice as an indispensable step towards the restoration of peace in Palestine (UN 1990). The conflictual situation in Palestine/Israel continued over the next three decades, erupting into open hostilities in 1956, 1967 and in 1973. A turning point in

Middle Eastern affairs was reached with the Six Day war of 1967 between Israel and Egypt, Jordan and Syria. By the time a ceasefire took effect, Israel had occupied Egyptian Sinai, the Gaza Strip, the West Bank (including East Jerusalem) and part of the Syrian Golan Heights. The Security Council, in resolution 237 (1967), called upon Israel to ensure the safety and welfare of inhabitants where military operations had taken place and to facilitate the return of displaced persons. The warring parties were asked to abide scrupulously by the 1949 Geneva Convention relative to the protection of civilian persons in times of war (UN 1997: 8).

The Security Council again adopted resolution 242 (1967), laying down the principles for a peaceful settlement in the Middle East. [6] It stipulated that just and lasting peace in the region should include the application of two principles:

1. Withdrawal of Israeli armed forces from territories occupied in the recent conflict, and
2. Recognition of every state in the area and their right to live in peace within secure and recognized boundaries. [7]

When another Arab-Israeli war broke out in October 1973, the council unanimously adopted resolution 338 (1973), calling for an immediate truce and asking the parties to start immediately after the ceasefire the implementation of resolution 242 (1967) "in all its parts". Following the 1967 war, the question of Palestine began to be understood in a broader political context than as a matter which related only to refugees. In November 1974, the General Assembly reaffirmed the inalienable rights of the Palestinian people, including the right to self-determination without external interference, the right of national independence and sovereignty, and the right to return to their homes and property. This resolution 3236 (XXIX) has been reaffirmed by the Assembly every year since (UN 1974). [8]

It was also in 1974 that the Palestine Liberation Organization, the primary Arab movement for the liberation of Palestine was invited by the Assembly to participate as an observer in its proceedings (UN 1974). [9] The item entitled "The Question of Palestine" has remained on the Assembly's annual agenda since 1974 (UN 1990: 144). [10]

American Perspectives on Zionism and Palestine

American involvement in Palestine dates back to 1832 when the first American consular agent in Jerusalem was appointed. The end of the Nineteenth century saw Palestine emerge as an issue engaging the attention of world Jewry and also the State Department (Foreign ministry) of the United States. This was as a result of the establishment of a new political creed called Zionism in 1897 at Basle, Switzerland. The World Jewish Conference comprising 104 delegates from 15 countries agreed that "Zionism aims at the creation of a home for the Jewish people in Palestine to be secured by public law" and accordingly they would encourage immigration to Palestine (Sachar 1976, in Neff 1995: 7).

At that time, Arabs represented 95 percent of Palestine's roughly half a million people and they owned 99 percent of the land (Khalidi 1997, in Neff 1995: 7). The first Zionist Federation was established New York in 1897. Zionism openly rejected assimilation and the whole melting pot metaphor dear to American hearts. Theodore Herzl widely regarded as the founder of the Zionist idea stated in his seminal pamphlet 'Der Judenstaat',

We have sincerely tried everywhere to merge with the national communities in which we live, seeking only to preserve the faith of our fathers. It is not permitted us (Sachar 1976, in Neff 1995: 7).

The fundamental rationale of Zionism was a profound despair that anti-Semitism could not be eradicated as long as Jews lived among Gentiles (non-Jews). It was out of this dark vision that grew the belief that the only hope for the survival of the Jews lay in the founding of their own state. The state department at first dismissed Zionism as merely a minority political group advocating an issue that was essentially an internal Jewish affair. But as Zionism increased in influence in Europe in the first decade of the twentieth century, it also began attracting a select group new converts in the United States. By the start of World War I, the American Zionists had in their ranks influential men like lawyers, professors and businessmen.

The American State Department established a Near East Division only in 1909. This new division covered on enormous region that included Russia, Germany, Austria, Hungary, the Balkans and the Turkish Ottoman Empire along with all the outlying areas that stretched from Persia to Abyssinia (Ethiopia). Rising Zionist demands for support of a Jewish nation were increasingly resented along US diplomats, who saw such requests "as an illustration of the purely Hebraic and un-American purposes for which our Jewish community seek to use this government" to quote a US diplomat of that period (Sachar 1976, in Neff 1995: 8).

First World War and After

The First World War and subsequent developments changed the states of the Middle East profoundly. During the war, an important factor was Turkey's involvement as an ally of Germany, Austria and Bulgaria against the allied powers such as Russia, Britain, France and other nations. Palestine, because of its strategic location, assumed great importance in the allied war strategy, especially for Great Britain whose predominant concern was the security of the Suez Canal (Manuel 1949, in Neff 1995: 9). The British instigated the Arabs of the Ottoman Empire to revolt against the Turks thereby compelling the British and French to invade and occupy Syria, Palestine and Iraq. In I9I7, the British Government issued the Balfour Declaration, stating that it viewed 'with favour the establishment in Palestine of a national home for the Jewish peoples (Tarner 2000: 915)'. Again in 1922, the League of Nations under British influence recognized 'the historical connection of the Jewish people with

Palestine' and 'the grounds for reconstituting their national home in that country (Europa 2001: 62-65)'.

In contrast, the US State Department defined its chief function as the protection and promotion of American interests abroad, not in endorsing or encouraging the efforts of a small group of Americans to help found another nation in a foreign land. It was against US policy to interfere in another country without any obvious American interests at stake and with a good chance of worsening relations. US-Ottoman relations were never quite easy and Zionist agitation against Ottoman rule in Palestine raised suspicions in Istanbul about broader US policies and goals in the region. At the Paris Peace Conference that convened in 1919, one of the most contentious issues was the future of the Fertile Crescent in general and Palestine in particular. The first action taken by the peace conference with regard to Palestine was to invoke article 22 of the Covenant of the League calling for the mandate system (Etheredge 2011: 52).

Both the Arabs and the Zionists sent their respective delegations to the conference to plead for their cause before the Supreme Council. The Zionist delegation demanded before the conference the inclusion of the Balfour Declaration in the peace treaty and the British being given the mandate over Palestine instead of making it an independent Arab state (Etheredge 2011: 47). The Arab delegation led by Emir Feisal (son of Sharif Hussein of Mecca and accompanied and helped by T.E. Lawrence of Arabia) demanded Arab independence as promised by the British during the course of the war. Feisal also urged that a Commission of Inquiry be sent to Syria and Palestine to know the wishes of the people (Etheredge 2011: 47). This proposal was supported by President Wilson (Etheredge 2011: 47).

The Supreme Council assigned the mandate for Palestine (including Transjordan that was later formed into the separate state of Jordan) to Great Britain on 25th April, 1920 (Etheredge 2011: 52). The final draft on the terms of the mandate was concluded by the League council on 22nd July, 1922 (RIIA

1946, in Pradhan 1994: 12). This decision was a victory for the Zionists and their compulsive diplomacy to keep the region open to Jewish settlement.

The last action America took with regard to the Palestine question, before returning to its traditional isolationist policy that continued till the Second World War, was to sign the Palestine Mandate Treaty (Anglo-American Convention) with Great Britain on 3 December 1924 whereby it recognized the legality of the British Mandate over Palestine (US-DOS 1924: 212-222). So from then until 1939, Britain ruled Palestine on its own.

As stated earlier, the League mandate not only recognized the historical connection of the Jewish people with Palestine but also make it the responsibility of the mandatory power "for placing the country under such political, administrative of a Jewish National Home" [Article 2] (Etheredge 2011: 52). It also provided for the recognition of the Zionist Jewish Agency "as a public body" to advise and cooperate "with the Administration of Palestine in such economic, social and other matters as may affect the establishment of the Jewish National Home" [Article 4] (Etheredge 2011: 52).

Again the mandatory power was ordered to "facilitate Jewish immigration under suitable conditions" [Article 6] (RIIA 1946, in Pradhan 1994: 12). So Britain assumed the mandate over Palestine pending the establishment there of such a national home. It was in accordance with this mandate that Jewish settlers were admitted to Palestine under the direction of Zionist settlement agencies. Naturally the native Palestinian Arabs resented this influx and there were anti-Zionists riots in 1921 and 1929 (Etheredge 2011: 51). During the period 1938-1939, a major Arab rebellion against the policies of the mandatory power vis-à-vis the Zionists was brutally suppressed by them (Etheredge 2011: 57-60).

Second World War and After

During World War II, Palestine remained by and large

peaceful. The moderate Jewish community supported the British. In September 1944, a Jewish Brigade attached to the British 8th Army was created (Etheredge 2011: 63). A total of 27,000 Jews enlisted in the British forces to fight against Rommel's Africa Korps in the North African desert (*Britannica* [15th ed.] 1974: 420). Equally important was the support won by the Zionists in the United States, to which they had shifted their major political effort after 1939. In May 1942, at a Zionist conference held at the Biltmore Hotel in New York City, David Ben-Gurion, the future prime minister of Israel, gained support for a program demanding unrestricted immigration and a Jewish army and the establishment of Palestine as a Jewish Commonwealth (Levitats 1943-1944: 206-207). [11]

Known as the Biltmore Programme, two of the eight resolutions adopted deserve special mention (Levitats 1943-1944: 206-207). Resolution 6 called for the fulfilment of the original purpose of the Balfour Declaration and the mandate which "recognizing the historical connection of the Jewish people with Palestine was to afford them the opportunity, as stated by President Wilson, to found there a Jewish Commonwealth" (Levitats 1943-1944: 206-207). Resolution 8 pleaded that:

The gates of Palestine be opened, that the Jewish agency be vested with control of immigration into Palestine...and that Palestine be established as a Jewish commonwealth integrated in the structure of the new democratic world. Then only then will the age-old wrong to the Jewish people be righted (Pradhan 1994: 40).

An increasing number of US Congressmen and politicians started making pro-Zionist statements. In August 1945, President Harry S. Truman requested Clement Attlee, the British Prime minister, to facilitate the immediate admission of 100,000 Jews into Palestine, and in December the US Senate and House of Representatives asked for unrestricted Jewish immigration to the limit of the economic absorptive capacity of Palestine (Khalaf 1991: 286).

All these measures contributed to the internationalization of the question of Palestine, already under way with the involvement of the Arab states since the 1930s. The Arabs of Palestine had remained largely neutral during the war, although some supported the Axis powers while others enlisted in the British forces. After the war, the neighbouring Arab countries began to take a more direct interest in Palestine. In March 1945, the covenant of the League of Arab States was drawn up with an annex emphasizing the Arab character of Palestine (Arab League 1945). [12] Again in December, the Arab League declared a boycott of Zionist goods (Weiss 2013: 1). [13] The pattern of the post-World War II struggle for Palestine was slowly emerging.

Proposal for Partition and After

In November 1947, the United Nations General Assembly passed a resolution calling for the establishment of a Jewish and an Arab state in Palestine. [14] Some after the UN resolution, communal fighting broke out in Palestine. The Zionists took all possible measures to increase their strength and to bring in new immigrants. In December 1947, the Arab League pledged its support to the Palestinian Arabs and organized a force of 3,000 volunteers (Khalaf 1991: 270). Civil war spread and external intervention increased as the dismantling of the British administration progressed.

By mid-January 1948, some 2000 casualties had resulted from the fighting. During this conflict, American policy in Washington and New York underwent changes that often alarmed the Zionist leadership and influenced their conduct of military operations in Palestine. At first, both the State Department and President Truman were of the view that the type of partition approved by the UNGA as per the recommendations of UNSCOP (United Nations Special Commission on Palestine) would be impossible to impose except by military force.

The American leadership was very much afraid that the former Soviet Union would seek to influence such a situation. Cold war calculations were already being imposed on every possible international affair. Yet the US would not and could not commit its own troops to Palestine, nor would the British do anything, but continue with their plans for withdrawal. The only solution seemed to lie in the UN Security Council and the means it might utilize for implementing the partition vote. In March, the UNSCOP reported its inability to implement partition because of Arab resistance and the attitude of the British administration. The US immediately called for the suspension of UNSCOP. On March 30, 1948, they appealed for declaration of a truce and the further consideration of the problem by the General Assembly (*Britannica* [15th ed.] 1974: 421).

US Recognition of Israel

The Zionists insisted that partition was binding on both parties to the dispute. As the date for the British withdrawal approached, they were busy in preparing for the proclamation of their own independent state. The White House, on the other hand was confronting the issue of providing recognition to the emerging Jewish state. On May 14, the last British High Commissioner, General Sir Alan Cunningham, left Palestine (Mann 2011). [15] On the same day, the State of Israel was proclaimed (MFA 1948). [16] The Truman administration decided to immediately extend 'de facto' recognition to the provisional government of Israel (MFA 1948). When it became clear that the new state had secured her future borders, 'de jure' recognition was given on January 31, 1949 (Truman 1956: 194). The US recognition of Israel just eleven minutes after the latter's formation was quite an unprecedented step. It was felt to be quite 'inconsistent with accepted principles of diplomacy' (Stevens 1970: 1-2).

There had been a divergence of opinion between the White House and the State Department on this issue. Truman's hasty and enthusiastic recognition of Israel was guided more by domestic political considerations (gaining a strong political base in the American Jewish community), then by accepted principles of diplomacy and foreign policy calculations. It was also a reflection of the success of the Zionist lobby in influencing American decision making with regard to Palestine. Already in 1946, US President Harry S. Truman had made a declaration where he stated that, "...the creation of a viable Jewish state ...in an adequate area of Palestine instead of in the whole of Palestine (would be acceptable)" (Truman 1946). This in turn had a definite bearing on future American policy towards Israel, first in the Arab-Israeli conflict and later in the Palestinian-Israeli conflict. It also affected the Palestinian Liberation Organization's perception of the US for years to come (Pradhan 1994: 49).

The *raison d'être* of American interactions with Israel can be traced back to some aspects of the collective American psyche in the immediate wake of World War II.

Factors Leading to US Recognition of Israel

1. **Guilt**: about the Nazi holocaust that nearly exterminated European Jewry while America and the western nations pretended that they did not know anything about it.
2. **Humanitarian Impulse**: the sense of guilt helped to ignite a general American humanitarian impulse towards arranging the resettlement of thousands of refugees displaced from the concentration camps of central Europe. This impulse did not however extend towards settling the refugees in the US. A second option such as Palestine was preferred by the American establishment and supported by the people.
3. **Duties**: Jewish donors and voters were very influential in American political life, particularly in the Democratic Party. Given the huge Jewish community in the US, American interest in Palestine was natural. American Zionist committees were among the largest benefactors of Jewish settlement projects in the 'promised land'. Allied to

these were the activities of Zionist lobbies in Washington such as the America-Israel Public Affairs Committee (AIPAC) which were constantly pressuring Congress and the Administration to be generous towards Israel. It was, in fact, during the administrations of F.D. Roosevelt and Harry. S. Truman that Zionist leaders were able to penetrate key White House department and sensitize the America ruling elite about the plight of Holocaust survivors.

4. **Idealism**: admiration for the founding of a new democratic state which proclaimed a Declaration of Independence complete with phrases drawn from that of the United States.
5. **Religion**: A common Judeo-Christian bible and heritage fired the enthusiasm of fundamentalist American Christians for this return to the holy land by an ancient nation of wanderers.
6. **Ignorance**: Americans have generally been ignorant of the region ant its original inhabitants, in particular the Arabs, a phenomenon that has continued for the last 50 years and is now so very evident in the post-September 11, 2001 scenario.
7. **Containment of Communism [Strategic Relationship]**: The so-called 'strategic relationship' between Israel and the US did not emerge as an openly declared policy statement till the 1970s and the Nixon era. Even then, it was only tacitly acknowledged for many years, developing slowly into today's virtual military alliance (Lewis 1999: 365). It was in October 1947 that American and British officials first met at the Pentagon to sketch out a geopolitical blueprint for the Middle East in the light of the new threats of Soviet expansionism and communist ideology. The 'reverse Monroe doctrine' of the interwar period had been finally abandoned. Though Britain still held the upper hand in the Middle East, US Secretary of State George C. Marshall was already contemplating on

eventual American leadership role in the region. It was for such an eventuality that support for the new state of Israel was deemed important. But in the 1940s and 1950s, the Israel-angle was not being projected by the state department (Hudson 1996: 330).

At the geo-strategic level, the US sought to contain the Soviets in the Middle East through military alliances, similar to NATO in Europe. This approach failed mainly due to American insensitivities about the area. Even the Baghdad pact (1955) generated more animosity than security in the Arab world. Looser political/economic umbrella projects like the Eisenhower Doctrine (1957) were no more successful. By securing arms deals with countries like Syria and Egypt, the Soviet Union and other Warsaw Pact nations were able to bypass American defences in the region. For most Arab governments, the real threat was Israel and not the Soviet Union. And it was here that American diplomacy vis-à-vis the Arabs always tended to malfunction.

The rise of Arab nationalism under the leadership of Gamal Abdel Nasser further complicated affairs for the Americans. Astute US field diplomacy and the respected non-governmental American presence to the region hoped to lessen the State Department's confrontation with Arab Nationalism. The Palestine problem lay at the heart of the pan-Arab cause, and American support for Israel was too big to allow for a compromise solution, a 'modus vivendi'. American diplomats always tried to avoid a head-on collision with the nationalist forces. The US tried to deal with the Egyptian President Gamal Abdel Nasser.

On the other hand, the US actively worked to suppress Iranian nationalism and also opposed the nationalist upheavals in Syria and Iraq. Even though Communism and Arab Nationalism did not mix well together, Soviet patronage enabled the nationalist anti-Israel camp to pose a serious challenge to US interests in the region (Hudson 1996: 332).

8. **Oil**: was another major reason for American interest in the Middle East. Saudi Arabia alone possessed some 25 percent of the world's known petroleum reserves. More may be waiting to be discovered. Combine this with the oil wealth of Kuwait, Iraq, the Gulf Emirates, Iran etc., and a formidable source of carbon energy comes into the picture. Oil did not acquire a strategic dimension until World War II. By then the Americans had started to see Middle East oil as a cheap supplement to their own declining reserves. Middle East oil became essential for the Western world's post-World War II economic development. Oil politics played a major role in post-war US strategy in the region (Kuniholm 1987: 11). The Americans were determined to exclude the Soviets from Gulf oil.. They were also dead against the nationalization of western oil companies operating in the region. This would result in the economics of price and production going out of their hands (Kuniholm 1987: 11).

So, the Americans and West Europeans always played their hand in such a manner as to maintain their influence in the region. This frequently included propping up authoritarian regimes (like the Shah of Iran) and despotic rulers (like Saddam Hussein before the Gulf war). The Middle East was a battlefield for Cold War forces. Both sides pumped an incredible amount of arms into the region. This resulted in many military conflicts that caused terrible sufferings to hundreds of thousands of civilians. The Palestinian struggle for self determination can only be seen in this context. It was essentially a victim of cold war machinations.

Suez War of 1956

Egyptian President Nasser's nationalization of the Suez Canal prompted a chain of events that eventually led to the joint Israeli- French-British attack on Egypt. Due to various reasons, all stemming from a violent hatred of Nasser and his policies, each of these powers were waiting for an excuse to attack Egypt. The Israelis under David Ben-Gurion held Nasser to be their worst enemy, not the least because of his demagogic popularity with the Arab masses and his equally scathing verbal attacks on Israel. The French held Nasser responsible for their Algerian problems (Golani 1998:43). The British felt that his calls for Arab nationalism and unity were undermining their traditional power base in the Middle East (Yaqub 2003). [17]

All these factors come to a head in July 1956 when Nasser nationalized the Anglo-French owned Suez Canal thereby breaking Egypt's last colonial bondage (Suez 2006). [18] The British and French immediately decided to attack Egypt and depose Nasser if possible. Israel on invitation was fully prepared to join them. The war started with an Israeli invasion of Gaza and the Sinai on 29th October, 1956 (Suez 2006). War planning and co-ordination between the three allies called for a joint Anglo-French ultimatum to both on 31st October to ceasefire and withdraw ten miles from the bank of the canal (Suez 2006). This call would, in effect give the Israelis the right to continue their attack until they reached that boundary, while the Egyptians would withdraw all their forces from the Sinai. Nasser would naturally not agree to the ceasefire and both the British and French could then blame him for continuing hostilities and thus justify their attack on him (Nye 1999: 158).

America Against the Suez War

The Israeli forces occupied Sinai and the Gaza strip as scheduled. Nasser's refusal of the Anglo-French ultimatum on the 31st resulted in British aircraft from Cyprus attacking Egyptian airfields (Suez 2006). This in turn caused Nasser to withdraw forces from the Sinai to defend mainland Egypt. The Egyptian withdrawal allowed the Israelis to occupy almost the whole Peninsula by November. A combined Anglo-French invasion of Port Said and Alexandria took place on 6th November (Suez 2006). The Americans had been totally against this operation from the very beginning. They preferred to deal with Nasser through peaceful means.

Both President Eisenhower and his Secretary of State Dulles were indirectly responsible for the Egyptian nationalization of the Suez when they had earlier refused Nasser any financial help from the West in the construction of the Aswan High Dam. Both were now infuriated by what they considered the appalling deception and stupidity of their allies. Although they disliked Nasser, they did not believe that armed force would resolve the matter. The situation was all the more serious because the rebellion in Hungary had taken place around the same time as the Suez crisis. Washington now found itself on-the defensive vis-à-vis the Soviets who soon invaded Hungary and crushed the uprising. Dulles, the great purist and anti-Communist moralist found himself unable to use the Hungarian crisis to prove the immorality of Communism and the need for all nations to rely on the West (Smith 1992: 172).

America too found itself appealing alongside the Soviet Union to the warring parties to end the crisis. British and French forces were forced to withdraw from Port Said by 23 December. The Israelis however were determined to remain in the Gaza Strip and at Sharm el-Sheikh. Pressure from the US finally forced them to withdraw but only on the condition that a UN force known as the United Nations Emergency Forces (UNEF) patrol the land border between Israel and the Gaza strip as well as the Egyptian Red Sea resort of Sharm el-Sheikh. This was ostensibly to prevent fidayeen attacks from these regions into Israel. Whereas for the British and French, Suez was an unmitigated disaster, the Israelis considered it to be a major success. They had achieved a significant military victory with relatively few casualties. They were able to free Israeli shipping from the blockade imposed by the Egyptians in the Red Sea. Finally, they secured for the next ten years a de-facto peace along the Israeli-Egyptian frontier which remained relatively quiet and patrolled by UN forces.

Nasser also emerged a victor despite the military defeat he

had suffered against obviously unassailable odds. Israel aligning with France and Britain to attack Egypt was again proof to the Arab world of the continuing Western collusion to try and impose outside control on developments within the Arab world. Nasser's defiance of the West during the Suez crisis only increased his hero status in the Arab world. The Suez War increased US influence in the Middle East. America now embarked on a period of active intervention in Arab regional politics that in the long run brought it closer to Israel (Smith 1999: 174).

Rise of Palestinian Nationalism

After the 1947-48 war, the Palestinian people become refugees in their own home land. Over 75 percent of them had to leave their homes and flee. They went to all the neighbouring Arab countries and also to the Egyptian-controlled enclave of Gaza and the Jordanian West Bank. Here these people were herded into squalid refugee camps that soon become more like concentration camps for the displaced people. The host States frequently placed these unwelcome guests under all sorts of inhuman restrictions. Many were even forbidden from leaving the camps. Political activity was also strictly prohibited. The refugees themselves trusted in Arab Nationalism and in the ability of the Arab states to eventually defeat Israel and regain Palestine for them. Thus, it was only after both the 1956 and the 1967 Arab-Israeli wars resulted in bitter defeat for the Arabs that the Palestinian people decided to take the full responsibility for struggle against Israel on their shoulders.

The Algerian revolutionary struggle that culminated in victory for the revolutionary forces, despite their defeat on the battlefield against the colonial French forces, was an eye-opener for the Palestinians. It revealed that an armed struggle, whatever the cost would be ultimately successful even in the face of overwhelming odds. In this context, it might be noted that it was Nasser's Egypt that gave a helping land to Palestinian nationalism when they conspired in the setting up of an organization known as the Palestinian Liberation Organisation (PLO) in 1964 with Ahmed al-Shukairy as its first chairman. The PLO was meant to be an outlet for the legitimate political aspirations of the Palestinian people, especially in the face of Western apathy and disinterest in their fate.

American Attitudes towards PLO till the 1970s

In the early years of the formation of Israel, the Americans seemed quite satisfied to leave the Palestinian refugees to the care of the United Nations Relief and Works Agency (UNRWA), the official UN body charged with looking after those people who had fled Palestine following the 1948 war. This body had been created with full US support. The Americans however did very little in the way of putting pressure on Israel to accept the refugees back. In this case, they fully supported the argument of the Israelis that to do so would be to negate the Jewish character of the State of Israel. After the formation of Israel, the US deliberately abandoned the UN partition resolution on Palestine. The creation of a Palestinian state was now out of the question, not the least because no Arab state (Jordan was violently opposed to such a state for historical reasons) was willing to support the idea of two states, Jewish and Arab, existing side by side. Moreover, American officials established a linkage between the refugee problem and the dispute between Israel and the Arab states. Thus, former Under-Secretary of State, Walter Bedell-Smith stated very clearly in 1953:

The refugee problem is the principal unresolved issue between Israel and the Arabs; outstanding issues are generally listed as compensation to the refugees, repatriation of the refugees, adjustment of boundaries, and the status of Jerusalem and the Holy places. None of the issues can be separated from the refugee problem (Pradhan 1994: 69).

This American approach was based upon the premise that solving the refugee problem would automatically lead to a solution of all the other issues, thereby bringing about a final settlement. This approach continued till 1967. At first, the Americans did not take the creation of the various Palestinian organizations seriously. They were just seen as isolated terrorist organizations. In this context, the US supported Israel's right of retaliation against these groups, but was frequently forced to protest the massive scale of revenge. In 1966, the US Congress passed a resolution after PLO Chairman Ahmad Shukairy's disclosure that Palestinian commandos were being trained by the People's Republic of China. The passing of the PLO leadership into the hands of the commando groups and their spectacular operations against Israel and other targets, compelled the Americans to take note of the existence of the Palestinian resistance movement. Naturally the view they took of this movement was a strongly pro-Israeli one. The PLO was perceived as a potential threat to vital American interests in the area, representing the faces of radicalism and anti-Westernism. It was definitely viewed as a terrorist organization with links to international terrorist networks (Pradhan 1994: 70).

The guerrilla organizations, on the other hand, rejected any political settlement that did not include the total liberation of historic Palestine and the return of refugees to their homes. PLO spokesmen always emphasized that their war was against the Zionist entity that was the state of Israel, and not against the Jews. The Charter of the PLO stated the aim of the organization in establishing a secular non- sectarian state in Palestine where Jew, Christian and Muslim would live in absolute equality. The Zionists and their American backers did not believe in the practicality of this goal and viewed the PLO as terrorists aiming to eliminate Jews.

US followed three main policies in dealing with the PLO:

1. Unless the Palestinians renounce terrorism, the Americans would have no direct contact or dialogue with it.
2. Non-recognition of the PLO while simultaneously fully guaranteeing the security and survival of Israel.
3. Full support (both military and political) for pro-US Arab

regimes that were threatened by militant Palestinian movements within their borders.

US support for Jordan during the black September crisis was on the basis of this strategy (Pradhan 1994: 71).

These policies lasted till the early 1970s. In January 1970, Assistant Secretary of State, Joseph Sisco ordered a "revaluation of major assumptions about American strategy" in the area because these assumptions had all turned out to be wrong. Some of these assumptions related to the Palestinians. To quote Henry Kissinger: We had assumed that the Palestinians could be dealt with in a settlement purely as a refugee problem. Instead they had become a quasi-independent force with a veto over policy in Jordan, and perhaps in Lebanon (Kissinger 1979: 573).

It was thus clear that the Americans would have to conduct a major reworking of their tactics and strategies vis-à-vis the Palestinian people and their armed groups in the Middle East.

1967 War and After

The war of 1967 was to prove as decisive in its consequences as that of 1948-49. All the land of original mandatory Palestine as well as the Egyptian Sinai peninsula and the Golan Heights of Syria passed into the control of the Israelis. The balance of power in the Middle East tilted firmly in the direction of Israel. The most important outcome of the war as far as the Zionists were concerned was the capture and annexation of the Old City of Jerusalem. A new concept of security took hold in the minds of the Israelis encompassing the whole Levantine area. The new 1948 armistice lines become as obsolete as the old UN partition borders. Again Jerusalem disappeared from the agenda as a negotiable item after the 'de facto' annexation of the former Jordanian sector. The problem of the 1948 refugees, whose population had become double due to natural increase, was made more severe due to a fresh exodus from the West Bank.

The humiliating defeat of the combined Arab armies at the

hand of the Israelis again exposed the weakness of the Arab world vis-à-vis Israel. The 1967 war was the final blow to Nasser's pan-Arabism. Henceforth, Jordan and Syria were to deal with Israel on their own calculation of interests and issues. The fate of the Palestinians changed radically as a result of the 1967 war. Till 1967, there was only a small marginalized Palestinian minority within the borders of Israel proper. After 1967, over a million Palestinian Arabs found themselves under Israeli control. In the new circumstances, the PLO sensed the possibilities of new forms of action, strategy and tactics. The war resulted in a marked increase in the degree of independence and broad-based popular support that the PLO movement enjoyed. The Palestinian people also come to realize that their fellow Arab nations could and would do very little for their cause. They realized that the fight for their home land would be solely on their own shoulders. Consequently some Arabs concluded that armed struggle in the form of guerrilla warfare and terrorism had become a more plausible course of action (Gresh 1983: 3).

By the mid 1960s the French had started to withdraw finally from Algeria. General de Gaulle therefore decided to end the special relationship that he had fostered with Israel to counter alleged Egyptian Nasserite support of the Algerian revolutionaries. The Germans also were stopping their post-war Holocaust victims' compensatory packages to Israel. The arena was thus becoming clear for a closer US-Israeli relationship. The US drew closer to Israel and began to play a more important role in assisting it. The US-Israeli relationship soon developed into a virtual alliance. Thus the Arab-Israeli problem moved to the centre stage in the Middle East policy of the United States. At a strategic level, the decision of the British in 1968 to withdraw from the area east of the Suez by 1971 posed new problems for the US. The Americans were compelled to fill what was perceived as a power vacuum. Thus from 1967 onwards, the US was to take on the mantle of a semi-permanent peace maker, at first under a multilateral UN umbrella in more or less cooperative ventures with the Soviet Union. Form the early 1970s, America relied on its own diplomacy vis-à-vis the Middle East with minimal attention to the UN Security Council and the Soviets (Lewis 1999: 367).

United Nations Security Council (UNSC) Resolution 242

The October war of 1973 was the fourth war between the Arabs and Israel since 1948. At the end of August 1967, Arab leaders meeting for a summit conference in Khartoum had reiterated their opposition to recognition or direct negotiation with Israel (Meital 2000: 64). [19] Naturally lack of negotiations would only lead to war. Israel's Prime Minister Levi Eshkol meanwhile declared that Israel would refuse to withdraw from any of the Arab territories occupied in June, 1967 without negotiations leading to peace treaties with all the parties concerned. Differences between the two parties prevented any of the early attempts by the UN Security Council to agree on resolution to address the crisis. The Arab world backed by the former USSR was determined that the UN should demand the withdrawal of Israeli forces from occupied Arab territory.

On the other hand, Israel and the Americans were opposed to draft resolutions that did not provide adequate guarantees of Israeli security. The minimum demands of both sides eventually found expression in UNSC resolution 242. [20] Adopted unanimously by the Security Council on 22 November 1967, it underlined the 'inadmissibility' of the acquisition of territory by war; and called for a 'just and lasting peace in which every state in the area can live in security' and for a settlement of the 'refugee problem' (Cossali 2001: 26). Resolution 242 also called on Israel to withdraw from territories occupied in the recent conflict, but strategically did not specify the extent of the withdrawal. The ambiguities and omissions in resolution 242 were to be a major source of conflict in the Arab-Israeli debate for years to come. [21]

US Position (1967-1973)

The United States fully backed Israel's stand of no withdrawal without peace agreement' following the 1967 war. However both the Johnson and the later Nixon administration expected Israel to withdraw from nearly all the lands it occupied in 1967, subject to minor border changes. Nevertheless, the US supported the UN resolution condemning Israel for unilaterally annexing East Jerusalem. After the 1967 war, there was a tremendous outburst of sympathy and support for Israel among the American public. American Jews were totally engaged in a *support Israel* campaign, both monetarily and politically. The American government was thus forced to express in public full support for Israel while at the same time privately trying to moderate its position. US diplomatic initiatives undertaken unilaterally (but also in cooperation with the USSR), frequently achieved terms that were usually closer to the Arab stand than the Israeli (Brecher 1975: 444).

In late 1968, Israel presented a nine-point plan for Middle East Peace to the United Nations General Assembly. The Levi Plan as it came to be known (after the then Israeli Prime Minister Levi Eshkol) did not directly offer an Israeli withdrawal, but proposed mutually agreeable 'boundary settlements' (ISA 1967). [22] The Arab world made no response to this plan. Arab public opinion had again hardened after the Jerusalem annexation as well as the establishment of the first settlements in the Palestinian Occupied Territories (OTs) in September 1967 (Nasser 1967). [23] In fact, in July 1969, after continued fighting along both the Suez and Jordan fronts (the so-called War of Attrition), Egypt's President Gamal Abdel Nasser publicly gave up hope of a peaceful settlement and predicted that another war would be necessary to dislodge Israel from the territories occupied in 1967 (Nasser 1967).

Attempts by the USA, the USSR, France and the UK to obtain an agreement from the warring parties on the implementation of resolution 242 made little progress

(Pedatzur 2010). [24] In December 1969, the US secretary of state, William Rogers, produced a set of proposals designed to steer a middle course between the two parties. Known as the Rogers Plan, its most important aspect was that it made clear the American stand that there should only be minor adjustments to the pre-June 1967 boundaries (Pedatzur 2010). In July 1970, Nasser accepted the Rogers proposals. The Israeli government followed suit a week later. Negotiations between the two parties were to be mediated by the UN through a Special Representative, Norway's Gunnar Jarring (Pedatzur 2010). The Jarring talks were suspended after a single meeting following Israeli withdrawal over a trivial military issue (Cossali 2001: 26).

Diplomatic initiatives between 1967 and 1975 were seriously handicapped by governmental and organizational factionalism among all the parties concerned. Israeli governments were often paralyzed by differences over what territories should be retained and what offered in exchange for peace. Nasser, in turn, attempted to balance his hope for negotiations with his army's desire for another deciding war. At the same time, he had to face increasing domestic unrest over the lost Sinai Peninsula.

The PLO opposed all efforts to attain peace, as it feared that its political objectives would be ignored. The Nixon administration's approaches to the Arab-Israeli conflict were severely affected by the rivalry between National Security Adviser Henry Kissinger and the Secretary of State William Rogers. The State Department, headed by Rogers viewed the issue mainly as a regional problem that should be solved through negotiations as soon as possible, along with the Soviet Union, if necessary. Kissinger had another view about the whole process of negotiations. His view was closer to the Israelis, in that he was primarily interested in ousting the Soviets from the region before undertaking any such talks. He wanted to establish total American dominance of the negotiating process which would in turn benefit Israel alone

(Smith 1992: 205).

Regional developments also seemed to be helping Israel, if not in the long run, at least in the short run. In September 1970 (known as Black September in Palestinian Diaspora terminology), civil war broke out in Jordan between the King's forces and the PLO fighters. Jordanian-Palestinian strife served to indirectly confirm Israel's value as an arm of American policy in the region, especially in the context of excluding the Soviets from the area. The Nixon administration took a secret decision that no further efforts would be made to stage Arab-Israeli peace talks until the Egyptians rid themselves of the Soviets and accepted US Influence in the region.

This policy which had a classic Kissingerian touch (he had became Secretary of State in 1973), remained unofficial US policy until the October 1973 Yom Kippur/Ramadan War. The new Egyptian President, Anwar al-Sadat played along with the US by expelling all the Soviet advisers in his country in July 1972. The outbreak of war changed all Kissinger's plans. He was forced to start talks between Israel and Egypt. These discussions and later negotiations between Israel and Syria led to agreements in 1974-1975 to disengage forces on the Golan Heights and in the Sinai. This also eventually resulted in the Camp David Accords between Egypt and Israel in 1978 (Smith 1992: 205).

Endnotes

1. Available at, http://www.wnyc.org/story/215677-ralph-bunche.
2. Refer Document VI in Appendices.
3. Refer Document I in the Appendices.
4. Refer Document II in the Appendices.
5. Available at, http://unispal.un.org/UNISPAL.NSF/0/57C45A3DD0D46B0980 2564740045CC0A.
6. Refer Document III in the Appendices.
7. Ibid.
8. Available at, http://unispal.un.org/UNISPAL.NSF/5ba47a5c6cef541b802563e 000493b8c/d442111e70e417e3802564740045a309?OpenDocu

ment#sthash.R04cRB0a.dpuf.

9. Available at, http://unispal.un.org/UNISPAL.NSF/5ba47a5c6cef541b802563e000493b8c/d442111e70e417e3802564740045a309?OpenDocument#sthash.R04cRB0a.dpuf.
10. Available at, http://unispal.un.org/UNISPAL.NSF/0/57C45A3DD0D46B09802564740045CC0A.
11. Available at, http://www.ajcarchives.org/AJC_DATA/Files/1943_1944_5_USCivicPolitical.pdf.
12. Available at, http://avalon.law.yale.edu/20th_century/arableag.asp#1.
13. Available at, http://www.fas.org/sgp/crs/mideast/RL33961.pdf.
14. Refer Document I in the Appendices on page 155.
15. Nir Mann, 'Zionist History: The View from the Commissioner's Palace', *Ha'aretz,* April 3, 2011. Review of (in Hebrew) 'Hageneral Sir Alan Gordon Cunningham 1945-1948' (The Last Commissioner: General Sir Alan Gordon Cunningham, 1945-1948), by Motti Golani Am Oved, Tel Aviv University (Hebrew). Available at, http://www.haaretz.com/culture/books/zionist-history-the-view-from-the-commissioner-s-palace-1.353825.
16. Available at, http://www.mfa.gov.il/mfa/foreignpolicy/peace/guide/pages/declaration%20of%20establishment%20of%20state%20of%20israel.aspx.
17. From the 'Introduction', available at, http://uncpress.unc.edu/browse/page/122.
18. The Suez Crisis: An Affair to Remember', *The Economist* (London), July 27, 2006, Special Report (From the print edition). Available at, http://www.economist.com/node/7218678/print.
19. Available at, Stable URL: http://www.jstor.org/stable/4329432.
20. Refer Document III in the Appendices on page 187.
21. Ibid.
22. Available at, http://www.archives.gov.il/ArchiveGov_Eng/Publications/Electr

onicPirsum/SixDayWar/

23. 'Egypt Will Fight, Nasser Shouts', *Associated Press* (Cairo), November 23, 1967 in *Pittsburgh Post-Gazette*, November 24, 1967. Available at, http://news.google.com/newspapers?id=EMdaAAAAIBAJ&sjid=mmwDAAAAIBAJ&pg=7158%2C4781942.
24. Reuven Pedatzur, 'Seeds of peace,' *Ha'aretz*, September 22, 2010. Available at, http://www.haaretz.com/weekend/week-s-end/seeds-of-peace-1.315172.

2

Carter, Begin, Sadat and Camp David-I

The Camp David Accords, signed by the President of Egypt and the Prime Minister of Israel on September 17, 1978, was an event of great historical importance in the modern Middle East. These agreements which were the result of the negotiations conducted over a period of some eighteen months, eventually resulted in the signing of a formal treaty of peace between Egypt and Israel on March 19, 1979. As a result, the strategic map of the Middle East was fundamentally altered. The Accords were also a tribute to the negotiating skills of the then US President Jimmy Carter who was almost singularly responsible for the agreement that was reached at Camp David, Washington in September 1978.

Prelude to the Accords

The process that culminated in the 1978 Camp David Accords had their origins in the Yom Kippur (Ramadan) War of 1973. This war which resulted in the Arab states of Egypt and Syria attacking Israel to avenge their 1967 defeat changed the negotiating strategies of almost all the major players in the Middle East, except perhaps the Soviet Union. Israel won this war but only after almost succumbing to a Syrian invasion and ultimately losing a lot of strategic Suez Canal territory to the Egyptians. It was left to the Nixon administration and in particular to his secretary of state, Henry Kissinger to broker a ceasefire between the two warring groups. The US was ultimately able to use the dominance that it had established during the war to broker three agreements among the combatants—two between Israel and Egypt and the third between Israel and Syria.

These agreements established dividing lines between the

military forces of both sides and strict limitations on their frontline deployments to reduce the danger of surprise attack (Kissinger 2001: 68). In fact, the Sinai II Accord between Israel and Egypt in 1975 was an important step on the path that culminated in the Camp David Peace Treaty of March 1979. This second Sinai agreement contained political elements that dealt with a durable peace between the two parties. However the commitment to non-recognition was still so great that the entire negotiations process had to be conducted entirely through an American mediator (Henry Kissinger). The two sides never met except at the military level at the very end of the negotiation to sign the documents. The Sinai-II agreement had political leaders' signatures which were added to the document separately in each country (Kissinger 2001: 68).

Arab Oil Embargo

It was the Arab world that was considered to have gained the most politically from the conflict. The war had convincingly demonstrated that the gap in military strength between Israel and the Arab countries had narrowed. The 1973 war also added a new dimension to the Arab-Israeli conflict. Soon after the outbreak of the war, there were demands from within the Arab world to deny oil to Israel's supporters in the West. In mid-October, Arab oil exporters, meeting in Kuwait, agreed to cut production, while the UAE took the lead in halting the export of oil to the USA. Western nations were soon experiencing rising fuel prices and growing shortages, showing the extent of their dependency on oil produced in the Arab world.

In early November, the member states of the European Community (EC), the forerunner of the present European Union (EU), endorsed a statement calling for an Israeli withdrawal from the territories occupied in 1967 and asserting the need for a settlement in the Middle East that did not ignore the legitimate rights of the Palestinian people (Cossali 2001: 27). It was the first time such a statement endorsing the right of the Palestinians was made by the Europeans. An outraged Israel accused Europe of surrendering to Arab blackmail. Before they could accuse the US of the same, President Nixon quickly deputed his Secretary of State, Kissinger to the region on a series of visits to Middle East capitals. It was the start of Kissinger's legendary shuttle diplomacy.

In June 1974, Nixon himself embarked on a tour of the region. America, in spite of having huge oil reserves, had experienced more inconvenience than expected by the Arab oil boycott. Nixon reassured Israel of continued US support. He was also able to please the Arabs by forecasting a new era of cooperation between the US and the Arab world. Arab leaders welcomed Nixon's overtures, believing that at last US influence would be used to promote an equitable settlement of the long festering Arab-Israeli dispute. American overtures resulted in the revoking of the embargo on the export of Arab oil to the US. Diplomatic relations between Syria and the US were also re-established. Israel's international position, on the other hand, was considerably weakened by the revelation of the extent to which the world was dependent upon Arab goodwill (Kissinger 2001: 28).

Palestinian Liberation Organisation (PLO) in the 1970s

The 1970s were a period during which the PLO made many sterling successes. In fact, by the end of the decade, the organisation had representatives, some with full Ambassadorial position, in more than 80 countries. On September 22, 1974, the UN General Assembly disregarding virulent Israeli and American objections, included on its agenda for the first time the Palestine question as a subject for debate rather than as part of the general question of the Middle East. And on November 13, 1974, the Assembly in a historic more, heard Yasser Arafat, the head of the PLO, plead for the Palestinian people's right of self-determination in his much quoted 'gun and olive' branch speech (Aburish 1998: 140-142). International recognition of the PLO had an important effect on the intra-state politics of the Arab world. The effect was felt at the Rabat conference of the league of Arab states in Morocco, in October 1974. The main item on the agenda was Palestinian representation at the proposed Geneva peace talks.

Prior to this, in November 1973, the Arab states excluding Jordan recognised the PLO as the sole, legitimate representative of the Palestinian people. The Hashemite Kingdom of Jordan, previously known as Transjordan till 1967 when it had also included the West Bank and East Jerusalem, had always been unwilling to allow the establishment of a Palestinian state on the Occupied Territories (OTs). Coupled with this was the traditional role of Jordan's monarchs as the custodians of all major Muslim holy places in Jerusalem, prime of which was the Al-Aqsa mosque, third holiest in Islam. The mosque itself was located on a raised platform called the Haram Al-Sharif, worshipped by Jews as being the site of their lost Temple, built by King Herod over 2000 years ago. Again the site was revered by Muslims as the place from which the *Prophet Mohammad (PBUH)* ascended to heaven. Naturally the ruling elite of Jordan were reluctant to give up all of this.

At Rabat, however, King Hussein was under the combined pressure of all the Arab states to accept the PLO's right to represent the Palestinians at all international fora. Finally, Hussain accepted a resolution that said that any liberated Palestinian territory 'should revert to its legitimate Palestinian owners under the leadership of the PLO' (Sela 2002: 158-160). This resolution helped to strengthen the position of moderate PLO elements led by Chairman Arafat, since they now had the backing of all the main Arab states to participate in negotiations as the legitimate voice of the Palestinian people. The elevation of the PLO to the state of a principal player on the Middle Eastern stage was welcomed by the Arab people. The Israeli Government however refused to have any dealings with the PLO, dismissing it as terrorist organisation responsible for the deaths of many of its citizens. The PLO's majority position on Israel itself underwent considerable change during the 1970s.

Though committed by its charter to the destruction of the Jewish Zionist state and its replacement by a secular democratic Palestinian state, the middle of the 1970s itself saw the majority of PLO members willing to accept the idea of a Palestinian state in the West Bank and Gaza with East Jerusalem as its capital.

In late 1975 and early 1976, the international position of the PLO was further legitimized though a series of discussions at the UN. In November 1975, the General Assembly adopted three resolutions concerning Palestine.

1. Establishment of a 20-nation committee to devise plans for the implementation of Palestinian self-determination and national independence.
2. Invitation to the PLO to take part in future debates on the Middle East.
3. And defining Zionism as a form of racism and racial discrimination (Cossali 2001: 28).

The United States by prior agreement with the Israelis (through Henry Kissinger) was committed not to recognize or to negotiate with the PLO. They therefore repeatedly blocked and vetoed resolutions aimed at affirming the Palestinians right to establish their own state. The Israelis themselves were not interested in the PLO at the moment. Their eyes were set on Egypt and Nasser's successor as president, Anwar el-Sadat. Sadat had evinced more than enough inclination that he was primarily interested in his land of Sinai and he was quite willing to sacrifice the Palestinians by establishing peace with Israel for the sake of that land.

Sadat, Egypt and the United States

When Sadat succeeded Nasser, who died in September 1970, he was a totally unknown quantity in the West. In appearance and nature, he seemed to be quite the opposite of Nasser. He lacked the pan-Arab aura of Nasser. Even his own people did not know him. Within three years of his rule, however, he was to change this perception completely by his momentous decision to attack Israel. Egypt and Syria's combined attack on Israel resulted in changing the negotiating spectrum of the Middle East considerably. Israel was brought down from a position of unassailable strength to that of a very vulnerable state committed to finding a durable peace with its neighbours.

The 1973 war and subsequent oil embargo resulted in a much more heightened consciousness among the world community about the plight of the Palestinians. Even before the war started, Sadat had showed his sense of 'realpolitik' by ditching the Soviets for the Americans. He carried this further in 1975 after the various withdrawals and military standstill agreements were negotiated with the Israelis by abrogating the Soviet-Egypt Treaty of Friendship signed in 1971. Sadat risked enmity with the Arab world and particularly from Syria, by aligning himself with the US. He knew that the Americans were committed (again through Nixon and Kissinger) to pursuing a hands-off policy vis-à-vis the Middle East. This action of Sadat resulted in Syria assuming temporary leadership of the Arab world.

Carter and the Arab-Israeli Dispute

The late 1970s were a period of more active negotiations on Arab-Israeli disputes. The Arab states supported Palestinian participation in an overall settlement providing for Israeli withdrawal from areas occupied since the 1967 war and establishment of a Palestinian state on the West Bank and Gaza strip. The US position towards the Palestinians also was changing. The new administration of President Jimmy Carter identified the Middle East conflict as a major foreign policy concern and promised more direct involvement in the region. In February 1977, President Carter sent his Secretary of State, Cyrus Vance, on a tour of the Middle East and invited Israeli and Arab leaders to visit him in Washington (Cossali 2001: 29). In March l977, Carter spoke of the need for a Palestinian homeland. He later stated that it was essential for the Palestinians to take part in the peace process. These were positions that were unthinkable during the Kissinger era. The Israelis in turn continued to reject direct participation of PLO representatives in the peace process, but were willing to allow Palestinians to sit in other Arab delegations like that of Jordan.

Begin and the Palestinian Issue

The May 1977 elections in Israel resulted in the victory of the rightwing Liqud party headed by the former Yishuv era (prior to the formation of the state of Israel) Jewish terrorist leader Menachem Begin. Begin as an individual and Liqud as a party were committed to maintaining Israeli control over the West Bank and Gaza, renamed in Biblical Jewish terminology as Judea and Samaria. In the approach to the 1977 election, Begin had campaigned hard for the expansion of Jewish settlements in the Occupied Territories (OTs) and permanent Israeli control over the West Bank. Begin was violently opposed to negotiation with the PLO which he dubbed a 'terrorist' organisation and refused to accept the notion of an independent Palestinian state. Begin was a Polish Jew who had been imprisoned in a concentration camp by the Nazis where he had lost almost all of his immediate family. This experience coupled with his later experience in Israel's war of independence served to create in him tremendous desire for security.

For him, no amount of sacrifice was sufficient to safeguard the security and territorial integrity of the Jewish state. He was also imbued with an equally great suspicion for the 'goyim' (non-Jews). He saw all land, whether of Israel proper or the Occupied Territories (OTs) including the Golan Heights captured from Syria, as the same sacred and holy part of the Biblical land of the Jews. Begin's long exclusion from governance in Israel and Israeli Labour's treatment of him as a 'pariah' had made him very bitter and created in him a burning determination to leave his mark on the polity of the Holy

Land. Almost immediately after the Begin govt. assumed office in 1977, it announced the extension of health, education and welfare services to the Palestinian populations of the West Bank and Gaza (Cossali 2001: 29).

Till then the Egyptians and the Jordanians along with the UNRWA had been fulfilling these needs of the Palestinian people. Arab fears that this was in fact the precursor to Israeli annexation of the two territories were deepened by the announcement of an accelerated program of Jewish settlement building on the West Bank along with the unveiling of a Israeli draft proposal for a territorial settlement that envisaged the maintenance of the occupation throughout the West Bank and Gaza. To counter the unnecessarily aggressive new Israeli government and to mollify the Arab world, the USA and the USSR issued a joint statement on October 1, 1977 urging a Middle East settlement that would ensure the legitimate rights of the Palestinians. The inclusion of such a phrase signalled an important shift in the official US attitude to the Arab-Israeli conflict and clearly troubled the Begin regime (Cossali 2001: 29).

Sadat's Attitude towards Israel

Egyptian President Anwar el-Sadat made the decisive break through in peace diplomacy with a dramatic visit to Jerusalem in 1977. He decided to take this radical and quixotic step because of his extreme dissatisfaction with the progress of the American mediated peace process in the Middle East. He was also afraid of what steps the rightwing Liqud government would take with regard to the Sinai, in particular, to expand and increase the existing number of settlements there. In a speech to the Egyptian Parliament on November 9, 1977, Sadat expressed his frustration with the lack of progress towards a peace settlement and announced that he would be prepared to go to Jerusalem to negotiate direct with Israel.

His offer was immediately taken up by Israel and on November 19, Sadat flew to Tel Aviv (Cossali 2001: 29). His initiative was welcomed in the West where it was regarded as a bold attempt to break with the sterile attitudes of the past. Within the Arab world however, Sadat's visit was seen with both scepticism and hostility. There was a general feeling that Sadat was prepared to undermine the cause of Arab unity for his own selfish purposes. Egypt's Minister of Foreign Affairs Ismail Fahmy resigned in protest at the proposed visit. In fact, Sadat's visit to Jerusalem had been planned a few months before during a secret meeting between Foreign Minister Moshe Dayan of Israel and Deputy Prime Minister Hassan Tuhamy of Egypt in Morocco. This meeting was primarily meant to explore the negotiating positions of both Egypt and Israel. President Sadat wanted to explore Israel's willingness to make serious concessions (Quandt 1986: 111).

As a case of pre-negotiation, this meeting helped to increase the confidence of both sides that negotiation was a credible option. At the meeting, Tuhamy told Dayan that Sadat was ready to meet with Begin, provided Israel gave a prior commitment to full withdrawal from all Arab territory. Moreover, he gave indication that the Egyptian President was ready to negotiate secretly and not in a multilateral forum like Geneva. Israeli leaders, on their part, stated a readiness to withdraw from almost all of Egyptian territory but were not prepared to return all Arab lands captured in 1967 (West Bank and Gaza) (Cossali 2001: 29). The subsequent failure of three months of direct negotiations between Egypt and Israel in which the United States was an observer rather than a participant helped to convince both parties that any further process of negotiation must involve the US as a full participant, if it was to succeed (Quandt 1986: 107).

American Mediation in the Camp David Peace Process

Jimmy Carter was unique among American presidents in his deep concern to find a solution to the issues dividing Israel from its Arab neighbours. In his first speech to the United Nations General Assembly in October 1977, he made these concerns clear: Of all the regional conflicts in the world, none holds more menace than the Middle East. War there has already carried the world to the edge of nuclear confrontation. It has already disrupted the world economy and imposed severe hardships on the people in the developed and developing nations alike (Stein 1989: 413).

When Carter came to the White House, he brought little more than a strong biblical knowledge and affection for the Holy Land. Being a devout evangelical Christian, he had a deep affinity for the state of Israel and the Jewish people. On the other land, he had next to no knowledge about the Palestinians except for the fact that they were obviously Arab. Throughout his tenure, his inability to deal with moderate Israelis as well as Palestinians coupled with absolutely no firsthand knowledge of the conditions in the Occupied Territories (OTs) made him blind to many facets of the dispute. It was only after his 1983 visit to the West Bank and Gaza that he could fully understand the Palestinian side of the argument. As far as American politics was concerned, Carter was on 'outsider', relatively new to Washington and its ways. He had been the former Governor of the state of Georgia (Quandt 1986: 30). So as far as he was concerned, it was a quick transition from local issues to those of great international significance.

Carter knows well enough that American interests would be best served if peace was brought to the Middle East. He came to know many of the leaders in the Middle East personally and established close relations with them. Most important of all, while showing a sympathetic face towards Israel, Carter was able to handle the Jewish lobby in New York and Washington relatively firmly. It must be acknowledged that Carter's achievements in the Middle East were built on the firm foundations laid by Henry Kissinger in brokering three Arab-Israeli agreements during 1974-75 (Quandt 1986: 320). Carter was also officially served by his Secretary of State Cyrus Vance who helped in drafting the Camp David Accords and the text of the peace treaty.

President Carter's original aim had been to promote a comprehensive Middle East peace that would be achieved through a series of negotiations that could conclude with the convening of a peace conference at Geneva. This was a highly controversial approach, especially after the failure of the 1973 Geneva Conference. A major point of discord about this approach was that Carter wanted to take the Soviets along, something that the Kissinger Doctrine strictly forbade.

The negative response to his policies, both at home and abroad forced Carter to reassess his priorities in the Middle East. He was forced to give up the Geneva conference paradigm of peace negotiations. Sadat's visit to Israel in November 1977 again forced the Carter Administration to change its Middle East policies (Quandt 1986: 18). The US concentrated now on meditating a bilateral peace agreement between Egypt and Israel. Ironically, this was the very approach that Kissinger had always dreamed of. Carter, who had always been a critic of Kissinger, finally ended up fulfilling the task left behind by him.

President Carter's decision to invite Sadat and Begin to Camp David was the result of his frustration at the slow pace of the Middle East peace negotiations during the later part of 1977 and early 1978. The two main actors, Begin and Sadat showed no signs of dropping their traditional animosity and sitting down to serious peace talks. At the same time, Carter realized that his continued involvement in the Middle East morass was costing him political breathing space and votes at home. With his re-election bid fast approaching, he could ill afford this. Moreover, Carter firmly believed that Middle East Peace, or at least an Egyptian-Israeli settlement, was both obtainable and necessary (Quandt 1986: 206).

He felt that the Egyptian and Israeli leaders suffered from distrust and lack of confidence which could be overcome by helping each to understand the other better. Carter felt that a summit meeting at Camp David would provide an ideal setting for Begin and Sadat to get to know and trust each other.

Invitations were therefore issued to both parties in early August 1978 for a summit in September. Both Sadat and Begin immediately accepted Carter's invitation to Camp David (Quandt 1986: 207).

Camp David: Course of the Negotiations

The main Camp David negotiations took place over a 13 day interval. During this time, both the Israelis and the Egyptians were kept negotiating in good faith by the presence of the Americans alone. The success of Camp David does not belong to Sadat or to Begin, but to President Carter and his team of mediators. Only Carter had the patience and influences to force two men who were of diametrically opposite nature to sit together and agree to a common purpose. The peace treaty between Egypt and Israel that arose out of the Camp David talks was a tribute to the skill and mediation of President Carter, his Secretary of State, Cyrus Vance and National Security Advisor, Zbigniew Brezinski.

The Camp David talks lasted from 5th to 17th September, 1978. [1] Two sets of agreements were produced. One established arrangements for determining the future of the West Bank and the Gaza strip. [2] The other elaborated principles whereby an Egyptian-Israeli peace treaty could be formulated bringing to an end the state of hostilities and establishing normal relations between the two countries. [3] The entire process was characterized by ups and downs. The progress of the negotiations was mostly related to Begin's ability to compromise. His tenacity in holding on to each and every bargaining point ensured that success came only at the very end. After ten days of intense discussion and negotiation, almost everyone at Camp David believed that the talks had reached an impasse (Quandt 1986: 234). Faced with the prospect of failure, Carter was obliged to reconsider his initial strategy. The political costs of leaving the summit empty-handed must have been apparent not only to Carter and Sadat, but also to Begin. If agreement was to be reached, one if not both parties were going to have to make major concessions.

One of the main areas of disagreement between the two sides related to the military/civilian settlements that Israel had planted in the occupied Sinai Peninsula. Egypt naturally insisted that these should be dismantled along with the airfields and all other infrastructure that Israel had built in the Sinai during their occupation. Begin refused throughout the negotiations to withdraw the Sinai settlements. He had made his political career protecting Jewish settlements on occupied lands. So he could not be seen as compromising on this very emotive issue. Finally, all that he would agree to was that the issue would be put to vote in the Knesset (Israeli Parliament) (Smith 1992: 225).

The Camp David Accords involved enormous skills on the part of all those involved in the negotiations. The talks would have achieved nothing had the participants not been able to demonstrate the will and ability to move away from extreme opening positions and compromise on the issues that sharply divided them. For example, President Sadat began the Camp David Conference on September 6, 1978 by presenting the text of a proposal entitled 'Framework for the Comprehensive Peace Settlement of the Middle East Problem'. It contained an eight-clause preamble and two articles. The major provisions of the plan were:

1. Withdrawal of Israel to international boundaries and armistice lines (the pre-1967 borders) in the Sinai, the Golan Heights, the West Bank and Jerusalem.
2. Removal of Israeli settlements from the Occupied Territories (OTs).
3. Supervision of the administration of the West Bank by Jordan and of the Gaza strip by Egypt 'with the collaboration of the elected representatives of the Palestinian people for a period not to exceed five years (the interim period)'.
4. The establishment of a national entity for the Palestinian people-linked to Jordan if the inhabitants so choose-after

they exercised their right of self-determination six months prior to the end of the interim period.

5. Recognition of the right of the Palestinian refugees to return or to claim compensation in accordance with UN resolutions.
6. Formation of a committee composed of equal number of resident Palestinians and Israelis to administer the Holy city of Jerusalem.
7. Implementation of these points within a framework of peace recognizing the principles of 'non-acquisition of territory by war'.
8. Finally, payment by Israel of full compensation for all damages caused by the operations of its armed forces and the exploitation of natural resources in the Occupied Territories (OTs) (Naaz 1991: 58-59).

As far as Begin was concerned, he was quite willing to sacrifice the Sinai for the sake of peace with Egypt (subject to negotiated conditions), but was totally unwilling to compromise on the status of the West Bank (Judea and Samaria) and Gaza strip. For him, these areas formed part of Eretz Israel (Greater Israel-the original homeland of the Jewish people). He was unwilling to even grant the indigenous Palestinian people basic human rights in their own land. Begin also refused to talk about Jerusalem, holy city of three religions, but holiest for the Jews. Jerusalem was a non-negotiable issue. It was the eternal and indivisible capital of the Jews.

Thus, Carter's role in helping to broker the agreements was central. Left to themselves, Sadat and Begin would never have overcome the accumulated legacy of decades of hatred and mistrust and would have broken off their talks over any number of issues. Carter's position on many issues influenced the final outcome. He wanted an Egypt-Israeli agreement on the Sinai, and he was prepared to press the Israelis hard on withdrawal and on the settlements to get it. However, Carter was less concerned about all agreement on the West Bank and Gaza (especially when he understood the strong Israeli and American-Jewish dislike for such an agreement). He did not think that any explicit linkage between Egyptian Sinai and the Palestinian question was desirable or necessary (Quandt 1986: 257).

The famous American political scientist and Middle East specialist William D. Quandt has stated that: In the end, it was Carter who made the final judgments on what to accept and what not to accept, and it was Carter who used his influence with Sadat to get him to stay and to sign an agreement that both men knew was imperfect (Quandt 1986: 257).

Egyptian Gains and Losses

Egypt's most important gain from Camp David was a commitment to full Israeli withdrawal from Sinai, including the oilfields, settlements and airfields. To get this commitment, Sadat had offered a period of three years to complete the withdrawal, security arrangements that would be monitored by the US and the UN, and a promise to 'normalize relations' with Israel once the first phase of withdrawal had been reached. The Accords contained general principles referring to the legitimate rights of the Palestinian people and the right of the Palestinians to choose their own form of government. All the details dealt with the procedures and arrangements for the transitional period and not for the final status of the Occupied Territories (OTs).

Again to quote Quandt: Israel had made no commitment to eventual withdrawal from the West Bank and Gaza; nothing was said about Jerusalem; and settlements in the Palestinian Occupied Territories (OTs) were nowhere mentioned, though the Americans were telling everyone that Begin had in fact agreed to a freeze in settlement construction for the duration of the negotiations on autonomy (Quandt 1986: 255).

Sadat thus gained for Egypt, but lost on the Palestinian cause. The Camp David accords finally ended Egypt's campaign on behalf of the Palestinians and Arab national unity. The Nasserite legacy was broken. It was revealed that on vital national issues, Egypt, like any nation, would only defend its own rights and not the rights of others, however just their cause may be.

Israeli Gains and Losses

The Camp David agreements were greeted in the West as a triumph of US diplomacy. There was also cautious approval in Israel, where there was satisfaction that a peace treaty could be completed with Egypt without substantial concessions on the issues of Jewish settlements and the continued Israeli control over the Palestinian and Syrian territories conquered in 1967. This view was reinforced by a speech made by Menachem Begin on the anniversary of the creation of the state of Israel in 1949 in which he asserted that 'no border would ever be drawn "through the land of Israel" and that we shall never withdraw from the Golan Heights' (Cossali 2001: 30).

Begin has been conceded by all to be the most able negotiator at Camp David. This former terrorist leader, associated with some of the most despicable war crimes committed during Israel's war of independence, made sure he fought over every word at the negotiating table. Begin had to concede the Sinai to Sadat, thus giving up something that for Israel was very valuable. There were extensive oilfields in the Sinai that were being utilized by Israel for their domestic oil needs. In return, Begin not only won a durable peace with Egypt, but also a comparatively free hand for Israel in dealing with the West Bank and Gaza. Begin protected himself from considerable US and Egyptian pressure on the key issues of the future of the Palestinian territories, and on any form of linkage between the Egyptian-Israeli agreement and the Palestinian question.

Crucial to Begin's victory was the fact that the Accords contained no controversial language like the 'inadmissibility of the acquisition of territory by war', the applicability of the principles of UN resolution 242 'to all fronts of the conflict', and the need for eventual Israeli withdrawal from the West Bank and Gaza. Israel's claim to sovereignty over all of undivided Jerusalem was not contested in the accord. Finally, Begin had only to promise a three month freeze on settlement construction in the West Bank and, Gaza. Israel's ultimate victory lay in that within nine months of signing a peace treaty with Egypt, and with Israeli troops still in the Sinai, diplomatic relations between Egypt and Israel were established and ambassadors were exchanged (Naaz 1991: 61-62).

Camp David Accords and the PLO

The Camp David accords were the first ever Arab-Israeli agreements that spelt out specific conditions for solving the Palestinian issue. Given the complexity of the issue, the only realistic approach to a solution was felt to be the establishment of a five-year transitional period for the West Bank and, Gaza. The first part of the Accords, entitled, 'The Framework for Peace in the Middle East' stated that Egypt, Israel, Jordan, and the representatives of the Palestinian people would participate in three-stage negotiations to determine the area's future.

1. Cairo and Jerusalem would negotiate and then supervise transitional arrangements for a maximum of five years. The current Israeli military and civilian administration would withdraw when the inhabitants of the areas had elected a self-governing authority in free elections.
2. Egypt, Israel and Jordan would determine the powers and responsibilities of the elected self-governing authority in the West Bank and Gaza strip. Israel would withdraw the IDF into specified locations. Local constabulary forces consisting of Israeli and Jordanian forces would patrol and thereby ensure proper border control.
3. After the establishment of the self-governing authority a transition period of five years would begin. Negotiations to determine the final status of the territories would begin no later than the third year. These talks must include Egypt, Israel, Jordan and elected representatives of inhabitants of the West Bank and the Gaza strip. The talks would be based on provisions of UN Resolution 242 and

include discussions of boundaries and future security arrangements. It was specified that the final 'solution would recognize the legitimate rights of the Palestinian people and their just requirements' (Friedlander 1983: 229).

On 18th September, 1978, an enlarged emergency session of the PLO-EC (Executive Committee) met to discuss the Camp David accords. The EC session gave a call to all Palestinians, inside and outside the Occupied Territories (OTs), to observe a general strike on 20th September to express 'resolute resistance' to the Camp David 'conspiracy'. Arafat in a message to the US President stated that the signing of the Camp David accords signalled the 'loss of US interests in the Middle East' (Pradhan 1994: 157).

To the PLO leaders, the accords only served to undermine the aim of Palestinian self-determination and their hopes of creating on independent state. In the eyes of the PLO, the United State's position on the question of autonomy had become a decisive factor. Thus after Camp David, the most important aspect of Palestinian diplomacy was to counter the American design to get closer to Jordan. This was to strengthen Jordan's opposition to Camp David as well as to strengthen the struggle in the Occupied Territories (OTs) (Gresh 1983: 219). They also targeted Western Europe.

The ground realities in Western Europe vis-à-vis the Palestinian question and the PLO were quite different from those in the US. The Europeans had supported the Camp David accords as a process though they had reservations over the provisions related to the Palestinian question. The European states had realized that their interests were being threatened by the continuing failure to solve the 'Palestinian problem'. The European countries recognized that their economic interests were tied to developments in the region. In July 1979, Arafat met with the Austrian Chancellor, Bruno Kreisky and the Chairman of the Socialist International, Willy Brandt, in Vienna. Following talks, they issued a joint statement in which the Palestine question was regarded as the central problem in the Middle East conflict (Pradhan 1994: 167).

The Arab countries opposition to Camp David was coordinated in the Ninth Arab summit meeting in Baghdad in November 1978. The final communiqué rejected the accords on the ground that these agreements 'had taken place outside the framework of collective Arab responsibility' and had harmed the Palestinian cause by violating the resolutions of the Algiers and Rabat summit conferences. It called for 'a just peace based on the total Israeli withdrawal from Arab territories occupied in 1967, including Arab Jerusalem' and for the establishment of an independent Palestinian state. The fourteenth Palestinian National Council (PNC) that met in Damascus in January 1979, also unanimously condemned the accords as 'a conspiracy that should be rejected and resisted by all means' (Pradhan 1994: 157).

Ultimately the US mediated initiative for a lasting peace in the Middle East met only with partial success. The Americans in the immediate Post-Camp David era did try to formulate a more specific peace formula that would help the Palestinians to achieve their aims short of an independent state. The Carter administration's frequently stated policy was that the Palestinian people must have the right for themselves and their descendents to live with dignity and freedom and with the opportunity for economic fulfilment and political expression. In a speech made before the Senate Foreign Relations Committee on 27th May, 1979, Secretary of State Vance stressed that the Camp David accords recognised the legitimate rights of the Palestinian people and their just requirements (Vance 1979: 27). What prevented the US from recognizing the PLO was the American stand on UN resolution nos. 242 and 335 and Kissinger's famous pledge to Israel not to deal with the PLO unless Israel did so first, as a guarantee for Israel's security and sovereignty.

The US, by allowing its policy on the issue of contacts with the PLO to be dictated by Israeli policy, ruled itself out as a credible actor in the search for solution to the Palestinian problem. Another reason why the Camp David framework was totally inadequate in dealing with the Palestine issue related to the ambiguities surrounding the concept of autonomy negotiations between Egypt and Israel that began in May 1979 and continued for over a year without any agreement over the format of autonomy for the West Bank. The Begin govt. reasserted its claim to the West Bank and Gaza as an indivisible part of 'Eretz Israel' and stated that any autonomy would not apply to land and water rights which would continue belong to Israel.

Israel announced plans in May 1979 for an ambitious programme of settlement construction in the West Bank and Gaza, and in September the ban on Israeli citizens purchasing Arab land in the Occupied Territories (OTs) was ended (Cossali 2001: 30). Sadat, on the other hand, called for full governing autonomy for the occupied territory, within a Jordanian entity, a stance that had the moral support of the Americans. The official American position at the end of the Carter presidency remained that Israeli settlements in occupied territory were illegal and that East Jerusalem was considered to be occupied territory despite its incorporation into Israel (Smith 1992: 257). The problem in American politics was that any party who stated this view openly would be sure to lose the influential Jewish vote and backing, thereby weakening their chances in any elections in the US. Carter achieved the Camp David accords and the Egypt-Israel peace treaty, holding to established American positions that, when declared openly, destroyed his chances for a second Presidential term. It was the costs of peace that he had to pay.

Endnotes

1. See Document IV in Appendices.
2. Ibid.
3. Ibid, 194.

3

Reagan, Clinton and the Oslo Accords

The Reagan and Clinton eras in US Politics were characterised by fast moving developments in the field of Israel-Palestine peacemaking. Many important events and landmarks such as the Madrid Peace Conference and the Oslo Accords took place during this period. While the basic contours of a future Israel-Palestine peace settlement were set during this period, an actual peace settlement remained elusive. Clinton was probably the last US President who tried to give his very best to solve the entangled imbroglio that is the Israel-Palestine conflict and failed to get an ultimate peace deal. The 'Carter moment' proved elusive in the search for peace in the fertile Levant.

Reagan Era

Ronald Reagan was elected U.S. President at the end of 1980. Strongly sympathetic to the Jewish state, his appointment of a team of pro-Israeli foreign affairs advisers caused protests from the Arab world. His assumption of the Presidency in January 1981 coincided with a time of increased regional strife throughout the Middle East. The Islamic Revolution in Iran during the last days of the Carter administration was followed by the Soviet occupation of Afghanistan which was again followed by the Iran-Iraq war in September 1980.

The Reagan administration saw the Soviet Union as an 'evil empire' which should be neutralized or eliminated if possible. All their actions were geared towards this perspective. After the fall of Shah's Iran, Israel was seen 'as perhaps the only remaining strategic asset in the region on which the US can truly rely...' (Smith 1992: 257). Reagan showed very little concern for the Palestine cause and had an entirely negative perception of the Palestinian Liberation Organisation (PLO). While the Carter administration had tried to involve the PLO in the peace process, the Reagan regime did the opposite by rejecting any PLO role in future negotiations. Reagan followed the typical Israeli line of discriminating between the PLO and the Palestinians, trying to marginalize the PLO.

Reagan Plan

In September 1982, President Reagan formulated new proposals to settle the Arab-Israeli conflict or the Palestinian-Israeli conflict as it would be more precise to term it. The 'Reagan Plan' envisaged the restoration of the Occupied Territories (OTs) to their Arab populations, but denied the creation of a Palestinian state. Instead it proposed Palestinian self-government in association with Jordan.

The plan also called for a freeze on Israeli settlement in the West Bank and denied Israeli claims of sovereignty over either that area or Gaza. It called for 'full Palestinian autonomy,' to be realised through confederation with Jordan in such a manner that the legitimate rights of the Palestinians would be realised without compromising the 'legitimate security concerns of Israel.' Reagan, in fact, denied both the basic PLO and Israeli positions. He stated that in America's view, 'the withdrawal provision of Resolution 242 applies to all fronts, including the West Bank and Gaza' (Smith 1992: 268). He also argued that Israel could not be expected to return to the narrow and indefensible borders it had before 1967.

The Reagan plan was formulated in the background of the Israeli invasion of Lebanon. They carried out this invasion with the purpose of destroying the PLO HQ in that country. The Israelis had secret American backing for their plans. Both the Americans and the Israelis were demanding the withdrawal of the PLO from Lebanon as the price for ending the invasion. The PLO, on the other hand, was demanding American recognition of the movement as the price for its departure. This position had strong support from many members in the Reagan administration. Reagan however refused to recognize the PLO as anything but a terrorist organization.

The plan aroused so much expectation among the Arabs that the 12th Arab League summit at Fez, Morocco (September 6-9, 1982) made it the prime focus of their deliberations. The Reagan plan was believed to be important because it was put forward by a state that was considered to be one of the most important actors in the region. In addition, the US was the sole country that was able to influence and pressurize the Israelis to make the necessary compromises for the sake of peace. In spite of all this, the Israelis rejected the plan outright.

Fahd Plan

On 7th August, 1981, the Saudi crown prince, Fahd bin Abdel Aziz, declared on eight-point plan as a basis for a 'Middle East peace settlement'. The plan was prefaced by a declaration in which the Saudi prime expressed regret for the support extended to the Camp David accords by the US. He stated that "we are not quite happy with the overall US policy in the Middle East, especially with regard to the Palestinian issue." The 'Fahd Plan' called for an Israeli withdrawal from all Arab territories occupied in 1967 and the creation of a Palestinian state in the West Bank and Gaza with its capital in Jerusalem (East). There was also a mention of the right of all states in the region to live in peace. The plan also provided for the recognition of the Palestinian people's right to return (to their homeland) and compensation for all who did not wish to do so (Pradhan 1994: 387).

The 'Fahd Plan' has been seen as an attempt to take over the mantle of leadership of the Arab world from Egypt after it was expelled from the Arab league following the Camp David accords. The plan contained no new provisions. What attracted everyone's imagination and aroused expectation was that it carried the name of the Saudi crown prince. The Arab world's richest and most influential nation was calling for a negotiated settlement between Israel and the Palestinians (Pasha 2000: 277). Interestingly, the plan envisaged placing the West Bank under United Nations supervision for a transitory period not exceeding a few months. This was in direct opposition to the Camp David accords and the so-called Reagan plan that fixed a transition period of not less than five years. The plan got a positive response from most of the moderate Arab states, Western Europe and even the US. However, the Arab summit called at Fez, Morocco, in November 1981, failed to endorse the plan.

Fez Charter

The Reagan plan gave the Arabs the necessary impetus to come up with a plan of their own. The 12th Arab League summit held at Fez in Morocco brought all the Arab league states (except Libya) together to produce a plan known as the 'Fez Plan'. It was essentially a reiteration of the Fahd Plan with minor amendments (Pasha 2000: 283). The text of the new plan was adopted by consensus of all the leaders including Arafat and Assad. It called for the creation of an independent Palestinian state in the West Bank and Gaza with Jerusalem as its capital. The Palestinian right to self-determination was mentioned along with the central role of the PLO in all future negotiations.

The controversial reference in the original Saudi proposals to "the right of all countries in the region to live in peace" was changed into a formula under which "the UN Security Council will guarantee peace for all the states of the region, including the independent Palestinian state" (Pradhan 1994: 198). This clause actually underlined the fact that for the first time the whole Arab world including the PLO agreed to a statement which recognized Israel's right to exist. The plan was thus a carefully drafted proposal fashioned to take into account the concerns of all including Arab moderates, radicals and the PLO. Israel again flatly rejected the plan, being vehemently against the establishment of an independent Palestinian state in the West Bank and Gaza (Pradhan 1994: 198).

If it was at Fez in 1982 that the Arab leaders endorsed the concept of guaranteed peaceful relations of Israel with 11 states in the Middle East, then it was at the Casablanca summit of the Arab league in 1989 that they approved the concept of partition (a two state solution) for the first time since 1947. The original UNGA resolution 181(II) on the Arab-Israeli conflict had been in favour of partition and the creation of a Jewish and Arab state. The Arabs had rejected this then. This naturally implied that UNSC resolution 242 was also collectively approved by the Arab Heads of State for the first time since it was passed by the council in 1967 (Khalidi 1990: 15).

Hussein-Arafat Accord

Meanwhile, repeated attempts throughout the 1980s by the PLO and Jordan to form a joint negotiating team to face Israel were blocked by the Israelis, who refused to deal with the PLO. Various American initiatives launched by successive Secretaries of State, George Shultz and James Baker failed to make any headway in the face of Israeli intransigence as well the inability of the US to engage in any meaningful dialogue with the PLO. No forward movement in solving the Israel-Palestine problem was possible until the PLO was recognized as the sole representative of the Palestinian people. The Hussein-Arafat Accord of February 1985, provided for Palestinian self-determination within the framework of a Jordanian-Palestinian federation. It also called for peace negotiations including all parties to the conflict along with the five permanent members of the UN Security Council. However general disapproval of the accord in the Arab world compelled the King in February 1986 to announce the end of political co-ordination with the PLO. The reasons he gave for this was the reluctance of the PLO to meet US pre-conditions for a dialogue, that it accept resolution 242 and ultimately recognize the state of Israel (Cossali 2002: 33).

Start of First Intifada

An intensified civil war in Lebanon during late 1985 and 1986 resulted in heavy fighting between the PLO and pro-Syrian militias. This in turn paved the way for the re-unification of the PLO which had been heavily ridden with factionalism. The 18th session of the PNC (Palestine National Council) held in Algiers in April 1987 resulted in Arafat re-establishing his authority over all the groups. Throughout 1987, there was a steady rise in political tension in the Occupied Territories (OTs). A large-scale uprising by the Palestinians in the OTs began on December 8, 1987. This 'intifada' came after more than 20 years of Israeli occupation when the Palestinians felt that there was no other way to accomplish their goals of self-government and national independence, other than to rebel. Israeli reaction was to try to suppress the rebellion using lethal force which soon came under international condemnation.

Shultz Plan

In February 1988, the US Government announced a new plan for the resolution of the Palestinian issue. The 'Shultz Plan' as it came to be known was presented at the far end of the Reagan administration. It called for negotiations between Israel and a joint Jordanian-Palestinian delegation to determine an interim form of autonomy for the OTs. The proposed transitional arrangement would last for three years and would provide for an Israeli military withdrawal from the West Bank and for municipal elections of Palestinian officials. Negotiations for a final settlement would run concurrently with the transitional arrangement and if necessary would be paralleled by an international conference including the five permanent members of the UN Security Council and all other parties to the conflict. All the negotiations would be conducted on the basis of UNSC resolutions 242 and 338. It also emphasised that negotiations between the Israeli and Jordanian-Palestinian delegation would proceed independently of any other negotiations (Maher 2002: 81).

This plan had the distinction of being rejected by all the parties concerned, including the Palestinians. The PLO rejected the plan outright because it failed to make provision for a Palestinian state or for their own participation in the peace process. King Hussein meanwhile announced in July 1988 that he was severing all official links, whether legal or administrative with the West Bank. His action paved the way for the PLO to emerge as the sole legitimate authority to represent the Palestinian people. As a result, in November 1988, the 19th session of the PNC culminated in the declaration of the independent state of Palestine, with the Holy city of Jerusalem as its capital. The Declaration of Independence cited UNGA resolution 181(II) of 1947, which partitioned mandate Palestine into two states, one Arab and the other Jewish, as providing the legal basis for the right of the Palestinian Arab People to national sovereignty and independence (Maher 2002: 81).

Israeli Peace Initiative

By the middle of 1988, the Intifada had spread throughout the OTs. The Israelis were determined that the intifada must be suppressed before any changes took place in the status of the occupied territories. Addressing the UNGA in December 1988, Arafat announced his recognition of Israel and renunciation of 'terrorism'. He also repeated his call for an international peace conference to be held on the basis of resolutions 242 and 338. The Reagan administration acknowledged the PLO's 'concessions' by holding the US's first official talks with Palestinians representing the movement. Under pressure from the PLO's diplomatic offensive, the Israeli government of Yitzhak Shamir which was a Liqud-Labour coalition came out with its own peace initiative in April 1989 for a negotiated end to the conflict.

The so-called 'Shamir proposals' provided for elections in the West Bank and Gaza in return for an end to the Intifada.

The elections would produce a Palestinian delegation to conduct negotiations on a final settlement. The delegation so elected should comprise solely of non-PLO members. A transitional authority was also envisaged during which a self - ruling authority might be established. The transitional period would serve as a test of co-operation and co-existence. Israel emphasized its willingness to discuss any option when negotiations on a final settlement were held. It soon because clear that Shamir was offering little more than recycled Camp David proposals. The 'Shamir Plan' was naturally unacceptable to the PLO and the Arab League. Attempts made by Egypt's president Mubarak as well as US secretary of state, James Baker III, to make the Israeli proposals more acceptable to the Arab world were not successful (Cossali 2002: 34).

Madrid Peace Conference

Theoretically, the Oslo Accord signed between the Palestine Liberation Organisation (PLO) and Israel on 13th September, 1993 was preceded by a long series of negotiations, between the two parties dating back to the Madrid conference held on 30th October, 1991. This conference established a new framework for multilateral negotiations that replaced the 1973 Geneva conference as the roadmap for future negotiations on the Arab-Israeli conflict.

It was for the first time that all the parties to the Arab-Israeli dispute, namely, Israel, Syria, Lebanon and a Jordanian delegation that was openly acknowledged to comprise of Palestinians from the west Bank and Gaza, sat down face to face for talks. Israel-Palestinian negotiations on the official Madrid track typically encountered many obstacles mainly due to the political fallout of Arab terrorist attacks and Israeli military incursions in the occupied territories. These factors influenced both parties to try out secret track-II model diplomacy similar to that carried out between Egypt and Israel in the late 1970s that led to the signing of the first Camp David Accords. The Israelis and PLO emissaries carried out secret talks in Norway under the able guidance of Terje Roed Larsen, a Norwegian social scientist. These highly secret negotiations led to the conclusion of a peace deal between the PLO and Israel known as the 'Declaration of Principles for Palestinian Self-Rule' in Washington on 13th September, 1993 (Azad 2000: 69).

Oslo Accords

...but if the enemy incline towards peace, do thou also incline towards peace, and trust in God (*The Holy Qur'an* (*Sura* 8:61). This verse from the Holy Quran is frequently quoted by Yasser Arafat to explain his reason for entering into a peace process with Israel. Another of his statements is as follows:

The Revolution will go on until an independent Palestinian state is established with Jerusalem as its capital. We will struggle on all fronts to prove that this land is Arab, Arab and Arab; we will defend every particle of Palestinian soil, and we will wage the battle of building a Palestinian state as we waged the liberation and peace battle (Yasser Arafat Interview in Saudi Journal *Al-Wasat*, January 9-15, 1995).

Yasser Arafat has for many years being making statements like the above, mixing the language of peace and compromise in his declarations in the Western languages, while saying in Arabic that Jerusalem is totally Palestinian and that not one acre of historic Palestine belongs to the Jews (Hertzberg 2001: 141).

In spite of all this, however, Arafat's stature as the undisputed leader of the Palestinian people began to slip after the signing of the 1993 Oslo Accords. The Accords formalised the legitimacy of Israel and ended Palestinian claims to Israeli land. The PLO also had to give up their claim to 30 percent of the territory that the original 1948 UN partition plan had defined as Palestinian. The so-called future state of Palestine was to comprise of littie more than 20 percent of what was once the British Mandate of Palestine (Hedges 2001: 134).

US Role in the Oslo Process

...the relationship between the United States and Israel is a special relationship for special reasons. It is based upon shared values, interests and a common commitment, to democracy, pluralism and respect for the individual (US Secretary of State. Warren Christopher, February 1993).

This statement by the top foreign policy official of the Clinton administration reveals the tilt, bias and interest of the Americans in any deal involving the prospect of a long-term peace between Israel and her neighbours. The Clinton Presidency itself when it took office was hailed as one of the most pro-Israel US governments to come to office in Washington for a long time. As an election candidate, Clinton had criticized the Bush administration for linking peace talks to humanitarian efforts to resettle Soviet immigrants. He often praised the Israeli Prime Minister Yitzhak Rabin for the steps he had taken to revive the peace process (the same Rabin who had brutally tried to crush the first intifada) and publicly appealed to the Arab side to respond. He was also quoted as repeatedly asking the Arabs to end their boycott of Israel. He promised to help Israel maintain its qualitative military balance in the Middle East (Flamhaft 1996: 98).

In March 1993, while meeting the Israeli Premier Rabin officially for the first time, President Clinton promised that he would prevent any measure to cut US military and economic aid to Israel. Clinton's affection for the Jewish state was best expressed in an interview given to the New York Times, the day before the Israel-PLO agreement was signed in Washington.

The only time I went to Israel was with my pastor, who told me after I got back that he thought one day I would be president and he said 'Just remember, God will never forgive you if you turn your back on Israel' (Flamhaft 1996: 98).

The above statement not only revealed Clinton's almost religious affection for the Jewish state (a must for all American presidents in their first term if they harboured ambitions for a second term) but also his almost childlike ego, a point that would again come to light at the end of the Camp David II summit. The Americans however had no direct role in the Oslo negotiations. They were only brought into the picture towards the end when it was sure that a deal could be signed. This in turn reflected the extreme secrecy under which the negotiations were conducted in Oslo. When the Israelis first intimated the Americans about the Oslo process, veteran Israeli politician and the then Foreign Minister Shimon Peres, reportedly told the US Secretary of State, Warren Christopher, that Israel was willing to publicly attribute all credit for the breakthrough to the Americans. More than making peace with the PLO, the Israelis wanted to get any commitment they made guaranteed by the US (Christopher 2001: 200).

The Oslo Accords consisted of two parts:

1. Mutual recognition between the PLO and Israel, and
2. Declaration of Principles (DoP) on interim Self-Governing, arrangements for Palestinians in the Gaza Strip and Jericho. [1]

It was the second part that was signed in Washington on 13th September, 1993. The DoP was signed on the White House lawns by Israeli Foreign Minister Shimon Peres and PLO Executive Committee member Mahmoud Abbas (Abu Mazen) in the presence of the US President Bill Clinton, Israeli Prime Minister Yitzhak Rabin, and PLO Chairman Yasser Arafat. It was witnessed by the US Secretary of state Warren Christopher and Russian Foreign Minister Andrei Kozyrev. The first part was in the form of two letters signed by Arafat and Rabin. Arafat's letter made far reaching commitments to Israel. The PLO recognised Israeli right to exist in peace and security, accepted Security Council resolutions 242 and 338, committed itself to the peace process and to a peaceful resolution of conflict between the two sides, renounced the use of terrorism and other acts of violence, and agreed to assume responsibility of all PLO elements and personnel to ensure compliance (Pradhan 2001: 415).

The PLO also agreed to change the relevant articles of the Palestine National Charter (PNC) denying Israel's right to exist and any other provision against the above stated commitments. Rabin's letter to Arafat stated that in the light of the PLO commitments, the government of Israel had decided to recognize the organization as the representative of the Palestinian people and to begin negotiations with it within the framework of the Middle East peace process.

A Palestinian Interim Self-Governing Authority (PISGA) which later came to be known as Palestinian Authority (PA) was to be set up in the territories of Gaza and Jericho (West Bank) following the withdrawal of the Israelis from these areas. The authority was to be extended to other areas of the West Bank later. To facilitate the extension of the PLO's power base, the projected agreement provided for a five-year programme of Israeli withdrawal from the occupied territories and troop redeployment. Negotiations on critical issues like the right of return of Palestinian refugees, the future borders of the projected Palestinian state, the future of Jewish settlements in the Occupied Territories (OTs) and the question of Jerusalem were all deferred, but it was specified that they should begin no later than the beginning of the third year of the interim period between the Government of Israel and the Palestinian Authority (Azad 2000: 70).

Palestinian Statehood and the Oslo Accords

It is interesting to note that nowhere in the wording of the accords does the question of Palestinian statehood figure. This was quite contrary to the PLO's oft-stated sole ambition of establishing a sovereign, secular state in historic Palestine or at least on the West Bank and the Gaza Strip. UNGA resolution 181 that clearly defines the legitimacy and necessity of a Palestinian state was never alluded to in the Oslo accords, whereas, UNSC resolutions 242 and 338 that refer to the Arab-Israeli conflict without any reference to the Palestinians, have constituted the base of the Oslo peace process. While no mention is made about a national home for the Palestinians in the Oslo process, there is a reference to the so called 'mutual legitimate and political rights of the Palestinians' in the preamble to the DOP.

There is no reference to the right of return of Palestinian refugees as enshrined in UN resolutions and concurrently, no mention is made of an end to the Israeli military occupation of the OTs. The so-called Israeli withdrawal from the West Bank city of Jericho and the Gaza strip was not a complete process in that the IDF was just redeploying from crowded population centres. As a result, Israel would continue to maintain its status as a de-facto sovereign even in Gaza and Jericho (Azad 2000: 71).

Israel, on the other hand, managed to get much more out of the PLO. Thus the PLO's recognition of Israel removed the raison d'être for the other Arab states to continue to withhold their recognition of the Jewish state. As a result of the Oslo accords, the PLO got official recognition from the US and European states. It also qualified for international assistance from donor organisations like the World Bank. Indeed as former US Secretary of State Henry Kissinger pointed out, "the outside world would increasingly endow that autonomous entity with attributes of statehood" (Heller 1997: 6).

Cairo Agreement

The Cairo Agreement also known as the Gaza-Jericho Agreement was signed on 4 May 1994. This provided for Palestinian self-rule in Gaza and Jericho as given in the DoP. It also required the Palestinians to accept a system of dual rights in the territories, i.e. a right for the settlers and a lesser right for the Arabs. The Cairo accords enshrined the Israeli right to fortify and defend its settlements in Gaza and Jericho, to reserve roads and highways for its exclusive use and to restrict the Palestinian population to strictly defined areas (Muralidharan 2000: 16). The US was supposed to have played the part of honest broker in these negotiations. In addition, a protocol on economic relations was agreed in Paris on 29 April 1994, and was added to the Cairo Agreement in May 1994. The new 'economic agreements' served to reduce the Palestinian economy to vassal status of the Israelis with import tariffs, trade taxes, import licensing and high standards being imposed on goods produced by the Palestinians. Israel could virtually dictate to the Palestinians in the economic field and bring about its unequal integration into a highly advanced Israeli economy (Pasha 2000: 254).

The Cairo agreement contained detailed arrangements for Israeli withdrawal from Gaza and Jericho and the deployment of a 9000-strong Palestinian police force. A newly appointed Palestinian National Authority (PNA) would be responsible for managing Palestinian affairs with the exception of security and foreign affairs. Elections were to be held in July 1995 in Gaza and the whole of the West Bank to choose members to a Palestinian Legislative Council. The Israelis also made a promise to extend self-rule to the remaining parts of the West Bank. Following the establishment of self-rule in Gaza and Jericho, Israel's position in the Arab world improved considerably. A formal peace treaty came into being with Jordan. This was followed by consular relations with other Arab countries like Morocco, Tunisia, Qatar, and Oman (Azad 2000: 82).

Clinton and the Arab-Israeli Peace Process

The Clinton administration's first term in office did not produce anything remarkable in the volatile peacemaking arena of the Middle East. The relationship with Israel was close but not to the extent of distancing Arab states and the Palestinians. The visibly genuine participation of Israel in the peace process further improved the US-Israeli relationship. Both Israeli Premiers, Yitzhak Rabin and Shimon Peres, enjoyed a good working relationship with the Clinton administration. In April 1996, President Clinton along with Israeli Prime Minister, Shimon Peres, issued a joint statement that set their 'strategic partnership' according to two main principles.

1. The natural US commitment to Israel, and

2. A mutual determination to achieve a comprehensive peace settlement (Rabil 2001: 431).

The United States was the only outside power that both Israel and the PA recognized could play a key role in the peace process. Israelis depended on the will and ability of the US to intervene even militarily if necessary should things go wrong for the Jewish state. American wealth and leadership was necessary for the international arrangements essential to maintain a peace agreement between two deeply distrustful combatants such as the Palestinians and the Israelis. The Palestinians, on the other hand, saw an active American role as the only way to maintain same sort of status quo in a situation greatly favouring Israel.

The Syrian Angle

After the heavy beating that Iraq received in the first Gulf war, Syria alone remained as the main threat to Israel in the neighbourhood. Both the Israelis and the Americans were determined to being Syria also into the peace fold on their terms. But their calculations were all foiled by the sphinx of Damascus, Hafiz al-Assad. For the United States, an Israel-Syria agreement would not only remove a major threat to Israel, but would improve the American strategic position in the region as well. While pursuing a dual containment policy vis-à-vis Iran and Iraq, the Americans were trying to improve their relations with Syria, banking on the recent Syria participation in 'Operation Desert Storm', against Iraq. In addition to sending his secretary of State, Warren Christopher to Damascus many times on shuttle diplomacy between Syria and Israel, Clinton himself met Assad twice in 1994. But he could not influence him to change his mind (Christopher 2001: 223).

The main issue for Assad was the Golan Heights that Israel had occupied in 1967. Assad rightly demanded a full and unconditional withdrawal by Israel from the area. Israel, on the other hand, was only interested in security guarantees from the

Syrians, which Assad was not prepared to give unless and until a withdrawal took place.

Oslo II Accord

It required a lot of prodding and mediation by the Americans as well as the Egyptians for the Israelis and the Palestinians to agree to the next stage of their peace process. Meeting in Washington on 18th September, 1995, the Israeli Foreign Minister Shimon Peres and the PLO leader Yasser Arafat put their signatures to a document known as the Interim Agreement on the West Bank and the Gaza strip or Oslo II. This agreement committed Israel to withdraw from 440 villages of the West bank and six of the seven cities, including Hebron. Civil authority would be transferred to the PNA in all these areas, but Israel would reserve the right to intervene militarily in the villages. In other words, no area in the West Bank was to witness Israeli withdrawal in the true sense as subsequent Israeli redeployment was to occur in the OTs. Oslo II was silent on the question of dismantling the Jewish settlements in the West Bank. Such a dismantling was antithetical to the Jewish conception of security. A major feature of Oslo II was the division of the West Bank into three zones.

Zone A consisted of the main towns (2.8 percent of total land area with 28 percent of the population) to be placed under direct Palestinian control. Zone B was to comprise of the remaining Palestinian population centres where civilian control resides with the PA and security control with Israel. This effectively placed Area B under Israeli jurisdiction. Zone C was composed of mostly rural land comprising nearly 70 percent of the total West Bank that included Israeli settlements and areas reserved for future Israeli infrastructural projects and military zones. In spite of so-called re-deployment, Israel always controlled over 80 percent of the land area in the West Bank.

With the Oslo-II agreement, Israel gained legal control over a majority of the West Bank. This was an aim, it had sought since 1967. In fact, the territorial divisions agreed to in the Oslo II accord, established the framework for a final settlement in the West Bank that would deny any territorial continuity to a future Palestinian state. Moreover, by accepting the division of the West Bank according to the provisions of the accord, Yasser Arafat accepted the legitimacy of Israeli settlement in the Occupied Territories (OTs) (Roy 2002: 12).

Arrival of Binyamin Netanyahu

The Clinton administration actively supported Shimon Peres in the May 1996 general elections in Israel that followed the assassination of the former Israeli premier Yitzhak Rabin. Clinton lived up to his promise of being the most liberal US President vis-à-vis Israel by granting huge amounts of military and technological aid together with the establishment of a formal defence treaty when Premier Peres visited Washington in April 1996. Arafat also helped the Peres campaign by presiding over the 21st session of the PNC (Palestine National Council) at which, the articles in the Palestinian National Charter denying Israel's right to exist were formally abrogated (Cossali 2002: 40). But none of this could save Peres from being defeated by Netanyahu.

Netanyahu's election represented a watershed in Israeli politics as it was for the first time that the people had directly elected a Prime Minister. Even though Netanyahu won by a slim margin, he was able to claim a political mandate independent of the outcome of elections to the Knesset (Israeli Parliament). Netanyahu's approach to the peace process was to modify it by the induction of two important concepts, that of security and reciprocity. Thereby he was aiming at bringing the Oslo process much more to the advantage of Israel. The underlying aim of this strategy was to prove that Israel would have the absolute right to stop withdrawing and if necessary re-occupy the territories on the pretext of lack of security (Azad 2000: 87). In this context, it may be noted that more than half of the West Bank was designated by the Netanyahu cabinet as necessary for Israel's security (Azad 2000: 88).

Hebron Protocol or Oslo III

Netanyahu's first foray into the previously untouchable (from a *Liqud* Party point-of-view) field of Oslo negotiations was the Hebron Protocol-signed January 15, 1997. This introduced some important changes from earlier accords and set new precedents for future negotiations. According to the protocol, the city of Hebron in the southern part of the West Bank was divided into two parts, H1 and H2. There was redeployment from 80 percent of Hebron where 100,000 Palestinians lived. However, Israel retained full control over the remaining 20 percent or H2, where same 400 militant Jewish settlers, protected by the Israeli Defence Force (IDF), lived among 30,000 Palestinians. These people were kept under almost continuous curfew, just for the sake of a few fanatic settlers. The Hebron Protocol contained no reference to UN resolution 242 or 338 as the legal framework for negotiations. Hebron's division into two parts created a new precedent for the further division of Palestinian lands into isolated enclosures. The PA's acceptance of an armed settler presence in a predominantly Arab population centre established another precedent for the permanence of Israeli settlement throughout the West Bank and Gaza and also for the bifurcation of Palestinian lands to make way for these settlements (Roy 2002: 12).

Wye River Memorandum (Oslo–IV)

In early 1998, the Clinton Administration proposed that those Israeli forces vacate 12-15 percent of the West Bank subject, of course, to commitments from the Palestinians to fight terror and prevent violence. The Palestinians were expecting a redeployment of 30-40 percent to make up for Oslo's missed deadlines. Netanyahu however, stated that a redeployment of more than 10 percent would jeopardize Israeli security. He refused to listen to Clinton's proposals for well over half a year, stating that they were 'neither desirable nor viable' (Cossali 2002: 41). Increasingly concerned by the lack of progress in the peace process, Clinton hosted a bilateral summit meeting between the Israeli Prime Minister and the PNA President Yasser Arafat at the Wye Plantation, Maryland on 15th October, 1998. The aim of the summit was to reach agreement on all the outstanding provisions of the interim phase of the Oslo accords, as defined in the Interim Agreements of September 1995 (Oslo II).

Negotiations between the Israeli and Palestinian teams concluded on 23rd October with the signing of the Wye River Memorandum. This committed Israel to withdraw from 13.1 percent of the West Bank in three phases, contingent on the security situation in the West Bank. Negotiation on the 'final status' issues—refugees, settlements and Jerusalem—were to commence in November 1998 and go on till Oslo's scheduled expiry date of May 1999. The PLO on its part agreed to weapons collection, security cooperation and other security measures in the occupied territories. A joint Ad-hoc committee was established to deal with certain bilateral economic issues. Discussions were started regarding the opening of the Gaza Sea Port. Israel also agreed to release Palestinian detainees in their jails and to facilitate the opening of Gaza International Airport as well as the Gaza-West Bank corridor.

The terms of the Wye Memorandum were much more favourable to the Israelis than the Palestinians. Thus, Palestinian negotiators were very much concerned that they had committed themselves to enter 'final status' talks with Israel still in control of over 80 percent of the OTs (Cossali 2002: 41). They need not have worried. Within a month of signing the Wye accord, and after only a minor transfer of land, Netanyahu suspended implementation of the agreement, under pressure from ultra-right parties and also in anticipation of Israel's national elections on 17th May, 1999.

Thus with each backward step, the dilemma produced by the Oslo Accords deepened. For over a decade, the Arab-

Israeli peace process has been based on the concept of building trust and keeping commitments albeit hesitantly. This gradualist approach had, in fact, been the original idea behind Kissinger's shuttle diplomacy in the mid-1970s. It resulted in two disengagement agreements along with a partial Israeli withdrawal from the Sinai. The Oslo agreements had seemed to be the logical endgame of this approach.

However, as progress had slowed down, the old concept was challenged. Ironically, the challenge had been first issued by Henry Kissinger. He had argued in 1996 that the time had come to face the facts, namely, statehood for the Palestinians; the definition of Israel's final borders; and the status of Jerusalem (Hyland 1999: 161). To quote him, 'The US must shift the discussion from procedures to goals. Israel must face the implications of its own policies, and the Palestinians, perhaps intoxicated by the heady wine of global solicitude must be reminded that they have no military prospects and that their people require not just co-existence, but Israeli cooperation in day-to-day living' (Kissinger 1996).

As both sides came closer to the core issues, slowing down of the Oslo process was inevitable. Frustration at this in Washington ultimately came to centre more on Israel than on the Palestinians. This again was a natural result of the intransigence of the Netanyahu government vis-à-vis the peace process. Clinton was regarded as a friend of Israel, but he was openly hostile to its government under Benjamin (Bibi) Netanyahu. Finally, the general elections held in May 1999 resulted in the defeat of Netanyahu and the victory of the pro-peace Ehud Barak as Prime Minister of Israel.

Endnote

1. Refer Document VI in the Appendices.

4

Clinton, Barak, Arafat and Camp David–II

Victory of Ehud Barak

President Bill Clinton's exasperation with the policies of Netanyahu and his *Liqud* party led him to openly back Israeli Labour Party candidate Ehud Barak in the May 1999 elections. He had made no secret of his inability to deal with Binyamin Netanyahu. The Netanyahu period had been one time when Clinton's traditionally close relations with the Israelis had come under tremendous strain. Traditionally, American Presidents had faced problems from *Liqud* premiers in Israel. Barak, on the other hand, as a former Chief of Staff of the Israeli Army had impeccable Labour party credentials.

During the election campaign, Barak worked on a platform guaranteeing both the security of Israel and the struggle against terrorism. Barak also promised to completely withdraw the Israeli Army from Lebanon and also to seek peace with the Syrians. He stood for the formation of a Palestinian state. In all his campaign speeches, he laid much emphasis on the concept of physical separation between Israel and the Palestinians in order to foster 'good-neighbourly relations and mutual respect' (Naaz 2000: 117). Barak's IDF-inspired obsession with strategic security was evident by all his pre-election emphasis on the conventional and nuclear strike capabilities of the Syrians, Iranians and Iraqis rather than on the Palestinians. Barak's role model was the former Israeli premier Yitzhak Rabin. He had served under him both in the Army and later as a Minister in his cabinet. Barak promised to secure peace with the Palestinians based on four security red lines. [1]

1. A united Jerusalem under Israeli sovereignty as the capital of Israel forever.
2. No return to the 1967 borders.

3. No foreign army would be allowed west of the river.
4. Most of the settlers in Judea and Samaria (West Bank and, Gaza) would be consolidated into settlement blocs under Israeli sovereignty (Weinburg 2000). [2]

Sharm el-Sheikh Memorandum (Wye-II Accord)

Though an admirer of Rabin, Barak had always been against the Oslo process which he felt compromised Israeli security (Shlaim 2005: 241-261). [3] He sought to replace Oslo's 'step by step' format with a direct all encompassing deal that would solve the problem once and for all. In this, he was supported by the Americans, in particular, President Clinton with the experience of the successful 1995 Dayton Peace Accords behind him. Barak however was more interested in brokering deals directly with the Arabs without the help of the Americans. In his first trip to the US, Barak is said to have asked Clinton to keep off unless asked to help out. It was in this context that the Sharm el-Sheikh summit cropped up, which was meant to get the suspended Wye agreement back on back. The Sharm el-Sheikh Memorandum signed on 4 September 1999, committed both parties to achieve a framework agreement on permanent status issues by February 2000 (Aronson 1999). [4] Israel also pledged to redeploy from 137 villages of the West Bank by January 2000. 'Final Status' negotiations were also scheduled to be completed by September 2000 (Aronson 1999).

The two sides also agreed on the starting of certain vital Palestinian infrastructural projects like the seaport at Gaza. Two 'safe passages' were also provided between the Gaza strip and the West Bank. On the security front, both sides decided to act to ensure the immediate, efficient and effective handling of any incident involving a threat or act of terrorism, violence or incitement whether committed by Palestinians or Israelis. To this end, they agreed to co-operate in the exchange of information and coordinate policies and activities (Naaz 2000: 118-119). The Memorandum also included a joint appeal to the international community to continue their support, both moral and economic to the Palestinian reconstruction efforts as well as the Israeli-Palestinian peace process.

As President Clinton approached the end of his second term in office, his desire to leave behind a legacy as a peacemaker propelled him ever deeper into the Arab-Israeli conflict. His first term in office brought the first major peacemaking success in the Balkans, when the three warring parties signed the Dayton Peace Accords. As far as the Middle East was concerned, Oslo-I and II, the Israel-Jordan peace treaty and same minor advances on the Syrian front was all that took place in Clinton's first term. The American role in all these affairs was relatively modest. The US acted more as a facilitator than as a mediator. Prior to Oslo, the Clinton administration never once forgot the Kissingerian dictum of avoiding all contact with the PLO unless otherwise authorized by the Israelis. Even after Oslo, the US refused to predict that a Palestinian state would rise out of the ongoing peace process (Quandt 2001: 26-27).

Camp David-II Summit

The Camp David-II Summit represented a radical break with the past as the Barak Govt. finally decided to jettison the moribund and unworkable Oslo peace process for a more radical 'make or break it' summit. The mood in which the summit was approached by all parties, including the hosts, can be gained from Clinton's statement on the eve of the summit: "We may not succeed, but we're sure going to get caught trying" (Friedman 2002). [5]

Prelude to the Summit

It was Barak's refusal to carry out the third stage of the army deployment; he himself had re-negotiated under the Sharm el-Sheikh agreement of September 1999 that acted as the main catalyst for the talks. Barak insisted on moving directly to final status talks. The summit model for these final status talks was itself a change in Barak's earlier stand that so-called 'final status' negotiations, might result in a series of long-term interim arrangements rather than a permanent settlement (Cossali 2002: 42). Initially, Barak's idea was to clinch a deal with the Syrians before ever turning to the Palestinians. To his military mind, the Palestinians were the lowest of the low, virtual scum because as an organized military force, they were almost nil. The Americans as always were more than willing to facilitate an Israeli-Syrian dialogue. This was in spite of the fact that they had burned their fingers in their previous attempt during Clinton's first term in office. US intermediaries were informed by the Syrians that negotiations would be resumed on the basis of the understanding that Israel was committed to withdraw from the Golan Heights (Cossali 2002: 42).

In December 1999, US Secretary of State, Madeleine Albright met with Israeli and Syrian leaders during a regional tour. Her visit was followed by an announcement that the Israeli Prime Minister, Ehud Barak, and the Syrian Foreign Minister, Faruq al-Shara, would be restarting negotiations from the point at which they had ended in February 1996. The two delegations met at Shepardstown, West Virginia from 3-10 January 2000 (Reinckens 2000). [6] President Clinton played an important part in these talks literally shepherding the two sides along to a mutually agreeable solution. The talks ended on 10 January with a mutual commitment to resume discussions on key areas of borders, water, security and diplomatic relations on 19 January. Following some misunderstanding, the negotiators never returned (Perlez 2000). [7] Another meeting that Clinton had with Assad in Geneva also ended in failure (Perlez 2000). Thus ended the Syrian track of Barak's ambitious peace programme.

Clinton's Gamble at High Wire Summitry

In mid May 2000, it came to light that both the PNA and the Israeli government had been involved in a secret dialogue in the Swedish capital, Stockholm. The negotiations were facilitated by a US administration anxious to conclude a peace settlement before the US presidential elections in November 2000. Clinton's plan was to invite both parties, Barak and Arafat to a brain storming session at Camp David, the presidential retreat situated in a secluded part of Maryland. If necessary, he would follow the pattern first practiced at Dayton and later finessed at Wye, namely, to apply intense pressure on the participants to conclude their negotiations in a successful manner. In mid-October 1998, both Arafat and Netanyahu were invited to meet Clinton for a couple of days at the Wye River Plantation in eastern Maryland. The plan was to resort to the Carter model of summit diplomacy. The president and his officers decided to play a direct role, even to the extent of full scale mediation, to bring the two parties to an agreement (Quandt 2001: 28).

However unlike Carter at Camp David, Clinton did not bother to remain at the negotiating site all the time. That was definitely not his style. After days of mutual recrimination and bickering, Clinton threw himself into the fray. He 'pulled an all-nighter', meaning he spent a whole night alternatively meeting each of the parties in the fray trying to get some sort of an agreement from them.

The result was the Wye River accord, signed on October 23, 1998 by Arafat and Netanyahu in the presence of Clinton and King Hussein of Jordan who had been quite literally plucked out of his deathbed to help in the process (Rhodes and Doherty 1998). [8] Clinton decided to repeat this process with Arafat and Barak. The only change he made was in the venue, choosing to go to Camp David with all its famous memories of another summit twenty years ago, when two bitter enemies had concluded a successful peace treaty. Clinton was evidently hoping to repeat Jimmy Carter's epoch making summit meeting at Camp David with Egypt's Anwar el-Sadat and the Israel's Menachem Begin in 1979.

Ehud Barak's Role in the Arab-Israeli Peace Process

Ehud Barak was elected prime minister of Israel in May 1999 on a platform of coming to peace with all of Israel's neighbours including the Palestinians (Sharrock and Hudson 1999). [9] He was immediately interested in a peace with the Syrians. But talks with the Syrians floundered over the conditions under which Israel was to withdraw from the Golan Heights (Perlez 2000). Barak then turned his attention to the Palestinians. It was Barak who signalled to Clinton his interest in a summit meeting with the PNA president Yasser Arafat (Morris 2002). [10]

His aim was to reach an agreement with Arafat by 13th September, 2000, which was the seventh anniversary of the Oslo Accords (Morris 2002). Clinton also was eager to seize upon this virtually last opportunity for him to make an impact on the Middle East peace process. Arafat, on the other land, was quite unwilling to appear for a summit meeting where he knew that he and his team would be forced to make compromises by the Israelis and the Americans. Arafat did not believe that the time was ripe for historic compromises, even for the sake of peace. The issues at stake were too vast and emotive for that. They involved the ambitions and aspirations of millions of Palestinian people, both resident and displaced refugees scattered around the world. In spite of his objections, Clinton and Barak decided to go ahead with the summit to be convened on 11th July, 2000, at the Camp David presidential retreat outside Washington (Cossali 2002: 43).

As per the Sharm el-Sheikh agreement of September 1999, Barak was committed to a phased 13 percent Israeli redeployment in the West Bank to be committed by January 2000 (Aronson 1999). Final status negotiations were scheduled to be completed by September 2000 (Aronson 1999). When it was decided to go ahead with the Camp David talks, all the revised Oslo deadlines were thrown into the dustbin. Barak also refused to carry out the redeployment that he had agreed to at Sharm el-Sheikh under the excuse that all these issues would be dealt with at the final status talks at Camp David (Bishara 2000). [11] Thus at the camp David summit, the Palestinians were forced to negotiate permanent status issues with only 42 percent of the 22 percent of historic Palestine that it was claiming, under its full or partial control. Also the PA had full control of only 18 percent of the 22 percent of the so-called area A. The remaining 24 percent was under joint control, constituting the so-called area B. In the pre-negotiation phase leading up to Camp David, the original Oslo understanding that withdrawal from the majority of the OTs during the five years transitional period (extended to seven years by the inaction of successive Israeli governments) was a prerequisite to final status negotiations, now became linked to major Palestinian concessions on final status issues (Hammami and Tamari 2001: 7).

In short, the Barak Government seemed out to kill two birds with one stone in the run up to the Camp David-II summit. One was the slow moving Oslo peace process based on a graduated process of incremental concessions by both sides. The second was the ability and power of the Palestinians to negotiate from a position of some strength having at least a majority of the land they were demanding. The Israelis from the very beginning seemed to have intended to impose the peace of the strong on the weak at Camp David. In this brute process, they had the full support of the Americans.

During the seven long years since the signing the Oslo Accords, the Palestinians had been forced to make innumerable concessions. They were witnessing the ongoing confiscation of Arab lands in the West Bank and Gaza. The existing Israeli settlements were being continuously expanded while new settlements were being established, contributing to the vivisection of Palestinian territory. The settler population had doubled in the last 10 years to over 200,000. The West Bank had been clearly divided into three distinct cantons by the Israelis, disconnected from each other by Jewish settlements.

Gaza was home to 6000 settlers occupying 40 percent of the territory, while the remaining 60 percent was populated by over 1.1 million Palestinians. Bypass roads built for use by the settlers alone, again served to further truncate Palestinian areas. The 'closure' policy in the West Bank and Gaza has become on institutionalized fact, thereby restricting the movement of the Palestinians and locking them into enclaves, besides totally destroying the economy. Again, the establishment of literally hundreds of police barricades and army checkpoints throughout the West Bank and the Gaza strip was a deliberate policy to further restrict and control the movement of the Palestinian people. In the creation of all these policies, Israel also indirectly relied on the Palestinian Authority (PA) and its huge 40,000 men strong security department to maintain control of the population and literally act to provide protection for Israel actions (Roy 2000: 14).

Given all these 'facts on the ground,' as the Israeli right was so proud of stating, the establishment of an adequately sovereign, resourced state in July 2000 was practically impossible. At Camp David, for the first time since the Oslo process began, the Palestinians refused to make any further concessions. The Palestinians had always made a stern distinction between the concessions they were forced to make during Oslo's transitional phase and the positions they would take on negotiating the 'final status' issues with the Israelis. Evidently the Israelis and Americans believed that the 'final status' talks would also witness heavy concessions by the Palestinians.

Palestinian negotiating positions at the start of the Camp David-II Summit were geared towards satisfying a people that had been tormented by any lack of progress in their liberation, years after the so-called Palestinian 'autonomy' had been established. In the popular perception, Palestinians had entered the peace process on the understanding that,

1. It would bring about concrete improvement in their lives during the interim period,

2. The interim period would be relatively short in duration, i.e., five years, and
3. That a permanent agreement would implement UN resolutions 242 and 338 relating to the return of the refugees and the establishment of a secure state (Hanieh 2001: 94). [12]

The peace process, as we have seen, did not deliver any of these things. On the contrary just before entering into the Camp David process, Israeli Prime Minister Ehud Barak publicly and repeatedly threatened the Palestinians that his 'offer' on the final status issues would be Israel's best and final offer. If not accepted, he said that Israel would seriously consider 'unilateral separation' by which he meant that Israel would forcefully impose a settlement rather than negotiate one (PLO-NAD 2000). [13]

Final Status Issues on Jerusalem

The stand of both the Israelis and the Palestinians on Jerusalem was radically different. Thus, the Israeli proposal at Camp David virtually required the Palestinians to give up any claim to the occupied portion of Jerusalem. The aim was to get Palestinian recognition of Israel's annexation of all of Arab East Jerusalem. In short, Israel wanted to annex the main settlements in and around East Jerusalem and would expand the greater Jerusalem area as far south as Gush Etzion near Hebron. They were prepared to grant full Palestinian sovereignty to the outlying Arab suburbs of East Jerusalem while the Arab neighbourhoods immediately outside the Old City would get on 'expanded form of autonomy'. The walled city of Jerusalem would remain firmly under Jewish sovereignty with the Muslim and Christian holy sites as well as the Arab neighbourhoods inside the Old City coming under the 'expanded form of autonomy' scheme. Metropolitan Jerusalem would again be divided into an Arab and an Israeli municipality within one open city with no borders or checkpoints marking the ethnic boundaries (Hammami and Tamari 2001: 6).

The Palestinian reply to this Israeli formulation was clear and forthright. Arafat declared that he would not be the first Palestinian leader to surrender Jerusalem (Hanieh 2001: 85). He also stated that Jerusalem was equally sacred to the Palestinians, both Christian and Muslim. For them, East Jerusalem including the walled city and the Arab districts must form the capital of their new state of Palestine. As part of the territory occupied in 1967, East Jerusalem in the Palestinian perspective was subject to UNSC resolution 242 (inadmissibility of territory acquired by force or war). [14] The Israelis and the Palestinians agreed on one point that Jerusalem should be an open city and that there should be free movement of people within the city. The future state of Palestine would be committed to maintaining the sanctity and dignity of the religious sites in the Old City that made Jerusalem so important. Freedom of worship and access would be guaranteed. [15]

At Camp David, the Israelis and Americans come up with a new proposal regarding the Haram al-Sharif (Temple Mount) which was the site of the Al-Aqsa mosque as well as that of the Jewish Temple, destroyed during Roman times. It was known as 'vertically divided' sovereignty in which the Muslims would control the ground level and the Israelis would control the area below the surface (Morris 2002). This proposal was striking given that no previous Israeli administration had ever advanced such a notion.

Settlements and Borders

These constitute a major point of disagreement between the Israelis and the Palestinians. Settlements had been built in the OTs since 1967 and now many extended right through the West Bank and Gaza. The Israelis wanted to annex three main settlement blocs (Ariel, Etzion and Ma'ale Adumim) which together had a combined population of some 250,000 settlers (Morris 2002).

The Palestinians were against this as around 80,000 to 100,000 Arabs in these areas would effectively become part of

Israel and would be disenfranchised. Such an arrangement would bring about the complete encirclement of East Jerusalem by Jewish settlements, sealing off the city from its Palestinian hinterland. It would also contribute towards effectively splitting the West Bank into two. They demanded the total withdrawal of all settlements in the West Bank and Gaza and the full restoration of the pre-1967 borders (Morris 2002). At Camp David, the Israelis were talking about annexing 10-13 percent of the West Bank (Morris 2002). They had no equal land swaps to offer to the Palestinians. In addition, the Israelis were interested in annexing West Bank land in such a way that all water resources would be under their control (Morris 2002).

As far as the Palestinians were concerned, accepting the January 4, 1967 borders itself constituted a major compromise on their earlier demand of all of historic Palestine (Morris 2002). They were not willing to accept the further cutting up of this territory, effectively rendering their claim to statehood null and void. In addition, the Palestinians opposed all Israeli demands for maintaining military infrastructure consisting of bases, troops and early warning stations and border posts along the Jordan River and in Gaza. A future Palestinian state was perceived by the Israelis to be essentially demilitarized with just lightly armed police forces (Hammami and Tamari 2001: 9). The Palestinians based their arguments on the promise that security relations between the future state of Palestine and Israel should be structured to reflect also the rights and interests of the Palestinian people.

Refugees

The refugee problem was a highly controversial issue for both sides. The Israelis were not even willing to acknowledge the issue. They saw the problem as not created by them. Instead they blamed the Arabs themselves, particularly the neighbouring Arab states for creating this issue. The Israelis were 100 percent against the return of the former Arab residents of Israel. This was perceived as a threat to the Jewish character of the state of Israel. In addition, they were also not willing to provide compensation to the refugees who were staying in miserable camps in the surrounding countries as well as in the West Bank and Gaza. The Israelis always linked any question of compensation to similar demands that the Jews that migrated from Arab states after the formation of the state of Israel be compensated.

For the Palestinians, the refugee issue was the primary issue. Without at least a symbolic acceptance by the Israelis that the refugees can return, a mutually acceptable compromise would be very difficult from their perspective. The Palestinian position on refugees was based on UN General Assembly resolution 194 (1948) that called for the return of the refugees and their compensation (Abbas 2001: 169). [16]

Camp David-II Venue and Conditions

Clinton's choice of Camp David as the venue for the peace talks between the Israelis was quite symbolic. Located over 50 hectares of forest land in the hills of West Maryland, Camp David had been a summer retreat for US presidents since 1942. It was at a distance of just 70 miles from the White House. Camp David had played host to many historical international meetings. During World War II, British Prime Minister Winston Churchill and US president Franklin D. Roosevelt planned the allied invasion of Europe while staying here. [17] In 1978, President Jimmy Carter chose Camp David for the meeting of two Middle East foes, Egyptian President Anwar el-Sadat and Israeli Prime Minister Menachem Begin. Within six months of this meeting, the first Arab-Israeli peace treaty was signed. [18]

Clinton evidently believed that the tranquil and peaceful surroundings of Camp David would help both parties arrive at a deal over the fateful issues concerning them. Towards this aim, the Americans took a number of steps to isolate the delegates that arrived to take part in the summit. They also wanted to ensure that all meetings took place in a friendly and informal manner. All delegates, upon their arrival, were assigned to cabins scattered around the thickly wooded retreat. The Americans expected nobody to wear suits and ties, but only formal clothing. The Americans seemed to have assumed that the absence of formalities would break down barriers between the two sides. Meals were generally taken together, allowing the delegations to mingle and chat informally. Even the negotiators leisure time was utilized to provide opportunities for informal meetings. The Americans hosts also attempted to build social relations between the negotiators. Secretary of State Madeleine Albright once invited delegates to a movie and on another occasion, the two sides were invited to play a basketball game (Hanieh 2001: 77).

Another main condition of the summit was to impose a near total media blackout to ensure the secrecy of the negotiations. There was only one telephone for each delegation and external calls were rarely transferred to the delegations. Telephones in cabins other than those of the leaders were for internal use only. The only official source of information was a White House spokesman and sometimes a State Department spokesman who held daily press conferences at a press centre some thirty minutes from Camp David. Palestinian and Israeli legal advisers and experts were not allowed to stay with the official delegations. A restricted number of them were permitted to travel daily to Camp David to meet their respective delegations for a specified amount of time.

The work format at the summit was quite interesting. There were full committee meetings, meetings consisting of two negotiators from each side, and meetings between Secretary of State Albright and each delegation on specific topics. The Americans also utilized informal contacts between members of their own peace team and delegates of both sides to explore positions on specific issues and try to bring about an agreement. They seemed confident that all the above conditions would create strong pressure on the negotiators to succeed in reaching an agreement. They just did not seem to realize that the reality of the conflict going on in the Israel/Palestine region was much more potent than the unreal world that they had created at Camp David (Hanieh 2001: 78).

Camp David II Summit: Proceedings on a day-to-day Basis

Israeli and Palestinian leaders began their summit at Camp David on Tuesday, July 11, 2000. The first day was given over to opening formalities with President Clinton as the host dominating the proceedings. Clinton, who was seeing visions of a Camp David-1978 repeat, ushered the leaders into the Presidential retreat. He certainly hoped that the chemistry of the place would induce a spirit of 'principled compromise' that would yield a substantive peace agreement. Mr. Clinton's speech on the occasion was couched in idealistic terms about securing a 'just and enduring end' to the conflict and about the 'gift of peace' that the leaders could give their children. Clinton tempered his speech by acknowledging that there was no guarantee of success. He however emphasized the point that 'not to try is to guarantee failure'. Officials on all sides acknowledged that a good partial agreement would represent a significant accomplishment and could in all probability mark the only realistic end to this rapidly scheduled summit meeting (Sontag 2000). [19]

Both Barak and Arafat had given strong indications of the highly principled and determined stand that each intended to follow at Maryland. Barak himself had come to the summit emphasizing his oft-repeated four red lines beyond which he was not prepared to budge. Another statement that he found himself constantly repeating was that 'it takes two to tango'. (*JPS* Fall 2003: 85). He was implying that without further Palestinian concessions, it would not be possible for the Israelis to conclude a peace agreement with the Palestinian Authority (PA). The negotiating table prepared by the Americans in the inaugural day of the summit was a rectangular one around which 21 American, Israeli and

Palestinian delegates sat to open the talks (*JPS* 2003: 85).

At the end of the day, all that the White House spokesman would say was that 'the atmosphere was good and the mood was serious (Lockhart 2000)'. [20] This was because both the principal actors in this drama (in addition to President Clinton), were under tremendous stress from their domestic constituencies to prevent a possible sell-out deal that would harm either side. At the press conference just prior to the start of the summit, both gave contrasting opinions of the projected summit that were intended as messages to placate their respective political constituencies. Thus, Shlomo Ben-Ami, the Israeli internal security minister, said on Monday that he felt confident that an agreement could be reached. In direct contrast, Abu Ala,' Speaker of the Palestinian legislature, said that he did not comprehend how Mr. Ben Ami could speak with such confidence. In an interview with the Voice of Palestine radio, Abu Ala' commented that 'the Palestinian position will never change. And the Israeli position has its well known "no's". So how can the minister talk about an agreement?' (Sontag 2000). [21]

The special nature of the Camp David summit was that it was expected to put all the highly controversial issues in the Israel-Palestine conflict on the negotiating table. Thus, the future borders of the Israeli and 'projected' Palestinian states, Jewish settlement in the West Bank, form of Palestinian statehood, water, the fate of the Palestinian refugees and the future status of Jerusalem were all to be discussed at the talks. It would be the first time in seven years that Jerusalem, a seemingly irresolvable point of contention .would be on the table, since the Israelis and Palestinians began talking publicly to each other.

Clinton was prepared to allow the two leaders to talk to each other for the first few days before engaging in any direct mediation. So he did not offer any specific proposals for the first few days, hoping instead to spend the first sessions airing all the issues. Administration officials stated that they expected the really important days for negotiations to be one week after the start of the talks, just before Clinton's scheduled departure for Okinawa to attend a summit meeting of the G-8 industrialised nations (Sontag 2000).

After two days of concentrated summiteering, Clinton on Thursday took a break by relinquishing authority to his Secretary of State, Madeleine Albright. The Americans continued to persist with their steadfast refusal to discuss the substance of the talks. Joe Lockhart, Clinton's chief spokesman, described Wednesday's meeting 'as a busy day between all parties, a day of engagement without any claim of progress'. Without any claim of progress, Lockhart warned against drawing any conclusions as to whether gaps were being narrowed in the talks. Without elaborating, the spokesman said that the two sides had been concentrating on core issues. Lockhart stressed that he did not expect any loss of momentum due to Clinton's absence from Thursday's deliberations, pointing out that Albright had already held talks with both leaders and presided at meetings of delegates from both sides (*Newstime* 2000). [22]

The Palestinians seemed to resent the enforced isolation more than the Israelis. Palestinian sources stated that Arafat wanted to hold a 'leadership meeting' with Palestinian officials who were not part of his delegation at Camp David. The rules of engagement laid down by the US State Department at the summit stated that each side could be permitted to bring in technical experts and lawyers as needed. Mr. Lockhart meanwhile stated that he knew of no planned arrivals at Camp David being cleared by security (*Newstime* 2000).

Meanwhile in a bid to inject more momentum and urgency into the summit, President Clinton delayed his departure to Japan to attend the G-8 summit, by a day (*Newstime* 2000). Apparently the main sticking point at the moment was the status of Jerusalem. According to an agency report, Barak apparently told Arafat that Israel would not recognize a

Palestinian state unless the Palestinians acknowledged total Israeli sovereignty over Jerusalem (*Newstime* 2000).

Arafat, on the other hand, threatened to unilaterally declare a Palestinian state by September 13 (Borger 2000). [23] He insisted on Arab East Jerusalem being the capital of the new Palestinian state. The Palestinians were however willing to cede to the Israelis, the Jewish Quarter and the Western Wall in the Old City of Jerusalem (Borger 2000).

By postponing his trip to Japan by a day, Washington was driving home both the seriousness and importance of the talks. Clinton, himself, referred to the ongoing process as the 'hardest ever' talks he had been involved in the last seven years of his Presidency (Krishnaswami 2000). [24] Eventually he was aiming to wrap up the outline of a final peace agreement before leaving for Japan. The round-the-clock negotiations had entered 'critical' stage on the seventh day of the summit at Camp David with Clinton almost continually involved in dialogue with Israel premier Ehud Barak and Palestine leader Yasser Arafat (Borger 2000). [25]

Meanwhile Speaker of the Israeli parliament, Avraham Burg told Israeli radio that Barak had told him that he was 'not really optimistic' about the summit's chance of success. (Borger 2000). The White House spokesman meanwhile commented that 'the peace and intensity of negotiations between Israel and the Palestinians have been stepped up in a bid to secure a West Asia peace agreement at Camp David by the Wednesday deadline' (*Newstime* 2000). Joe Lockhart added that 'there have been two straight very long nights between the sides working through the difficult issues here. There are a number of negotiators who have been awake for a long time over the last two or three days' (*Newstime* 2000). Clinton and his team seemed to be trying the famous 'Wye river technique' in which the delegates would be compelled to sign on the dotted line out of sheer tiredness and exhaustion. But Barak and Arafat proved to be more resistant than Netanyahu and Arafat in 1998.

For all practical purposes, the summit had failed by the time Clinton had to leave for Japan for the G-8 summit on the island of Okinawa (*Newstime* 2000). Before leaving, he persuaded the two leaders to stay on at Camp David. The US Secretary of State, Madeleine Albright deputized for him (Hanieh 2001: 91). [26] The last-ditch effort to save the talks began only after Clinton returned home. He immediately entered into intensive discussions with all the parties concerned. But the gaps between their positions was really too wide to be successfully or even partially filled. At this stage, Clinton even made proposals of his own to bridge the gap between Barak and Arafat (Hanieh 2001: 87). He even joined second-rank negotiations for an all-night session in the hope of formulating proposals that the two leaders might then consider. But that was not to be. The talks had to be abandoned after 14 long and strenuous days. Despite this, both the leaders, the Israeli Prime Minister Ehud Barak and the Palestinian Authority President Yasser Arafat, promised to work towards a negotiated settlement and to avoid violence (Agha 2000). [27]

It was not possible for either side to bridge the gap on core issues, none of which they had earlier discussed, in just 15 days. Also all the issues under discussions at Camp David were highly emotive and had the potential to trigger violence. The two leaders could not make any gains towards that purpose.

Camp David-II Summit Failure

Ehud Barak blamed Arafat for the collapse of the peace talks and Arafat declared that he could not be forced to make any further compromises (Sontag 2001). [28] He said that what the Palestinians were asking was only 22 percent of the historic Palestine that existed till 1948 (Shamir n.d.). [29] Arafat's refusal to sign a peace deal and bow to the US-Israeli pressure was considered a Palestinian victory in the West Bank and Gaza and other parts of the Arab/Muslim world (Bahaa 2000). [30] Thus, the Camp David outcome enhanced Arafat's prestige in the entire Arab World. Arafat had been under pressure from the entire Islamic Ummah not to cave in on the issue of Jerusalem, home of Al-Aqsa, Islam's third holiest site (Mubarak 2000). [31]

It would have been politically suicidal for him to have compromised on Jerusalem, home to over 200,000 Palestinians (Mubarak 2000). UN Partition Resolution 181 (II) of 1947 had granted special international status for the Holy city of Jerusalem to 'protect the interests' of the Jewish, Christian and Muslim communities. [32] After the creation of Israel in 1948, it occupied West Jerusalem. East Jerusalem remained with the Arabs till the 1967 war. Arafat was not prepared to sign a partial accord which did not give him full sovereignty over East Jerusalem, which was envisaged as the capital of the future Palestinian state (Agha 2000).

Another contentious issue between Israel and the Palestinians on which Barak and Arafat could not make much progress was the question of the 3.6 million United Nations registered Palestinian refugees scattered throughout the Middle East. The Palestinians wanted Israel to recognize UNGA Resolution 194 which demanded for the refugees the right of return to their homes in Palestine and Israel proper. [33] Israel maintained that it would neither grant them the right to return, nor accept moral responsibility for them. Barak stated that he was willing to accommodate 100,000 Palestinians back in Israel under a programme of 'family reunification' (Agha 2000). Israel also favoured an international fund to rehabilitate refugees in the countries they occupy now (Agha 2000).

The issue of Jewish settlements in the Occupied Territories also remained unsettled at Camp David. There were over 200,000 Jewish settlers in the West Bank and Gaza in 2000. The Israelis were not interested in pulling back the settlements. On the other hand, they were behaving as if the settlements were there to stay finally and for all time. The Palestinians were demanding the opposite. They insisted that under UNSC resolution 242, they had the right to all the Arab territory occupied by Israel in 1967. [34] The Palestinians rightly argued that Israel maintaining its sovereignty over the settlement blocs scattered all over the territories would rob them of a state of geographical continuity.

Sharing of water and delineating the borders of the future Palestinian state were two of the other core issues that came up for discussion at Camp David. On borders, Israel demanded control over Palestinian borders with Jordan and Egypt. Israel also asked to control 15-20 percent of the Jordan River and a sector of the Jordan Valley. This was in addition to a proposed annexation of around 10.5 percent of the West Bank to absorb the settlements. The Palestinians rejected any such moves. Minor borders changes and an exchange of lands equal in quantity and quality that did not exceed 2 percent was acceptable to them (Mazen 2001: 168-169).

There were thus too many contentious issues to be discussed and resolved in too short a period of time. The negotiators found themselves dealing with extraordinary difficult issues that required a great deal of discussion and compromise. Ultimately they were not up to the mark. The failure of the Camp David-II summit must also be linked to the failure of the Oslo approach to Middle East peacemaking. The Oslo process was based on the premise that the way to peace was one step at a time. It was assumed that the experience of working together on each succeeding stage of agreement would create better chances for the next stage. The holistic successful culmination of this experiment was the hypothesis that by the time the two sides reached the hardest issues at the end, these would no longer be so hard after all (Lewis 2000: 6). [35]

The negotiators at Camp David-II from both sides of the spectrum have maintained that if the hard issues like Jerusalem had been active topics of discussions during the last seven years and not suddenly brought up as a serious topic on the penultimate day of the summit, the chances of a successful settlement would have been such higher. The understanding at Camp David that nothing was final until everything was agreed ensured that no agreement was reached on anything. In actuality however, the conditional compromise positions that were considered and accepted at Camp David-II on many of the controversial issues ensured the prospect of a continuation of the dialogue process and a benchmark for negotiators whenever talks resumed (Quandt 2001: 26-28).

Clinton's Role at the Camp David II Summit

Did President Clinton play an important role at the Camp David-II summit, other than his natural role as the host, embellished with the theatrics that are a part and parcel of his nature? Or was he following Henry Kissinger's advice to 'stay calm and just be available as a facilitator. And I would tell him not to be more interested than the parties themselves' (Quandt 2001: 30). Clinton had been exploring the possibility of a three-way summit in early June when he met Arafat at the White House. Arafat intimated that he was not interested, but Barak seemed to be, given the fact that his coalition government seemed about to collapse, paving the way either for a national unity government or new elections (Franklin 2000). [36] All accounts of the proceedings at the Camp David-II summit have agreed on one respect, that Clinton's own role there was surprisingly strong (Hanieh 2001: 78-79). Both parties to the conflict, namely the Israelis and the Palestinians had a large degree of confidence in him. For the Israelis, this was natural, given Clinton's traditional affinity for the Jews and the Jewish State.

As far as the Palestinians were concerned, Clinton had been the only American President to date to show any genuine concern for their fate. His visit to the territories in 1998 had been the first ever by a sitting American President (*CNN* 1998). [37] His address to the Palestinian National Council (PNC) during that visit helped him to gain many friends among the Palestinians (Clinton 2000). [38] Moreover Clinton developed a personal relationship with Arafat since their first meeting in 1993 during the signing of the Oslo Accords

(Friedman 1993). [39] The Netanyahu interlude helped Clinton to draw much closer to the Palestinians than would ever have been possible given the normally close ties between Israel and the US.

Most important of all, Clinton remained hugely popular at home, which, given the fact that he was technically a lame-duck President at the far end of his career, was a huge plus point. He was able to handle the all-powerful Jewish lobby in Washington that was keeping an eagle's eye on the proceedings. In fact, Clinton could count on bipartisan support short of pressuring Israel on sensitive issues or asking Congress for a large aid package (Quandt 2001: 31). Given Clinton's history, he had avoided taking stands on many of the most controversial issues, urging the two opposing parties to reach compromises themselves. The two delegations went to Camp David sure in the belief that Clinton could be relied on to preserve the 'peace'.

F.D. Roosevelt once said that 'the President of thc United States should also be the best actor in the country'. All Clinton's acting skills were early visible at Camp David. However, from the beginning it was clear that the American President was determined to succeed and that he had done his homework. At the inaugural session itself, Clinton emphasized his determination to work intensively. Interestingly and perhaps amusingly, the American president started to apply pressure on the participants from the very beginning itself. He tried in his opening speech to create a link between Camp David and the G-8 summit in Okinawa that he would be soon attending; promising huge financial support from the G-8 for any agreement the two sides would reach. Evidently the 'carrot and stick' policy would also be used at Camp David.

A Palestinian negotiator who was present at Camp David has described Clinton's personality in the following words: Watching him (Clinton) in action, one also sees a man who is very intelligent, hardworking, persistent, and endowed with a strong memory and overwhelming charisma. Besides all this there is also a broad cultural background, numerous human interests, and a driving interest in a range of issues. He is also good at breaking barriers (cultural). He would carry his own tray at Camp David village's Laurel restaurant, serve himself from the buffet, and sit-as he twice did-with members of the Palestinian delegation having dinner on the balcony. He would easily initiate conversations...(Hanieh 2001: 78).

As far as the Palestinians were concerned, they saw in Clinton a person who could listen and understand. In spite of the wholly pro-Israeli bias of the US Middle East team, they were banking on Clinton's 'objectivity' and 'neutrality' to make Camp David succeed. Unfortunately they were soon to be terribly disappointed.

Talks opened at Camp David on July 11, 2000 and continued for 15 days. These fifteen days were characterized by exhaustive negotiations, brinksmanship and a virtual news blackout. Ultimately however all ended in vain as the summit broke up in acrimony, with the Israelis and the Palestinians accusing each other about who was responsible for the failure. The Americans, supposed to be the hosts and impartial mediators clearly showed who they were partial to, by openly supporting the Israelis. After the end of the summit, President Clinton made it quite clear in numerous interviews and speeches that he believed Israeli Prime Minister Ehud Barak to have been more flexible in the negotiations, and that Chairman Arafat bore the greater responsibility for the collapse of the summit (Baumgarten 2004: 31). [40] Significantly all parties in the process stated that permanent status talks had been adjourned rather than ended.

The collapse of the Camp David-II summit process can be attributed to three factors:

1. The inability of the American mediators, including President Clinton to understand the depth of feelings of the Palestinian side about the issues at stake.
2. Circumstances were not ripe and the Palestinian people or their negotiators, including Chairman Arafat, were not

willing or capable to make any 'historic compromises' for the sake of peace.

3. The Israeli side came to Camp David in a 'Versailles' frame of mind, ready to impose the peace of the victors on the vanquished. They did not make any preparations to modify either their views or that of the Israeli public regarding any far-reaching compromises that could be made for the sake of peace (Baumgarten 2004: 16-17).

Ultimately only Arafat made any measure of gain out of the Camp David-II meeting. He was warmly commended both in the Arab and Muslim world and among his own people for having resisted US and Israeli pressure to conclude a 'dishonourable peace' (Cossali 2002: 13). Clinton soon had to vacate his post at the end of his second term and Barak was soundly defeated in the Israeli general elections paving the way for the rise of Israel's greatest hardliner, Gen. Ariel Sharon, as the new Prime Minister of Israel. All peace moves were conclusively at an end.

Endnotes

1. Details regarding the four security red lines of Ehud Barak can be accessed from the *Information Regarding Israel's Security* (IRIS) article 'Ehud Barak's Vanishing Red Line,' available at, http://www.iris.org.il/red_lines.htm.
2. David Weinberg, 'Arafat Has Us on the Run', *The Jerusalem Post*, July 9, 2000. This article can be partly accessed through the *Information Regarding Israel's Security* (IRIS) website article 'Ehud Barak's Vanishing Red Line,' available at, http://www.iris.org.il/red_lines.htm.
3. Available at, http://users.ox.ac.uk/~ssfc0005%20/The%20Rise%20and%20Fall%20of%20the%20Oslo%20Peace%20Process.html.
4. Available at, http://www.thejerusalemfund.org/www.thejerusalemfund.org/carryover/pubs/19991014ib.html.
5. Thomas L. Friedman, 'Middle East leaders running out of time,' *The Baltimore Sun*, April 25, 2002. Available at, http://articles.baltimoresun.com/2002-04-

25/news/0204250090_1_saudi-arabia-crown-prince-abdullah-sharon.

6. William B. Reinckens, 'Israel And Syria Open Peace Talks In Shepherdstown, West Virginia (Secretary Albright says there is "no done deal")', *Washington File*, United States Embassy Press Section, Tel Aviv, Israel, January 3, 2000. Available at, http://www.usembassy-israel.org.il/publish/peace/archives/2000/january/me0103c.html.
7. Jane Perlez, 'Clinton's Effort Fails To Get Syria To Resume Talks', *The New York Times*, March 27, 2000. Available at, http://www.nytimes.com/2000/03/27/world/clinton-s-effort-fails-to-get-syria-to-resume-talks.html?pagewanted=all&src=pm.
8. Chet Rhodes and Jude Doherty, 'The Wye River Accord for Mideast Peace', *The Washington Post*, Friday, October 23, 1998. Available at, http://www.washingtonpost.com/wp-srv/inatl/longterm/me_peace/me_voices.htm.
9. David Sharrock and David Hudson, 'Peace First, Barak Tells MPs as he Unveils Dovish Cabinet', *The Guardian* (London), Wednesday, July 7, 1999. Available at, http://www.theguardian.com/world/1999/jul/07/israel.
10. Available at, http://www.nybooks.com/articles/archives/2002/jun/13/camp-david-and-after-an-exchange-1-an-interview-wi/
11. Available at, http://www.thejerusalemfund.org/www.thejerusalemfund.org/carryover/pubs/20000920ib.html.
12. Available at, http://www.jstor.org/stable/10.1525/jps.2001.30.2.75.
13. Available at, http://www.nad-plo.org/etemplate.php?id=156.
14. Refer Document III in the Appendices.
15. Ibid.
16. Refer Document II in Appendices.
17. Available at, http://www.whitehouse.gov/about/camp-david.
18. Refer Document III in Appendices.
19. Deborah Sontag, 'Israel, Palestine Summit under way,' *Deccan Herald* (Bangalore), July 13, 2000.

20. Available at, http://www.usembassy-israel.org.il/publish/peace/archives/2000/july/me0717c.html.
21. Deborah Sontag, 'Israel, Palestine Summit under way'.
22. 'Albright Takes Over the Reins of West Asia Summit,' *Newstime* (Hyderabad), July 14, 2000. Available at, http://www.aparchive.com/metadata/usa-albright-replaces-clinton-at-camp-david-talks.
23. Julian Borger, 'Camp David Negotiators Burn Midnight Oil; Special Report: Israel and the Middle East,' *The Guardian*, Wednesday, July 19, 2000. Available at, http://www.theguardian.com/world/2000/jul/19/israel/print.
24. Sridhar Krishnaswami, 'Clinton Delays Japan Trip', *The Hindu* (Madras), July 20, 2000. Available at, http://hindu.com/2000/07/20/stories/03200009.htm.
25. Julian Borger, 'Camp David Negotiators Burn Midnight Oil; Special Report: Israel and the Middle East'.
26. Available at www.palestine-studies.com/files/pdf/jps/2759.pdf.
27. Qamar Agha, 'Peace in West Asia,' *The Hindu*, August 10, 2000. Available at, http://www.hindu.com/2000/08/10/stories/05102524.htm.
28. Deborah Sontag, 'And Yet So Far: A Special Report; Quest for Mideast Peace: How and Why It Failed', *The New York Times*, July 26, 2001. Available at, http://www.nytimes.com/2001/07/26/world/and-yet-so-far-a-special-report-quest-for-mideast-peace-how-and-why-it-failed.html?pagewanted=all&src=pm.
29. Shimon Shamir, 'The Enigma of Camp David'. Available at, http://tau.ac.il/institutes/diplomacy/TheEnigmaOfCampDavid.doc.
30. Sherine Bahaa, 'No Deal is a Good Deal,' *Al-Ahram Weekly* (Cairo), August 3-9, 2000, Issue No. 493. Available at, http://weekly.ahram.org.eg/2000/493/re1.htm.
31. 'Mubarak: Jerusalem Compromise Will Lead to Violence,' *ABC News (abcnews.go.com)*, Cairo, Egypt, August 12, 2000. Available at, http://abcnews.go.com/International/print?id=82907.
32. Refer Document I in Appendices.
33. Refer Document II in Appendices.
34. Refer Document III in the Appendices.

35. Flora Lewis, 'Danger mounts, but the Mid East Time Isn't Ripe', *International Herald Tribune* (Bangkok), August 1, 2000, 6.
36. Stephen Franklin, 'Israeli Political Crisis Deepens For Barak', *The Chicago Tribune*, August 3, 2000. Available at, http://articles.chicagotribune.com/2000-08-03/news/0008030409_1_prime-minister-ehud-barak-new-elections-knesset.
37. 'Palestinians Affirm Israel's Right to Exist; US, Palestinians, Israelis to Hold Summit,' *CNN.com*, December 14, 1998. Available at, http://edition.cnn.com/WORLD/meast/9812/14/clinton.gaza.03.
38. Archived at the United States Embassy in Israel (Tel Aviv) Section at, http://www.usembassy-israel.org.il/publish/peace/archives/2000/august/me0811b.html.
39. Thomas L. Friedman, 'Rabin and Arafat Seal Their Accord as Clinton Applauds Brave Gamble', Old Warriors Now Face Task of Building Upon Foundation, *The New York Times*, Washington DC, September 13, 1993. Available at, http://www.nytimes.com/learning/general/onthisday/big/0913.html.
40. Available at, http://ialiis.birzeit.edu/fmru/eprintnews.php?id=115.

5

Camp David-II Dilemma

Moonis Ahmar has opined that: A peace process is a mechanism or a set of negotiations where the parties involved attempt to avoid war or a war-like situation and wish to settle conflicts peacefully by using techniques such as diplomacy, bargaining, secret negotiations, open negotiation, trade-offs and mediation (Ahmar 2001: 19).

Again Harold Saunders has written that: The peace process is more than conventional diplomacy and negotiation. It encompasses a full range of political, psychological, economic, diplomatic, and military actions woven together into a comprehensive effort to establish peace between Israel and its neighbours. Progress towards peace depends on breaking down the barriers to negotiation and reconciliation-the other walls. If we ignore the politics of breaking down these barriers, the mediator and negotiator may never have a chance (Saunders 1991: 3).

And C. F. Joel Peters writes that: The peace process has been framed primarily on the political issues that lie at the heart of the Arab-Israeli conflict, namely territorial withdrawal, border demarcation, security arrangements, and the political rights of the Palestinians. The architects of the peace process, which opened with the Madrid conferences of October 1991, recognized the need to address simultaneously the economic, social, and environmental problems which cut across national boundaries. To this end, they created a set of multilateral talks to run in parallel with the bilateral negotiations. The aim was to bring together Israel, its immediate Arab neighbours, the Gulf Arab states and the Maghreb to discuss issues of regional concern within a framework for dealing with the issues of mutual interests which might also serve as confidence-building measures and facilitate progress at the bilateral level (Peters 1960: 2).

The Arab-Israeli peace process has seen many ups and downs since the 1973 Geneva conference and the 1991 Madrid Conference. However, it was the two Camp David Summits that focused full attention on the role of the US in the Arab-Israeli peace process. America was now the only power with sufficient leverage on both sides to have a say in the final solution. The role of the American government and bureaucracy in the Arab-Israeli peace process has always been a controversial one. Generally, the US Congress has always taken a pro-Israeli stand. This phenomenon has always forced US administrators to be sensitive to the possibility of adverse Congressional reactions if it seeks to pressure Israel (Quandt 1986: 7).

US Presidency and Arab-Israeli Relations

Even a strong American President can find difficulty in dealing successfully with a Congress opposed to his views. In any crisis situation, he can appeal to the American public for support. The main power of Congress lies in its control of the federal budget. For example, US Congress must approve aid levels to Egypt and Israel. As a result of U.S. commitments to Israel and post-1979 (Camp David) obligations to Egypt, this aid programme had a net value of over 6-7 billon dollars annually (Quandt 1986: 7).

When confronting issues of vital national interest, narrow domestic political considerations often lose much of their usual importance in decision-making. The President can be assured of bipartisan support in Congress during such crises, especially if the issue involves friends and allies of the US like Israel. However, if the crisis drags on for too long and especially if there is a military casualty dimension also, the President's room for manoeuvre will be drastically reduced. The standard case is Vietnam. In the Middle East, America's Lebanon policy has always suffered from this syndrome. In such circumstances, in addition to popular demand, Congress itself will take the lead in pressing for rapid disengagement

(Hyland 1999: 138).

A US President will feel more ready to try new initiatives in the first year of his first term than he will in his fourth year. By his late second or early third year in office, a President will generally want to limit the effects of any partisan approach he is following on a foreign policy issue. This scheme of action has been visible in the Arab-Israeli context with successive Presidents from John. F. Kennedy following this pattern. Recently, this phenomenon was visible during the tenure of Bill Clinton. Clinton was by all accounts the most pro-Israeli US President ever, but even he felt the need to tilt towards the Palestinian side. He was compelled to follow this policy during the hardliner *Liqud* government of Benjamin Netanyahu. Taken in this context, both the Camp David summits on the Middle East were similar. Both were held towards the end of Presidential tenures. Unfortunately for Carter, his first tenure of service was also his last.

The first Camp David summit held in 1978 was in the second year of the Carter Presidency. The success of this peace summit between Egypt and Israel was over shadowed by the failure of the Carter administration in dealing with the revolution in Iran and the subsequent hostage crisis. Carter thus lost his bid for re-election in 1979. The second Camp David Summit involving the leaders of the newly formed Palestinian Authority and Israel took place twenty years later in the last year of the Clinton Presidency. The main issue at stake for President Clinton here was the legacy he hoped to leave as the 'peace-maker' President of the USA.

The Jewish lobby in New York and Washington was another factor that all American Presidents had to actively consider and contend with. Some of American's most powerful non-governmental organizations and lobbying interest groups are Jewish-controlled. Active Jewish and pro-Israeli lobbing groups include the AIPAC (America-Israel Public Affairs Committee) and the Anti-Defamation League (ADL). Coupled with this is the major stake that American Jews have in the business, entertainment and media scene. Major newspapers like the New York Times and the Wall Street Journal are Jewish owned and are generally pro-Israel in their coverage of the Middle East. The over six million strong Jewish voters are very crucial in American elections. The swing between the two major political formations in the US was always decided by the minority vote, either Jewish, Latino or Afro-American.

In addition to all this, the massive financial clout that wealthy American Jews are willing to expend on election campaigns, make then very valuable participants in the American political process. 'Jewish power' is thus a very potent force in the US. All parties and their Presidential or congressional candidates seek to gain by adopting a pro-Israeli stand, especially when an election is around the corner (Uzer 2002: 127). Jewish lobbyists and pressure groups exert a lot of pressure on the government to support the state of Israel both politically and financially. US support for Israel was guaranteed in the UN. Massive yearly US military and economic aid to Israel was also guaranteed.

Corresponding Arab influence in American politics was very weak. Arab-Americans as a group were not powerful when compared to the Jews. Arab influence in US politics and foreign policy was primarily restricted to the Saudi Oil barons and their American collaborators. Arab-Israeli issues in American foreign policy consideration would be controversial because the stakes would be high and public interest would be equally high. Presidential involvements at the highest level were generally required in the resolution of these issues. In a cyclic process, Presidential involvement ensures that political considerations deeply influence the conduct of American Middle East policy. In short, American involvement in the Middle East (particularly in issues involving Israel) cannot be separated from domestic political considerations (Uzer 2002: 136). All the above factors must be taken into consideration when trying to analyse the Camp David-II summit.

Ultimately, it was Palestinian Authority President Yasser

Arafat who made the most gain from the summit meeting. He was able to resist the combined pressure of both the US President and the Israeli prime minister to surrender to an unjust peace, by standing firm at Camp David. The compromises agreed to by the Palestinians during Oslo and after, had led them (the Judaeo-American lobby) to believe that the time was ripe for a settlement, naturally to be in favour of the stronger party (Israel) in the conflict. This led to the calling of the summit, the timing of which had virtually no support among the Palestinians. Indeed, the experience of Oslo, and post-Oslo had only served to legitimize the partiality and bias of Western, particularly American interlocutors in the minds of the Palestinian people.

Palestinian Experience

The Palestinian people's experience in the last ten years since the so-called peace effort started had been a rapidly progressing ghettoization that seemed programmed to ultimately result in their being made prisoners or expelled from their own land. The Zionist land appropriation and settlement programme had been progressing at such a rapid pace that now almost every Palestinian city, town, village, refugee camp or rural community was cut off and isolated from each other. The Palestinian people were not longer allowed to travel on the main roads. All these were for the use of settlers only.

The whole West Bank had been cut into parcels and strips of land by 'settler-only' roads. The Israeli army surrounded almost all Palestinian places of habitation, ready to impose a total blockade at short notice. Curfews could be imposed at any moment in Palestinian areas to add to the misery of the people. Even as Jewish settler homes spring up all over the place, Palestinians were subject to the strictest regulations in building houses or any other forms of normal developmental activities. Jerusalem, the focal point of all Palestinian aspirations was now out of bounds for people of the West

Bank and Gaza.

The Gaza strip had been separated from the rest of Israel and indeed Palestine by an electrified fence that effectively imprisoned the 1.5 million people of this coastal desert area. Israel had long been thinking of doing the same with the West Bank, i.e. building a fort-like wall to separate Palestinian populated areas from Israel proper and thereby deter suicide bombers from attacking the Jewish State. They have more or less completed this project which also meant the de-facto annexation of many areas of pre-1967 Palestine to Israel proper. Coupled with all this was the rampant and shameless siphoning of the water and natural resources of the West Bank and Gaza for the use of Israelis alone. Palestinians had to put up with massive shortages so that their neighbours could enjoy all the luxuries that a European lifestyle requires in a traditionally parched land.

Barak's Dilemmas at Camp David

At Camp David, Yasser Arafat and his team fought tooth and nail to defend Palestinian rights (Hanieh 2001: 77). As a result when Camp David-II ended without an agreement, both Barak and Clinton raised questions about Arafat's willingness to negotiate in good faith. Still no one was ready to declare the peace process dead. Secretly (and in public) all parties seemed to agree that some progress had been made. But this was not enough for the Americans and Israelis. Ehud Barak had staked his whole political future on making peace with the Arabs of whom the Palestinians were by far the smallest entity. But being small did not make them less conspicuous. They were, by far, the most painful thorn in Israel's side. In fact, Barak's decision to give more importance to the Syrian track of the peace process over the Palestinian one during his first year in office has been considered by many as one of the major mistakes he made in his foreign policy (Waxman 2001: 77).

The main problem for Barak was that Israel's political system made it next to impossible to make peace with the

Palestinians. Over the years, Israel had developed a political system based on coalitions which gave a lot of power to small fringe parties. These parties were the main advocate of Israeli expansion and militarism, confiscation of Arab lands and building of settlements in the occupied territories. Whenever the chances of making peace with the Arabs arose, these ultranationalist organisations would withdraw their support to the Government. In the present context, no coalition in Israel could survive without the support of these groups. Just before leaving for Camp David, Barak's government was reduced to a minority in the Israeli parliament. Later, Foreign Minister David Levy resigned accusing Barak of making too many concessions to the Palestinians. Even if an agreement was reached at Camp David, it would not have been ratified by the then Israeli parliament. It was to overcome this difficulty that a decision was taken to put a final peace accord to a referendum (Agha 2000).

The turning point in Israeli-Palestinian relations in the present context was the failure of the Camp David summit in July 2000. This was also the turning point of Ehud Barak's political career, in general. Barak risked his political future at Camp David and lost. It goes to the credit of Barak that he was not deterred by this and continued to determinedly pursue the goal of reaching a final settlement with the Palestinians till almost the end of his time in office. It can be said that Barak acted as a statesman and not a politician. He followed what he sincerely believed was in Israel's best interest and not his own. Unfortunately he was dealt the hard hand by history (Clinton 2000: 2). Barak was forced to leave office before he could recover from his loss of face at Camp David.

Clinton's Choice

US President Bill Clinton was certainly the most frustrated man to emerge from the Camp David-II Summit. His last hope of ensuring 'a legacy for all time' had been shattered. When Clinton called Arafat and Barak to Camp David, his personal experience at the successful Dayton talks between the warring Yugoslav factions was probably uppermost in his mind. He overlooked some crucial differences. The Yugoslav issue was a European problem and a leftover of the Second World War and the Cold War. The Israel-Palestine issue on the other hand, was basically a neo-imperialist and colonial issue and something that grew out of deep-rooted regional politico-religious animosities and hatreds. By the time of Dayton in 1995, each side in the conflict had basically fought itself to a stand-still. The peace that followed was the inevitable result of war exhaustion almost similar to the Taif Accords that ended the Lebanese civil war. Conversely, the multiple combatants in the Israel-Palestine issue were by no means exhausted and looked as though they were quite willing to fight for as many more years as it took to attain their legitimate ends.

Clinton was ill advised on his decision to call the summit. There was no way that the Palestinian leadership, already discredited for submitting to the Israelis on a large number of issues that had brought only increased humiliation and suffering to the Palestinian people, would agree to further concessions. The Israelis on the other hand had nothing to lose and only to gain from such a summit meeting. If the combined Israeli-American initiative was successful in getting Arafat to agree to a settlement that would guarantee peace and security to the Israelis at the cost of just a few cosmetic changes in the political status of the West Bank and, Gaza, so much the better. But Clinton and Barat just did not understand that the Palestinians were well prepared to deal with all their tricks. Before arriving at the summit, the Palestinian side led by Yasser Arafat had made the strategic decision to reject any all-embracing deal, if their basic demands wave not considered (Hirsh 2002: 33). [1] Even Clinton's 'Wye river strategy' could not break their determination. The Palestinians had after all not fought for a hundred years just to see all their bargaining chips disappear in a single summit meeting. Clinton himself is quoted as saying that:

The Arab-Israeli conflict is not just a morality play between good and evil. It is a conflict with a complex history, whose resolution requires balancing the needs of both sides, including respect for their national identities and religious beliefs (Clinton 2000: 3).

He again adds that talks must be accompanied by acts which show trust and partnership. Goodwill at the negotiating table cannot survive forever with ill intent in the background. It is important that each side understands how the other reads actions (Clinton 2000: 3).

For Clinton, Camp David was a transformative event, because the two sides faced the core issue of their dispute in a forum that was official for the first time. And they had to debate tradeoffs required to resolve the issues. Just as Oslo forced Israelis and Palestinians to come to terms with each other's existence, the discussions of the past six months have forced them to come to terms with each other's needs and the contours of a peace that ultimately they will have to reach (Clinton 2000: 3).

And, in fact, more than two years after Camp David, despite the bloody reality on the ground, many of the participants who negotiated at the summit and subsequently (until the arrival of Ariel Sharon), believe that a permanent peace agreement was possible in the not-so-distant future. Such a peace agreement would no doubt have to be based on the proposals formulated at Camp David together with those put forward by President Clinton in December 2002 that were conditionally accepted by both Barak and Arafat. Arafat later even went to the extent of giving an unconditional yes to these proposals.

American Diplomatic Priorities

One plus point of Palestinian-Israeli negotiations in the last decade has been the 'reframing' of the conflict in nationalist terms. This was in direct contrast to the earlier ethno-religious (Arab-Jewish) prism through which events in the Middle-East were seen. It was the idea that the dispute was between a Jewish state, albeit, one accepted by the Palestinians and a Palestinian national movement seeking a state of its own that created the possibilities of territorial compromise as a solution for the problem. Full negotiations during the last ten years, including Camp David II have been based on this understanding.

Thus for American diplomacy, the priority would always be the preserving of the nationalist framework of the conflict and separation of religion from issues of political sovereignty. Even proposals to resolve core issues such as Jerusalem and the Palestinian refugees should be made on the basis of the above confliction framework, though agreement on these issues may not be achievable in the short term (Telhami 2001: 14). The Camp David summit clearly showed that the peace envisioned by the Palestinians was not the peace Israel was prepared to offer. Israel was prepared neither to acknowledge the Palestinian right of return as laid out in UN resolution 194 (thereby accepting responsibility for the '*Naqba*,' the large scale expulsion of Arabs from Palestine in 1948 by the Hagannah and other Jewish militias), nor to accept more than token return of Arab people to Israel under family reunification and not legal provisions. [2] Israel insisted on maintaining sovereignty over most of East Jerusalem, including the old city. Most of the West Bank Jewish settlements would not be dismantled, but would be annexed to Israel thereby depriving the future Palestine state of territorial continuity (Parry 2002). [3]

Viewed in each side's perspective, both Arafat and Barak made remarkable concessions at Camp David. Barak broke all previous records in agreeing to eventually withdraw from over 90 percent of the West Bank and to surrender control of some East Jerusalem neighbourhoods. In return, Arafat can be said to have offered stunning concessions. The Palestinians allowed that most Jewish settlers on the West Bank could remain in settlement blocks in parts of the West Bank that would come under Israeli sovereignty. In exchange Palestinians should be compensated with new territories near Gaza. It was agreed to separate the issue of the 'right' of the Palestinian refugees to return to their names from the actual settlement of such rights. On the highly volatile Jerusalem issue, the Palestinians agreed that the Jewish Quarter and the Western 'Wailing' wall would fall under Israeli sovereignty (Telhami 2001: 14).

So where did the two sides go wrong? One can only trace the failure of the summit to the negotiating tactics and strategy followed by the opposing parties and their so-called 'neutral' mediator.

Barak's Failures

Ehud Barak had developed a deep dislike for the concept of gradual normalization that was the basis of the 1993 Oslo accords between Israel and the Palestinians. In his view, the recalling of Israeli forces from parts of Gaza and the West Bank along with the simultaneous partial rearming of the Palestinians during the last seven years had forced Israel to pay a heavy price without getting anything tangible in return (i.e., peace in the territories and in Israel proper) The scope of the Palestinians final demands was also not clearly known (at least in the Israeli perspective). Barak also seemed to be under the delusion that the Palestinians would be willing to make a historic compromise for peace only after they had exhausted all other possibilities (other than the negotiation table).

After the fatal Rabin experience, Barak's team had to be extra-sensitive to the domestic political scene in Israel. They were convinced that the Israeli public would ratify an agreement with the Palestinians (even one that provided for far reaching concessions), as long as it was final and brought peace to the country. It was thus necessary to minimize any domestic political tension before the conclusion of such an agreement. Keeping these principles in mind, Barak undertook a number of steps that went against the provisions of various agreements concluded between Israel and the Palestinian Authority. These included a third partial redeployment of troops from the West Bank, the transfer to the Palestine Authority of three villages outside Jerusalem, and the release of prisoners imprisoned for acts committed before the Oslo agreement.

But Barak's main failure was his inability to prevent the rapid spread of West Bank settlements. He apparently saw no reason to alienate the settler constituency. To Barak's mind, Arafat and the Palestinians had to be made to understand that there was no other way to peace. Oslo's 'interim' approach had been abandoned once and for all by the Israeli establishment. In front, there was now a corridor leading either to an agreement or to renewed confrontation (Malley and Agha 2001: 64).

Barak's 'all or nothing' approach might have succeeded if it was accompanied by confidence-building measures towards the Palestinians (like keeping all previous deadlines and agreements) and building good relationships with Arab leaders, especially Chairman Arafat. During almost two weeks of talks at Camp David, Barak refused to hold even one personal meeting with Arafat (Sontag 2001). [4] So under the circumstances, Arafat's distrust of Barak was not a fact to be astonished at. Arafat was even once quoted as saying that 'Barak is worse than Netanyahu' (Arafat 2000). [5]

Like most Israelis, Barak remained highly suspicious of the Palestinians. He was unconvinced that Israel had a true partner for peace in the Arafat leadership. This made him unwilling as far as practical confidence-building measures on the ground were concerned to do what was necessary to prove his 'good' intentions to the other side. While Barak himself was prepared to go all the way to reach an agreement and to make the minimum concessions required for this, his political statements remained hard-line (Malley and Agha 2001: 64).

Barak's negotiating strategy was completely wrong. There was also no clear Israeli negotiating position at Camp David. This was in direct contrast to the Palestinians who clearly knew what they wanted and the extent to which they were willing to make compromises to achieve their goals. Barak should have presented the principles underlying what eventually became his proposed solutions (primarily regarding the amount of territory Israel was willing to the Palestinians). Abu Mazen, the Palestinian architect of the Oslo accords, had repeatedly recommended that the general principles guiding the Permanent Status Agreement be established at the beginning itself. Unfortunately Barak refused to do so, fearing to expose his positions too early in the game.

However doing so would have provided the Palestinians with an incentive to move forward and also have given the talks a sense of purpose and urgency. The trouble with Barak was that his long years in the army seemed to have programmed him to see civil political life also in military strategic terms. He treated the whole field of negotiations like a major military exercise in which he was the sole general officer commanding (GOC). When he exposed his masterstroke (the territorial compromise, including Jerusalem) at the end of the negotiations, it was too late. The Palestinians did not trust him and had no confidence in what he was offering. Barak ended up weakening the Israeli position by offering too many concessions for virtually nothing in return (Pundak 2001: 39).

Palestinian Negotiation Positions

As far as the Palestinians were concerned, they had already made the most important territorial concession, that of accepting a Palestinian state on just 22 percent of British mandatory Palestine. In contrast to this, the initial Israeli offer at Camp David was based on a map which had included an annexation of approximately 12 percent of the West Bank without any compensation. Naturally, there was no way the Palestinians were going to accept such a proposal.

The Palestinian position at the Camp David talks was based on three basic realities:

1. They were not prepared to complete the final status

negotiations in a single summit that took place three to five months before the date set in the Sharm el-Sheikh agreement for the end of negotiations. This was in direct contrast to Barak's ideas. The Palestinians were opposed to the proposed summit from the beginning and had to be virtually dragged into them by US Secretary of State, Madeleine Albright and President Clinton. When forced into attending the summit, Arafat requested that it be the start in a series of such summits that would enable him to build a coalition for an agreement, within the Palestinian political class and the public at large. However, neither the Israelis nor the Americans sufficiently appreciated this requirement.

2. The Israeli concessions offered (very far-reaching from the Israeli point of view) were far from the minimum that would have enticed the Palestinians to sign an agreement.
3. Trying to trap Arafat into conceding an agreement was a tactical mistake, almost certain to push him into actions at odds with the requirement for successful negotiations. Once he felt that a trap was being set for him by the Israelis along with their American allies, Arafat's primary objective become to cut his losses rather than maximize his gains. Reaching a final settlement become only the second best option at that point of time. Arafat himself had been interested in attending a summit meeting scheduled for November 2000. In his point of view, July was too early to reach an agreement. His aim had been to continue with the secret negotiations till the end of summer 2000 in the hope of producing a joint document that would leave only a few issues for the leaders' decision. Then he planned to hold a number of summit meetings with his Israeli partner that would have culminated after the American elections in December (Pundak 2001: 39). Unfortunately the Israeli-American alliance had other plans in mind.

American Role at Camp David

America had many roles to play in the two week long 'drama' at Camp David. It had responsibilities as the chief broker of any future peace deal between the Israelis and the Palestinians. The US also acted as the guardian of the peace process. But America's main role was as Israel's one and only strategic ally and its cultural and political partner.

As the broker of the peace deal, Clinton was expected to present a final agreement that neither party, particularly the Palestinians could refuse. In practice, Americans proposals were so near the Israeli stand that it was next to impossible for the Palestinians to accept them even as a basis for negotiations. The Americans tended to have an acute sensitivity of Israel's domestic political concerns and a totally exaggerated appreciation of each and every Israel move. The US strategic relationship with Israel resulted in what was known in popular diplomatic parlance as the 'no surprise rule', namely an American commitment to vet each and every one of its 'ideas' with the Israelis, in advance.

As a result, the Americans often ended up presenting Israeli negotiating positions as their own and underwriting them as red lines beyond which Israel would not go. This sort of negotiating behaviour resulted in a substantial depreciation of the Palestinians confidence in Clinton, US credibility and America's ability to exercise effective pressure (Malley and Agha 2001: 73). Still the Americans had an important role to play in shaping the contents of the proposals. Frequently President Clinton would have to work to convince Ehud Barak to accept what he had refused till then, mainly issues like the principle of land swaps, Palestinian sovereignty over at least part of Arab East Jerusalem and the Haram ash-Sharif (this was after the camp David Summit) as well as a proposal to significantly reduce the area of Israeli annexation in Jerusalem and other parts of the West Bank.

Bill Clinton was known for his pro-Israeli views and he also had an almost Zionist devotion to the state of Israel. His two terms in office had seen American-Israeli relations flourish as never before. But Clinton was also the first US President to show himself to be openly sympathetic to the Palestinian cause and their desire for a separate state of their own. Ehud Barak once commented that, on matters of substance, the US was much closer to the Palestinians than to Israel.

The relationship between Washington and Tel Aviv was a friendly yet complex one. The inability to understand this relationship cost Arafat dearly. Americans saw the Palestinian position in terms of foot-dragging, passivity and contradictory positions within their delegation. They were even described as exhibiting a 'bunker mentality' at Camp David. This behaviour obviously left a bad impression on Clinton who contrasted it with the perceived huge steps taken by Barak, disregarding old Israeli taboos and at the risk of great personnel and political danger. Clinton's public statement at the close of the talks-openly blaming the Palestinian side for the failure seems to have been motivated by this impression, though there was also the aim of helping Ehud Barak to recover some sort of political mileage at home (Pundak 2001: 41).

By failing to put forward clear proposals, the Palestinians left the Americans without any means for pressing the Israelis to compromise. This led them to question both the seriousness of the Palestinians and their genuine desire for a settlement. The cut-throat attitude of the Israelis and their American cohorts at Camp David certainly played a major part in putting Arafat and his team on the defensive. Though Arafat had spent a decade building a relationship with Washington, he proved incapable of using it when he needed it most. As for the Americans, their performance at Camp David was certainly not up to the mark. Though the hosts, they never fully took control of the situation. Pulled in various directions, the Americans never fully figured out which way to go and instead of using their authority to good purpose, frequently allowed themselves to be used by others.

Ultimately the negotiation path set out by the Americans-to agree on a proposal with the Israelis, present it to the Palestinians; get a counter-proposal from them; bring it back to the Israelis-just did not work. The Israelis were never willing to lay down their final proposal, the Palestinians never put a counter proposal and so finally no deal was able to be struck.

Whatever are the consequences and aftershocks, the negotiations that took place between July 2000 when the Camp David Summit was held and the final effort at finalizing a deal at the Egyptian Red Sea resort of Taba in January 200I mark an indelible chapter in the history of the Israeli-Palestinian conflict. To quote an American participant at Camp David, 'taboos were shattered, the unspoken got spoken and, during that period, Israelis and Palestinians reached on unprecedented level of understanding of what it will take to end their struggle' (Malley and Agha 2001: 75).

The beginnings of a foundation for a comprehensive, just and lasting peace have been laid. Poor management of the process alone has kept the Israelis and Palestinians from reaching the agreement. Bill Clinton's desired legacy, which of presiding over a comprehensive Middle East peace may ultimately be reflected in an eventual reconciliation between those two peoples and peace and good harmony between their two states in the future.

Endnotes

1. Michael Hirsh, 'Blowing the Best Chance', *Newsweek Magazine*, April l, 2002. Available at, http://www.highbeam.com/doc/1G1-84191321.html.
2. Refer Document II in Appendices.
3. Nigel Parry, 'Misrepresentation of Barak's Offer at Camp David as "Generous" and Unprecedented', *The Electronic Intifada*, March 20, 2002. Available at, http://electronicintifada.net/content/misrepresentation-baraks-offer-camp-david-generous-and-unprecedented/3991.
4. Deborah Sontag, 'And Yet So Far: A Special Report; Quest for Mideast Peace: How and Why It Failed', *The New York Times*, July 26, 2001.
5. 'Arafat: Barak worse than Netanyahu', (Reuters-Cairo), *New*

Straits Times (Singapore), April 11, 2000. Available at, http://news.google.com/newspapers?id=1lNIAAAAIBAJ&sjid=bBQEAAAAIBAJ&pg=6802%2C2325675.

6

Palestinian Politics in Historical Perspective

Arab Nationalism

One of the defining attributes of the Arab world since the end of the Ottoman Empire after the First World War has been the rise and growth of Pan-Arabic nationalism (*al-Qawmiyya al-`arabiyya*) in the region. Arab Nationalism was an ideology that sought to restore the lost glory of the Arab people based on their ancient heritage and culture, with an emphasis on modernisation and secularism in the present world context. The emphasis in Arab nationalism was on political union, reminiscent of the Arab world as it had been once united under the Abbasid and Umayyad Caliphs of the early Islamic era. While Arab nationalists were overwhelmingly exposed to Western culture and European rationalist education, they sought to be fiercely nationalistic and independent in that they were extremely critical of Western interference and proxy-control in the Middle East. However, one of the defining drawbacks of Arab nationalism was an inability to institute lasting democratic transformation within their respective territories in the Arab world. The continuance of European colonialist/mandatory policies in the Middle East post-World War 1 also impacted negatively on the hopes and aspirations of Arab nationalists.

The creation of the predominantly Jewish state of Israel out of the crucible of the Second World War as a homeland for European and other Jews of the Middle East, Africa and Asia also created a point of conflict with Arab nationalistic aspirations in the region. The presence of the Jewish state which was perceived as a colonialist 'European' implant in the region, encouraged the overt (and covert) militarisation of the region as both sides, Jews and Arabs sought to take sides in the post-World War II Cold War to gain the necessary military advantage over each other. Militarisation benefited the 'new' state of Israel the most as they were able to benefit from a largely well educated 'European' origin population that could well adjust to the usage of Western arms and technology in the region. Israel also benefited from Western support, first that of France and the UK, and later that of the US in their wars with the neighbouring Arab powers such as Egypt, Jordan and Syria.

In fact, the Arab-Israeli War of June 1967 and its implications and consequences resulted in the death-knell for Arab nationalism as the pre-eminent 'ruling' ideology of the Middle East. It was Arab Nationalism that sought to define Palestinian Nationalism as the basis for a new Palestinian identity. The Palestinian National identity was comprehensively defined in the 1988 Independence Declaration which stated that Palestine was: An Arab state, an integral and indivisible part of the Arab nation…in heritage and civilisation. It is the state of the Palestinians everywhere where they enjoy their collective national and cultural identity...under a parliamentary democratic political system which guarantees freedom of religious convictions and non-discrimination in public rights of men or women, on grounds of race, religion, colour or sex (Passia 1997: 331-332).

The Palestine Liberation Organisation's (PLO's) aim was to establish a secular state in the entire present 'land' west of the Jordan, a land where Christians, Jews as well as Muslims would enjoy equal rights and be able to co-exist in peace (Passia 1997: 331-332).

Muslim Brotherhood

Ever since the fall of the Ottoman Empire, there has been a movement in the Middle East that has sought to re-instate Islam as the main idea behind the modern Middle Eastern nation-state. One of the earliest of these organisations in the Levant was that of the Muslim Brotherhood, founded in Egypt in 1928 by Hassan Al-Banna (Mura 2012: 62). He emphasised the link between faith and creation, something that Muslims in general take very seriously indeed. All forms of secularisation and westernisation, particularly on the Turkish Ataturk model, were rejected as inconsistent with the true practice of Islam. There should be no separation between Church and State. Al-Bana revived the emphasis on a world-wide Islamic state or Empire. He stressed the 'international' bond of the Islamic *Ummah* (brotherhood). He exhorted his disciples to be willing to die for the actualisation of the Islamic Empire, thereby giving rise to the whole phenomena of Islamic Jihad. The rise of many independent Arab states after the end of the Second World War also resulted in the rise of Arab nationalistic regimes in many Arab nations (Mura 2012: 75).

The subsequent, successful attempts by the West to destroy Arab nationalism as a step towards Arab unity resulted again in a rise in Islamism in the Arab world. The post-1967 revival of Islamist attitudes in the light of the Arab defeat of 1967 was also accompanied by a simultaneous emphasis on the modern-day validity of Islamic law or *Sharia* as the 'sine qua non' of Islamic rule in the Muslim world. The prime exponent of this ideology was the Egyptian ideologue Sayyid Qutb. Qutb was a revolutionary in the Arab and Islamic worlds in that he advocated the *Qur'an* and the *Sharia* as the sole basis on which modern rule may be maintained in the Arab-Islamic world. It was Qutb's call on the people of the Islamic world to confront and get rid of their individual oppressive and corrupt rulers that caused his ultimate death at the hands of the Egyptian ruler Nasser. Qutb emphasised the importance of the rule of Islamic Law, the *Sharia*. He also produced a reworking of Islamic history while in prison in Egypt, arguing that the secularisation of Egypt meant that it was not an Islamic state, but was still in a state of *Jahiliyya* (religious ignorance), approximately similar to the situation of the Arabs before the advent of Islam (Mura 2012: 70).

He was strongly against any kind of individualistic rule,

believing in the supremacy of the rule of God through the medium of God's Law. He declared that all problems in the Islamic world were because rulers did not act according to the rule of *Sharia*. Active steps should be taken to overthrow such rulers and the existing political order, in favour of a *Sharia*-based one (Mura 2012: 78). Inspired by Qutb's teachings, two groups broke away from the mainstream Brotherhood to form the *Takfir wal-Hijra* and *al-Jihad* organisations, which were committed to achieving the Islamic state by violent and immediate means, thereby forsaking the gradualist approach of the parent organisation. These two organisations were together known under the title of *al-Gama' at al-Islamiyya* (the Islamic Groups) and actively resorted to terrorist tactics to achieve the projected Islamic state. Their argument was that these were the only methods to lead from a state of *Jahiliyya* to a society controlled by *Sharia* law and *Shura* (consultation) between the leaders and the people (Sofer 2001: 152-153).

Palestine as an allied territory of Egypt, both largely controlled by the British after the First World War, was particularly susceptible to developments in Egypt. The Muslim Brotherhood established a Palestine branch rather late in 1946, towards the end of the British Mandate (Mura 2012: 69). The Brotherhood managed to spread quite fast, with chapters in many Palestinian cities, due to support from the Mufti of Palestine, Haji Amin al-Husseini, who was a close friend and confidante of the Brotherhood supreme Hassan al-Banna (Cohen 1982: 144). Membership in the Muslim Brotherhood was a common bond that united many of the early leaders in the Palestinian national movement in exile (Forman Summer 2010). [1] The Brotherhood was particularly active in Gaza, because of the Egyptian influence there (Abu Amr 1994: 20).

Brotherhood in Palestine

Among the early Palestinian resistance leaders drawn to the Brotherhood in the first instance was a 20-year old engineering student in Cairo University called Muhammad

'Abd-al-Ra 'uf al-Qidwa al-Husayni (alias Yasser 'Arafat) and one of the lions of the resistance Khalil al-Wazir (alias Abu Jihad) (Aburish 2012: 29). The Brotherhood had a military wing, in keeping with its ideology listed above and this proved to be highly attractive as well as beneficial for many Palestinians in exile as well as those in Gaza and the West Bank (Sayigh 1999: 80-81). Later political Islamic organisations like the Brotherhood managed to get a considerable footing in the Palestinian refugee camps of Transjordan (including the West Bank) in the 1950s. The Brotherhood's emphasis on Jihad against the Israelis and the need for Palestinians to themselves take up arms in defence of their own country, without relying on outside support, struck a sympathetic chord in the hearts of many refugees.

The Brotherhood in Palestine placed an emphasis on sports and scout activities, mock military training, and other such activities. This was based on their experience as a mass-based party in Egypt, whose main support base was among the rural peasantry and urban under-classes. The Brotherhood focused on Arabism and Arab unity, but only as a tool towards a greater Islamic unity. They were opposed to Arab nationalism, as a tool that was been used by secularists so as to divide the Arab and non-Arab Islamic worlds. For the Brotherhood, it was anathema to worship the modern nation as a counterpart or even competitor to the attentions of the people, in place of God (Segesvary 2000: 194).

The so-called Islamic Liberation Party was another competitor for the attention of the Palestinian Muslim peasantry, which recognised Islam as the sole basis for statehood and taught that a unified Islamic state must be set up before a jihad against Israel could be launched. Both parties actively sought recruits among police and paramilitary forces in the West Bank and Jordan. Palestinian peasants of Muslim background readily accepted the 'fusion' of Arabism and Islam propagated by these respective political parties (Sayigh 1999: 49). Many of the traditionalist parties of the Arab world and of Palestine were unable to expand their base beyond the relatively restricted group of educated urban dwellers in the cities and towns of Palestine.

One of the reasons for this was the division prevalent in Palestine and throughout the Arab world, between 'educated' urbanites and the rural masses. In addition, many of the Arab nationalist parties had a disproportionate number of Christians in their membership as well as secularised urban elites (Sayigh 1999: 50). Coupled with all this was the fact that the Muslim Brotherhood was the only accepted socio-political organisation that was accepted in Jordan, after the official banning of all political parties in April 1957 (Sayigh 1999: 52).

International Jihad

The 1967 War resulted in discredit to the concept of a trans-national Arab state and gave a fillip to Islamist tendencies among the Arab masses. Coupled with this was the Oil Crisis of 1973-74 that propelled the oil-rich Arab states into the world limelight, with their use of oil as a bargaining tool in the political and military crises of the early 1970s. The Gulf Kingdoms and Emirates were all conservative Islamic Sheikhdoms where the more austere Islam of the Arabian Desert was in practice. Increased oil-money meant that these states were able to attract hundreds of thousands of Arab and other workers to their countries in search of work, which in turn meant a spread in radical Islamic values through these people further abroad. The same period also saw the Afghan Civil War that resulted in the almost total destruction of that country under first the Soviet occupiers and their local allies and late under the Western and Arab-Islamic backed Mujahidin that resulted in the overt Islamisation of Afghanistan with its consequent spill-over effects in Pakistan and throughout the Arab and Islamic worlds in the 1970s, 1980s and 1990s of the 20th century.

The 1970s saw the revival in calls for a worldwide Muslim state where the *Sharia* would be the sole determining and controlling factor. There was a revival in grassroots work among Islamist groups and parties in the Palestinian territories and also within the state of Israel, which paved the way for the later formation of parties like Hamas and Islamic Jihad. There was tacit Israeli support for this as Islamists were regarded as a counterweight to the 'secular' Palestinian nationalist forces. The Islamic Revolution in Iran, while inaugurating a professedly *Shi'ite* regime, was an additional boost to the Islamists as they saw how Iran under the clerics managed to devise a completely new theocratic state, that nevertheless had democratic attributes.

The 1980s also witnessed the catastrophic Iran-Iraq war that was again another Cold War-sponsored proxy war that was fought between the then powerful Baa'thist dominated Iraq on the one side and the newly formed Islamic republic of Iran on the other side. The weakening of Arab nationalistic states that took place throughout the 1980s, particularly after the signing of the Camp David Accords between Israel and Egypt, resulted in the Palestinians having to weigh their own options regarding the viability or success of ever establishing a Palestinian state on all of the former territory of the Mandate of Palestine. US and Israeli refusal to acknowledge or talk with the Palestinian Liberation Organisation as the sole representative of the Palestinian people and their voice for independence also played a role in weakening the Palestinian resolve vis-à-vis the state of Israel. The existence of the state of Israel slowly came to be accepted by the Palestinian people and their supporters as a *fait accompli.*

In 1988, the PLO as the premier organisation, embracing many different factions working towards Palestinian liberation, took a public commitment towards accepting the so-called two-state solution as the basis for the resolution of the decades old Israel-Palestine imbroglio (Ibrahim 1988). [2] The Islamist parties in Palestine and Israel, have on the contrary never accepted the reality of the state of Israel on the soil of the 'Holy Land', made holy, according to them by the purported

'*Qibla* of the Prophet Mohammad' (his reputed 'journey' from the 'Temple Mount-Dome of the Rock' precincts to 'heaven,' via the medium of a mythical white horse) (Hamas 1988). [3]

The Palestinian political organisations espousing Islamist views such as Hamas and Islamic Jihad, in addition to a number of other organisations currently active (including those with supposed links to *Al-Qaeda*) have also rejected the secular orientation of Palestinian national politics and struggle as it has been historically practiced (Hamas 1988). Hamas spent the entire period of the late 1970s and 1980s building up its social service network in the Occupied Territories and they were particularly well placed to render useful services to the people of Gaza and the West Bank during the First Intifada of 1987-1993. Palestinian Islamists have been widely noted as gaining in influence since the early 1980s.

Hamas and Islamic Jihad

Hamas (*Harakat al-Muqawama al-Islamiyya*) which grew out of the work of the Islamic Brotherhood in the Gaza Strip has always been strong in this region, while the corresponding Islamist militia known as Islamic Jihad (*Harakat al-Jihād al-Islāmi fi Filastīn*) has been strong on the West Bank (Mannes 2004: 203). The founding head of Hamas was the late Sheikh Ahmad Yasin, who was a refugee in Gaza born in undivided Palestine in 1938 (Amayreh 2004). [4] Palestine was considered a Muslim land and the Palestinian problem a Muslim problem of concern primarily to the Islamic world. Islamic Jihad too had a similar early development as an off-shoot of Palestinian Islamist activists that had grown close to the Muslim Brotherhood after the comprehensive Arab defeat of 1967. Many of their early cadre had been born in Gaza and were educated in the Strip as well as in Egypt, where they came under the influence of the Brotherhood. The Islamic Revolution in Iran was a major influence on the Palestinian Islamists as they were increasingly disillusioned with the Brotherhood's resistance against organising armed activities against the state of Israel, probably in deference towards the wishes of the Egyptian state against needlessly provoking the Israelis.

The early leaders of Islamic Jihad were influenced by *Shi'ite* Islamist theology coming from Iran, particularly the thought of Ayatollah Khomeini, with its emphasis on rebellion against tyrannical authorities. Islamic Jihad grew throughout the 1980s, thus making it a major influence poised to take an important role in the first Intifada, along with its brother Hamas organisation. Both these groups made extensive reference to the writings of both Hassan al-Banna as well as Sayyid Qutb in their writings (Emerson 2008). [5]

They also make extensive references to Sheikh Izz ad-Din al-Qassam, the great Palestinian leader of the Arab Revolt of the 1930s (Segev 1999: 360-362). References to Qassam as well as Khomeini show the reliance of these groups on Palestinian Nationalism as well as the Jihadist roots of political Islam. Islamic Jihad, in particular, was disillusioned with the Islamic Brotherhood over their espousal of 'faith' as praxis without Jihad (holy war or struggle), while the PLO took the path of Jihad, without sufficient faith and belief. Both these groups took an essentially philosophical attitude towards the conflict with the Israelis, emphasising the 'essentially unchanging' nature of conflict with the Israelis and seeking the destruction of the Zionist state as a corrupting influence in the heart of the Arab and Islamic world and its substitution with an Islamic state of Palestine. Both these movements drew their membership primarily but not exclusively from the lower middle class populations of Gaza and the West Bank, a population mainly scattered in the numerous refugee camps in the region.

Hamas and Islamic Jihad have focused on the transformation of Palestine into an Islamic society as a preliminary step in the liberation of the whole undivided land of Palestine from the Zionist Jewish forces. The two Islamic groups listed above have always emphasised the interdependence of faith and politics in every aspect of the life of the people of the country (Sayigh 1999: 625-631). Palestinian politics has thus since the late 1970s been increasingly polarised between an upper and educated secularised and Westernised urban class that supported the PLO and other secular Palestinian and Arab Nationalist parties while, the lower classes, made of the large refugee populations, plus the rural residents and the urban 'uneducated' classes largely supported the Islamist parties such as Hamas and Islamic Jihad.

Hamas was the more popular of these two groups having taken the pains to develop a vast social movement and base among the impoverished refugees as well as rural and poor urban Muslims of Palestine. They emphasised a strict following of Islamic guidelines as regarding piety, good familial settings, a sound Islamic based education network and awareness of the need to supersede Israel with an Islamic state. When Hamas was first founded, they emphasised what was termed 'sensory isolation' in Arabic *(al-in 'izal al-shu 'uri)*, as a must for good Muslims to be able to live in a non-Islamic society. By this they were referring to what they saw as a non-Muslim ruled society where Sharia law was not enforced as was the situation in the Israeli-occupied West Bank and Gaza in the 1970s (Sayigh 1999: 625-631).

Against a reflection on their Muslim Brotherhood roots, early Hamas activists sought to get involved in armed actions against Israel using the military-political framework of Fatah (the premier PLO organ). The Muslim Brotherhood and Hamas kept out of direct military confrontations with the state of Israel (and as a result, were encouraged to function and grow by Israeli military commanders in the Occupied Territories, as a non-violent and anti-national counter to the influence of the PLO) till the outbreak of the First Intifada in 1987 (Higgins 2009; Levitt 2007: 24). [6] This was in keeping with the prerogative of the Islamic Brotherhood to keep out of direct military action in the two decades after 1967 (Sayigh 1999: 625-631).

Hamas refused to cooperate with the nationalist leadership

of the PLO and the First Uprising, on the grounds that it was focused on creating an Islamic state, and not a secular one, while refusing any kind of compromises with the Israelis. In August 1988, when the organisation openly published its founding charter for the first time, the Hamas Covenant called on all Palestinian Muslims to wage holy war on the state of Israel as the only solution to the Palestinian problem (Hamas 1988). The founding Charter of Hamas, a document that the organisation has never changed since then or modified in any way, despite widespread demands from Israel and the West, over a proviso calling for the destruction of Israel, confirmed the movement as a branch of the Muslim Brotherhood (Hamas 1988).

It was Islamic Jihad along with a faction within Fatah that professed Islamist leanings that was led by the one-time PLO Planning Centre director as well as Christian-born Munir Shafiq (a close relative of the former Anglican Bishop of Jerusalem, Riah Abu el-Assal) that first started military actions against Israeli targets during the mid-to-late 1980s before the start of the popularly inspired First Intifada. Armed attacks were initiated by the Hamas organisation from August 1988 onwards and though severely suppressed by the Israelis, Hamas was able to survive due to their unprecedented network of social service organisations, based mainly in mosques and Islamic institutions that helped to maintain the momentum and Islamic ideology of the group, even when a majority of Hamas leaders were in jail or exile (Sayigh 1999: 625-632, Sofer 2001: 161-162).

Hamas and Palestinian Christians

It should be noted in this context that since March 1993, as a result in the upsurge in suicide-terrorist attacks due to the widespread resistance to the Oslo Accords among Islamist and radical Palestinian circles, Palestinians both Christian and Muslim, from the West Bank and the Gaza Strip have been prevented from freely entering Jerusalem and the territories of the state of Israel in general, thereby inhibiting the rights of the people to worship freely at their holy sites such as the Church of the Holy Sepulchre and the Al-Aqsa Temple Mount Compound. This in turn has made its impact on the Christians of Palestine, especially in the wake of recent Hamas victories at the 2006 polls in Palestine, both on the West Bank and their own regional powerhouse of Gaza.

Many Christians reported how Hamas operatives visited Churches and Christians institutions before the defining Palestinian parliamentary elections in 2006, reassuring them that if elected, the radical Islamist party would do nothing that would jeopardise their continued existence, lives and religious and social rights and status in the Occupied Territories as well as in any future state of Palestine, ruled by the group. [7].

Nationalist Christians did not express any surprise at the victory of Hamas, as the widespread disillusionment with the Palestinian National Authority was very evident in Palestine during this period (Sideras 2009). [8] The overwhelming consensus was that the democratic decision of the people must be respected. As a respected Palestinian nationalist Christian put it: I am utterly confident that the Palestinian government headed by Hamas will not distinguish between a Christian and a Muslim. All citizens will be equal before the law and their religious freedoms will be respected as they are respected until now. Hamas will cooperate with them for the good of the homeland and the citizens. We are not afraid of those who believe in God, the compassionate, the merciful, but rather we are afraid of all those who wrongly exploit religion, politicise it and interpret it according their interests. This is what is practiced by many religious Jews. I am certain that the prophetic voice of we Christians will not be silent under any Palestinian government. Rather it will remain loud demanding right and justice and criticising falsehood. We will not be silent if injustice is done to anybody be he a Christian or a Muslim. At the same time, we have to cooperate with the authority and to help in building the bridges of religious and cultural dialogue with the Western societies and with the Christians in particular (Khoury 2006: 183). [9]

The failure of secular nationalist Arab states to build viable and stable societies with responsible democratic frameworks has meant that a large proportion of the people of the region, and especially the vast majority of those who have not progressed materially under these regimes, have suffered disillusionment with these forms of regimes. The corresponding rise of Jewish fundamentalist forces after the 1967 war as well as the rise of Islamic fundamentalism coupled with the collapse of the Soviet Union left many secular or left-leaning Arab Christians in a quandary. After fighting for over 150 years for a separation of 'Church and State,' these people were faced with a novel situation demanding their adjustment to predominantly theocratic regimes in the region in the future. Faced with the Islamist current in the Middle East, with its insistence on combining religion and state so that each complements the other, Arab secularists, Muslims as well as Christians have been faced with a stark choice of assimilation-coexistence and migration from the region (Chesler 2010: 41).

Politics of Hamas

Legislative and presidential elections have been held consecutively since 1996 in Palestine. [10] The first presidential election in 1996 was won by the late former Chairman of the PLO, Yasser Arafat. [11] Following his fall from favour with the West and in particular with America and the state of Israel, the incumbent President Mahmud Abbas was first elected as Palestinian Prime Minister and later on the untimely death of Arafat, was re-elected as Palestinian President (Seddon 2004: 2). In 2005, Palestinian municipal elections to various town and area councils were held after a long lapse. The 2006 legislative elections were held on 25 January 2006 (Wilson 2006). [12] For the first time ever in the history of Palestinian democracy, the radical Islamist grouping Hamas won 74 seats out of the 132 seats in the Palestinian

Legislative Assembly that were in the public electoral sphere (Khoury 2006: 174).

Fatah, the main Palestinian Liberation Organisation grouping along with the US and Israel sought to sideline, boycott and deny Hamas its electoral victory in the January 2006 elections and the right to form the next Palestinian government. The resulting clash between the two rival Palestinian factions led to Hamas taking over the Gaza Strip in June 2007. Palestinian internal politics since then has been characterised by a fractured polity, with Hamas's control of the Gaza Strip meaning almost total isolation for the people of the Strip from the outside world, as Israel has enforced a strict blockade of the area from both land as well as sea to put pressure on the radical Islamist grouping, thereby putting the people of the Strip under incredible economic and social hardship and suffering.

Hamas's control over the Gaza Strip and virtually half of the Palestinian political spectrum has also given the Israelis a good excuse to desist from serious or meaningful peace negotiations with the Palestinians on the pretext of not having a suitable partner for peace in the region, Hamas being ideologically committed to the establishment of an Islamic state on all of the historic territories of Palestine, much of which is now the state of Israel. The founding Charter of Hamas mentions that the state of Israel would be eventually destroyed by Islam (Hamas 1988).

Hamas has never to date formally repudiated this founding Charter of principles that seek to guide the Palestinian Islamic Movement (Hamas 1988). Hamas and Fatah have periodically sought to bury their differences and come together in a show of unity to form a pan-Palestinian national government of unity, but these efforts have also been stoutly opposed by Israel and also by the US under the pretext of having nothing whatsoever to do with a 'fundamentalist' Islamist grouping such as Hamas. It remains to be seen whether Hamas and Fatah will really be able to cooperate together in forming a national government as being envisaged in the present-future as the two parties have never had a history of collaborating effectively with each other and indeed have only had an experience of intense political and sometimes fratricidal rivalry and conflict.

Hamas' leadership at present appears seriously divided over the post-effects and impact of the ongoing Syrian and Iranian crises in the region. Iran is a serious backer of both Hezbollah in Lebanon as well as Hamas in the Gaza Strip and the West Bank. The external top leadership of Hamas led by Khaled Meshaal were based in Damascus till recently (Akram 2012). [13] However the Civil War-like situation at present in Syria with the Alawite Baa'thist regime of Bashaar al-Assad fighting against a predominantly Sunni-majority Free Syrian Army rebels, with the consequent large-scale deaths and bloodshed that have been going on since the uprising broke out in 2011, has meant that Hamas has had to re-evaluate its ties with the Syrian regime (Greenwood 2012). [14] In fact it has been rumoured that Meshaal's attempt to make up with the Mahmud Abbas-led Fatah controlled Palestinian National Authority in the West Bank recently did not have the executive authority of the Hamas internal leadership based in the Gaza strip (Yaari 2012). [15]

The reconciliation process with Fatah and the PLO is at present deadlocked over multiple procedural tangles and leadership issues. The Hamas leadership that have been internally based in the Gaza strip for many years now under a siege of virtual isolation are almost pathologically suspicious of the 'liberal' views of the secular Fatah movement in the West Bank. On the other hand, they derived considerable encouragement from the upsurge in the fortunes of the Islamist parties in the recent free elections that were held in Tunisia and Egypt. The fall of the last maverick of the old guard Arab nationalist revolutionaries, Colonel Mu'amer Gaddafi in Libya was also another boost in the armpits of the Islamists. The Syrian regime was and is the last old-guard 'republican' socialist Baa'thist regime still surviving in the fertile Levant.

Mahmoud al-Zahar, who was a senior Hamas leader in Gaza, has gone on record as stating that: The changing factors around us are in our favour…they are not in favour either of Fatah's project or those with whom it cooperates, including the Israeli enemy...It all depends on Fatah's policy now…If Fatah wants the (unity) agreement to be accomplished, we will be ready. If they do not want, then we are sitting here and the future is ours (Al-Mughrabi 2012). [16]

Zahar also opined that he foresaw the rise of Islamism and Islamic parties such as the Muslim Brothers in Egypt (which was the mother organisation of Palestinian Islamist groups such as Hamas and Islamic Jihad) as being of great advantage for the Palestinian cause, as invariably these parties would reflect the widespread public opinion in the streets of Cairo, Tripoli and Tunis in their domestic and foreign policy calculations. He again stated that what is coming is a thousand times better than in the past. Therefore we have to invest in these achievements by the Arab street for the sake of achieving the fundamental goals of the Palestinian people, the liberation of land and the return of (refugees) (Al-Mughrabi 2012).

Whatever the current travails vis-à-vis Israel or Fatah in the West Bank, Hamas sees itself as being on the right side of history as regards the its current status in the Arab and wider Islamic worlds. It views the present crises in the Arab and greater Middle Eastern world as being in the nature of a passing 'crisis of existence' that will stabilise with the passage of time. After that, and after waiting with fortitude (Sumud in Arabic) through the present difficulties, the Hamas leadership believe that their view will emerge triumphant in the Palestinian context. However, the present internal leadership in the Strip does not believe in making any present compromises with either Israel or the Fatah-led PNA for future gains.

Endnotes

1. Available at, http://www.thejerusalemfund.org/ht/a/GetDocumentAction/i/26807.

2. Youssef M. Ibrahim, 'P.L.O. is Expected to Declare an Independent State', *The New York Times*, November 11, 1988. Available at, http://www.nytimes.com/1988/11/11/world/plo-is-expected-to-declare-an-independent-state.html.
3. Available at, http://avalon.law.yale.edu/20th_century/hamas.asp.
4. Khaled Amayreh, 'The Martyr Sheikh', Obituary: Sheikh Ahmed Yassin: 1938-2004, *Al-Ahram Weekly Online*, 25-31 March 2004, Issue No. 683, available at, http://weekly.ahram.org.eg/2004/683/re2.htm.
5. Available at, http://www.investigativeproject.org/documents/testimony/353.pdf.
6. Andrew Higgins, 'How Israel Helped to Spawn Hamas', *Wall Street Journal*, January 24, 2009. Available at, http://online.wsj.com/news/articles/SB123275572295011847.
7. Comments recorded by the researcher in conversations and interviews with Palestinian Christians during my July-August 2007 field trip to the region.
8. Available at, http://www.thejerusalemfund.org/ht/a/GetDocumentAction/i/6716.
9. Comments recorded by the researcher in conversations and interviews with Palestinian Christians during my July-August 2007 field trip to the region.
10. Refer, 'The 1996 Palestinian Presidential and Legislative Elections', available at, http://www.elections.ps/Portals/0/pdf/Resultselection1996.pdf.
11. Ibid.
12. Scott Wilson, 'Hamas Sweeps Palestinian Elections, Complicating Peace Efforts in Mideast', *The Washington Post Foreign Service*, Friday, January 27, 2006, available at, http://www.washingtonpost.com/wp-dyn/content/article/2006/01/26/AR2006012600372_pf.html.
13. Fares Akram, 'Hamas Leader Abandons Long-time Base in Damascus,' *The New York Times*, January 27, 2012. Available at, http://www.nytimes.com/2012/01/28/world/middleeast/khaled-meshal-the-leader-of-hamas-vacates-damascus.html?_r=0.

14. Phoebe Greenwood, 'Hamas Risks Damascus Base to Support Syrian Opposition', *The Telegraph* (London), February 26, 2012. Available at, http://www.telegraph.co.uk/news/worldnews/middleeast/syria/9107218/Hamas-risks-Damascus-base-to-support-Syrian-opposition.html.
15. Ehud Yaari, 'The Agony of Hamas', *Times of Israel*, February 27, 2012. Available at, http://www.timesofisrael.com/the-agony-of-hamas.
16. Nidal al-Mughrabi, 'The Future is Ours', says Hamas Gaza leader, *Reuters*, Gaza, January 9, 2012. Available at, http://www.reuters.com/article/2012/01/09/us-palestinians-hamas-idUSTRE8081MQ20120109.

7

Clinton Parameters and the Road Map to Peace

The Israel-Palestinian peace process has taken shape over the years, in spite of the violence that has been ongoing ever since the start of the conflict over 60 years ago. The term 'peace process' itself owes its origin to the Israeli-Palestinian or the Arab-Israeli conflict as described by William B. Quandt in his book 'Peace Process.' He writes:

Sometime in the mid-1970s the term peace process began widely used to describe the American-led efforts to bring about a negotiated peace between Israel and its neighbours. The phrase stuck, and ever since it has been synonymous with the gradual, step-by-step approach to resolving one of the world's most difficult conflicts. In the years since 1967 the emphasis in Washington has shifted from the spelling out of the ingredients of 'peace' to the 'process' of getting there. Much of US constitutional theory focuses on how issues should be resolved, the process rather than on substance, what should be done. The United States has provided both a sense of direction and a mechanism. That, at its best, is what the peace process has been about. At worst, it has been little more than a slogan used to mask the marking of time (Quandt 2005).

The Presidency of George W. Bush was noted for its enunciation of the 'Road Map' to peace as the means by which a lasting solution could be reached for the Israeli-Palestinian imbroglio. The November 2007 Annapolis Conference also reiterated that the preferred solution for the conflict would be the 'Two-State' solution (Uni, Ravid and Benn 2007). [1]

Clinton Parameters

Prior to the Bush regime's policies on Israel-Palestine, we

find what became known as the Clinton Parameters from the far end of the Clinton Presidency. The Clinton Parameters were guidelines for Permanent Status Agreement to resolve the Israel-Palestinian conflict and were proposed under the name of President Bill Clinton in late 2000, towards the end of his second term as US President. The background for the Clinton Parameters was the failure of the Camp David Summit of June 2000 coupled with the outbreak of the Second Intifada, the so-called '*Al-Aqsa Intifada*' which broke out as a result of the controversial visit of the Israeli *Liqud* Party strongman former General Ariel Sharon to the holy Al-Aqsa, Dome of the Rock Compound on September 28, 2000.

The Parameters were also produced in the light of an upcoming Israeli general election where exit polls indicated a defeat for the incumbent Ehud Barak and victory for the hard-line Liqud Party, under the leadership of the even more hard-line Ariel Sharon. Clinton was also looking to end his eight years of involvement in Middle Eastern peacemaking on a successful note. The Clinton Parameters were presented on December 23, 2000. The leaders of both parties to the conflict accepted the Parameters with certain reservations. These reservations were felt by the Americans to be acceptable within the confines of the Parameters which left space for continued negotiations on many of the most controversial issues like land swaps, and the question of Jerusalem and the refugees (Swisher 2004: 402).

Territory

According to the Parameters, Israel would gain sovereignty over the Jewish prayer zone know as the Western Wall that falls just below the Temple Mount complex. The Palestinians would be awarded sovereignty and the Israelis would be accorded 'symbolic ownership' over the actual Temple Mount structures. The two parties would share sovereignty over the excavations that were going on below the Temple Mount. East Jerusalem and the Old City would be divided according to ethnic lines with Israel gaining sovereignty over the Jewish Quarter and the Jewish settlements in East Jerusalem and the Palestinians getting sovereignty over the Palestinian inhabited areas.

As regards territory, the Parameters envisaged a Palestinian state comprising 94-96 percent of the combined territories of the West Bank and the Gaza Strip. Israel would be allowed to annex all the remaining land which would comprise almost wholly of the Israeli Settlements (and around 80 percent of the Settler population). Israel would in return cede 1-3 percent of its land to the Palestinians in return for the annexations. There should be adequate provision for a contiguous Palestinian state and particular care would be taken to ensure that the areas annexed to Israel from the present Palestinian Territories had as few Palestinians as possible (Clinton 2000). [2]

Refugees

As far as the refugee issue was concerned (which was and is one of the most emotive issues as far as the Israel-Palestinian conflict is concerned), the Parameters again envisaged the Palestinians giving up their 'right of return' so as to speak, waiving their claim to an unlimited return of refugees to the territory of Israel proper. Israel in return was required to make the symbolic concession of 'acknowledging the moral and material suffering caused to the Palestinian people by the 1948 war, and the need to assist the international community in addressing the problem' (Clinton 2000). An international commission would be established to implement all aspects dealing with the refugees as part of a permanent peace agreement. The Palestinian state would accept all refugees willing to settle in its territories. Another group of refugees would be rehabilitated in the host countries and a third group would be allowed to emigrate to third-party countries while a limited number would be able to return to Israel proper if Israel would be willing to accept them. Both parties would agree that United Nations General Assembly Resolution 194 had been implemented (Clinton 2000).

Security

As part of Israel's security presence in the West Bank, the Clinton Parameters proposed that Israel would keep a military presence in the Jordan Valley, under the authority of an international force for the first 36 months which could be reduced, should the threat perception to the state of Israel be felt to have been reduced. Israel would also be allowed to set up three radar facilities in the West Bank. These facilities would be provided with a Palestinian liaison and would be subject to review every ten years, with any changes to be mutually agreed by both parties to the conflict (Clinton 2000).

The Palestinian state would gain sovereignty over its own airspace, with special facilities for Israeli training and operational needs. The Palestinian state would have to be a non-militarised state and would not be allowed to possess conventional military forces, but would be allowed to have a 'strong security force'. The Palestinian state would also be provided with an international force for border security and deterrence. In the event of a serious military threat to Israel's national security requiring a state of emergency and the mobilisation of armed forces, the IDF would be allowed to deploy to certain areas and routes within the West Bank and Gaza, according to a pre-drawn map and after the relevant notifications was issued to the international forces before any such deployments (Clinton 2000).

The Clinton Parameters required that the Israel-Palestinian conflict be brought to an end as a result of these provisional agreements. This could be implemented through a United Nations Security Council Resolution declaring that resolutions 242 and 338 had been implemented (Clinton 2000).

Acceptance of the Parameters

Both sides had significant reservations about the Clinton Parameters. Prime Minister Ehud Barak, while provisionally accepting the Clinton Plan, sent President Clinton a 20-page letter of 'reservations' about the Plan. Barak's main issues of contention stood with the 'proposed transfer of sovereignty of the "Jewish" Temple Mount to Palestinian hands', and that 'no Israeli Prime Minister would be willing to accept even one Palestinian refugee on the basis of the so-called "right of return" for Palestinian refugees of the 1948 and 1967 wars' (Clinton 2000). The Israeli side also had minor reservations as regarding various security arrangements as mentioned in the Parameters including deployment areas and control over passages. Barak also demanded that Israel be allowed to retain sovereignty over the so-called 'Sacred Basin'—that is the whole area outside the Old City that included the so-called 'City of David' and the 'Tombs of the Prophets' on the road to the Mount of Olives that was not mentioned in the Parameters (Swisher 2004).

On the Palestinians side, PLO Chairman Yasser Arafat also sent a letter to President Clinton outlining the Palestinian reservations to the proposed Parameters. The Palestinians were basically concerned whether the proposals so-outlined in the Parameters would enable the establishment of a viable state for the Palestinian people. Arafat also opined that without adequately addressing the concerns of the Palestinian people in their conflict with the Israelis, there could not possibly be a 'pragmatic resolution of the conflict'. In the end, Arafat also gave his qualified approval of the Parameters while making reservations for his requests for clarifications on certain aspects of the Plan. The White House meanwhile released an official statement in which they stated that both sides had accepted the Parameters with reservations (Shavit 2002). [3]

The talks that were later held at Taba in the Sinai Peninsula were based in part on the Clinton Parameters. Some more progress towards a compromise was made at Taba, though the timing of the talks just before major general elections in Israel meant that the talks were doomed to be unfruitful. Barak's opponents in Parliament claimed that his government lacked the public and political support of the Israeli people, the Parliament (Knesset) and taking into consideration the upcoming polls, he (Barak) was submitting Israel to what amounted to a 'liquidation sale' to the Palestinians with American help (Pressman 2003: 42).

Taba Talks

The Taba conference talks that were held between January 21 and January 27, 2001 were practically the last attempts at resuscitating the Oslo Process and bringing the Israel-Palestinian Conflict to a close, by aiming at talks on reaching the 'final status' negotiations. The Taba talks are believed to the closest that the two sides ever came to reaching a final settlement than any previous attempts at peace negotiations (PLO-NAD 2001). [4] This was mainly because the Taba talks built on what had previously been achieved during the long drawn-out Oslo Process and the Camp David-II Summit meeting as well as what had been laid out in the Clinton Parameters, the release of which had preceded the Taba talks. The Clinton Parameters was by itself the main motivation for the Taba talks. The tragedy of the Talks was indeed their timings, scheduled just before major Israeli general elections in early 2001 that held no prospect for the victory of the incumbent Labour Premier Ehud Barak and as a result would by themselves carry no weight or any compulsion to follow up on the part of the newly expected Liqud Party hard-line incumbent Ariel Sharon, who had indeed already expressed his opposition to the negotiations path that Barak was leading vis-à-vis the Palestinians and the Peace Process as a whole.

In many ways, it seemed as if the negotiators at Taba, whether Israeli and Palestinian were functioning in a vacuum, as their home bases and particularly the Israeli home base was decidedly wobbly, given the context of the change of regime that was imminent in the country within a very short time. However given the numerous shortcomings of the summit meeting, there was still extensive and extremely valuable work done at Taba on all the permanent status issues like territory, Jerusalem, refugees and security, so that ways could be found to come to joint positions. The Taba talks also showed that there were still serious gaps and differences between the two sides that would have to be sought to be overcome in future negotiations. As far as the controversial issue of territory was concerned, both sides initially agreed that in accordance with UNSC 242 (text of resolution given in the appendices on page 187); the June 4 1967 lines would be the basis for the borders between Israel and the Palestinian State.

As far as the West Bank was concerned, both sides presented their own maps on the Territory which served as a basis for discussion on the OTs and the Settlements. The Israeli side presented two maps and the two sides engaged in discussions on the basis of these maps as well as a couple of illustrative maps that the Palestinian side provided as representing their understanding of Israeli interests in the West Bank (Clinton 2001). [5] The Israeli side presented proposals based on the Clinton Plan for the annexation of whole settlement blocs in the West Bank, areas that only had a minimum number of Palestinians in them. The Palestinian side however could not agree to the annexation of settlement blocs, stating that such annexation would cause definite harm to the Palestinian interests and would also jeopardise the livelihood of those Palestinians that continued to live near these settlement blocs (Matz 2003).

Gaza Strip

As far as the Strip was concerned, neither side provided any maps and the understanding that the area would be under complete Palestinian sovereignty. The Gaza settlements would be evacuated and what was debated was the time that it would take to complete this process with the Palestinians stating that six months would be more than sufficient for this process and the Israelis disagreeing with this view. There was provision as per the old Oslo Accords for a so-called 'safe passage' between the north of Gaza and the Hebron district that was the closest part of the West Bank. This fact was again agreed to by both parties along with the proviso that there should be some sort of territorial continuity between the West Bank and the Gaza Strip (Matz 2003).

Jerusalem

As far as Jerusalem was concerned, there was agreement in principle as per the Clinton Plan that Israel should have sovereignty over the Jewish neighbourhoods of East Jerusalem and the Palestinians should be given sovereignty over the Palestinian neighbourhoods. Both sides favoured the idea of an open city. The Israeli side accepted for the first time that Jerusalem would be the capital of two states, namely Yerushalaim, present Capital of Israel and Al-Quds, capital of the state of Palestine. As regards the Holy Sites regarded as holy by each side, it was agreed, again in principle, of respective territorial control of each side's respective holy sites. While Israeli sovereignty over the Western Wall was accepted, the whole question of the Haram al-Sharif/Temple Mount was left unresolved as a holy area contested by both sides to the dispute (Matz 2003).

Refugees

As regards the question of refugees, both sides agreed that a just solution to the refugee issue should be in accordance with UNSC resolution 242 which should lead to the implementation of UNGA resolution 194 (the text of relevant UNSC and UNGA resolutions provided at the end of this work as appendices). The Israeli side acknowledged its understanding that the wish to return of the Palestinian refugees should be within the framework of one of the following programs:

1. Return and repatriation to: (a) Israel proper, (b) to Israeli swapped territory, and (c) to the territories of the future Palestinian state.
2. Rehabilitation in host country.
3. Relocation to third country (MFA 2001). [6]

Both sides agreed that the United Nations (Palestinian) Refugee Works Agency (UNRWA) would be phased out gradually once the status and rehabilitation of the registered refugees was decided and solved. A provisional timetable of five years was agreed to as a target period. The Israeli side raised the issue of the compensation of Jewish refugees from various Arab countries be recognised while in turn recognising that this was not a responsibility of the Palestinian side or indeed a bilateral issue. The Palestinians raised the issue of the restitution of Palestinian refugee property within Israel which was promptly refused by the Israeli side (Taba 2001). [7]

Security

Security was an issue of particular concern to the Israelis given that from their point of view, they had historically fought the Arabs for almost a century since the reestablishment of Jewish settlement in the so-called 'Holy Land' over this very same issue. Particular emphasis was placed at the Taba talks over this issue. The Israeli side as well as the Palestinian side raised a number of issues pertaining to the post-Palestinian independence set-up in the OTs and Gaza.

1. The Israeli side requested to have three early warning stations on Palestinian Territory.
2. The Israelis insisted that the Palestinian state must be a non-militarised one as per the Clinton Plan. The Palestinians on the other hand were willing to accept limitation of the acquisition of arms and to be defined as a state with limited arms.
3. The two sides agreed that the future state of Palestine would have sovereignty over its airspace. The Israelis agreed to honour all Palestinian civil aviation rights under international regulations, but sought a unified air control system under overall Israeli control. The Israelis also requested access to Palestinian airspace for future military operations and training.
4. The Israeli side sought a 36 month period for withdrawing

from the West Bank plus another additional 36 month period for withdrawing from the Jordan valley in conjunction with an international force that would be stationed there as per Clinton Parameter recommendations. The Palestinian side rejected the 36 month time-limit as they saw this period and too long and liable to inflame Israeli-Palestinian relations, based on their experiences of previous Israeli withdrawals and refusals to withdraw during the Oslo Process.

5. The Israeli side requested to maintain and operate five emergency early-warning stations on Palestinian territory in the Jordan Valley. The Palestinians were only prepared to allow two stations that would be conditional on a time limit or dismantling. The Palestinian side also declined to agree to the stationing of Israeli armed forces on Palestinian Territory during emergency situations, but was prepared to consider ways in which international forces might be used in that capacity, particularly within the context of regional security cooperation arrangements.
6. Both sides were prepared and willing to commit themselves to promoting inter-security cooperation and fighting terror on a joint basis.
7. The Palestinian side seemed pretty confident that Palestinian sovereignty over borders and international crossing points would be recognised and adhered to in the agreement (*Ha'aretz* 2002). [8]

Results

The Taba Talks ended with a joint official statement by both parties that unequivocally stated that the two parties had never been so close to reaching an agreement as they had been at Taba over the previous week or so (Matz 2003). They expressed the hope that they would be allowed to meet after the Israeli elections to conclude their negotiations and reach an agreement that would pave the way for a genuine peace between the Israelis and the Palestinians. One of the main points highlighted by both parties in the joint statement was the rebuilding of trust between the two parties at Taba, trust that had been severely tested during the Camp David II Summit that had ended in bitter acrimony for all concerned and without any agreement, whatsoever (Matz 2003).

The breakdown of talks after Taba is often attributed to the change of government both in the United States and Israel with conservative hard-liners taking power in both countries and thus having very different priorities from the previous administrations. The negotiators at Taba had run out of political time. They could not conclude an agreement with President Clinton out of office and Israeli Premier Ehud Barak soon to face his fortunes at the election table. To quote two deeply involved men at the Taba talks, "We made progress, substantial progress. We are closer than ever to the possibility of striking a final deal", said Shlomo Ben-Ami, Israel's negotiator. Saeb Erekat, Palestinian chief negotiator, said, "My heart aches because I know we were so close. We need six more weeks to conclude the drafting of the agreement" (Matz 2003).

The Israeli general election was won as predicted by the hard-line hawkish former Israeli Army General Ariel Sharon on 6th February, 2001. Sharon's government as expected did not choose to go ahead with the high-level negotiations that had ended at Taba without complete agreement. Meanwhile the Israeli Foreign Ministry on 8th February, 2001 brought out a statement in which they confirmed that any commitments as regards the Israeli-Palestinian peace process made by the previous Barak regime would not be mandatory for the new Israeli Government under Sharon (MFA 2001). [9] This commitment by Ehud Barak effectively negated any and all the gains that Israeli and Palestinian negotiators had so painstakingly cultivated over the last couple of years since Barak came to office and in particular the progress in the peace talks that had been achieved under the auspices of President Bill Clinton's direct involvement in the negotiations via the

Camp David Process, the Clinton Parameters and the later Taba Talks.

Mitchell Report

On 28th September, 2000, prospective Israeli Premier Ariel Sharon and a posse of over a 1,000 Israeli policemen visited the Temple Mount Complex, where the Dome of the Rock Mosque and the Al-Aqsa Mosque are situated thereby creating a highly volatile situation in the region and providing the spark that was necessary for the Second Intifada, the so-called *Al-Aqsa Intifada* to break out (Greenberg 2000). [10] The day following this visit, large-scale clashes broke out across the West Bank and particularly in the environs of the Mosques themselves (Greenberg 2000). There were soon many dead and injured across the West Bank and the Gaza Strip as well as within the state of Israel among the Israeli Arabs.

The Israelis claimed that the *Al-Aqsa Intifada* had been planned months in advance by Chairman Arafat and the Palestinian Authority to regain the diplomatic hand that they had lost in the public perception after the failure of the Camp David-II Summit in July 2000. President Bill Clinton deputed Senator George J. Mitchell on a fact-finding mission to the region to study the reasons for the flare-up in the Palestinian-Israeli conflict during the period from late 2000 to early 2001 and the report produced by Senator Mitchell and published on April 30, 2001, is known after him as the 'Mitchell Report' or the 'Sharm El-Sheikh Fact-Finding Committee Report' (Mitchell 2001). [11] The Mitchell Report stressed the need for the Israelis to stop settlement building and expansion activities in the Occupied Territories (OTs) and the Palestinians to abjure violence, for the situation to calm down. The Report called for decisive action in three phases:

1. An immediate cessation of all violence.
2. Rebuilding confidence by a full-scale effort by the Palestinian Authority to prevent terrorism against Israel and the simultaneous freezing of Israeli settlement activity

(and other confidence-building measures).

3. The restarting of the negotiations process between the Israelis and the Palestinians (Mitchell 2001).

While both the Israeli Government as well as the Palestinian Authority accepted the Mitchell committee recommendations, with some reservations, there was no move by either party to implement the letter and spirit of the report on the ground in the Occupied Territories and in Israel. It was in fact the Mitchell Committee Report that became the basis for the so-called Road-Map for Peace in the Israel-Palestine region devised under the Presidency of George W. Bush. The Mitchell Report stated that:

The Sharon visit did not cause the "*Al-Aqsa Intifada*". But it was poorly timed and the provocative effect should have been foreseen; indeed it was foreseen by those who urged that the visit be prohibited. More significant were the events that followed: the decision of the Israeli police on September 29 to use lethal means against the Palestinian demonstrators; and the subsequent failure, as noted above, of either party to exercise restraint (Mitchell 2001).

It is interesting to note in this context that an Israeli domestic commission of enquiry into the events of October 2000, the so-called Orr Commission found the Israeli police wanting by being unprepared for dealing with the rioting among Israeli Arabs and Palestinians and using excessive force to disperse the mobs that resulted in the deaths (in one particular Israeli case) of 12 Israeli Arabs, one Jewish and one Palestinian citizens (*PMC* 2003). [12]

Sharon as Prime Minister of Israel

Sharon was elected Prime Minister of Israel in February 2001 (Whitaker 2001). [13] In May 2003, he endorsed the Road Map for Peace in the Middle East, the latest plan put forward by the United States, the United Nations, the European Union and Russia, the so-called Quartet that have been concerned with Middle Eastern affairs ever since on the world stage (Weisman 2003). [14] Sharon started a dialogue with the Palestinian Prime Minister Mahmud Abbas and announced his commitment to the creation of a Palestinian state in the future (Jeffery 2003). [15]

Arab Peace Plan

The Arab Peace Initiative (API) was first proposed in 2002 at the Beirut Summit of the Arab League by the then-Crown Prince and later King Abdullah of Saudi Arabia (Podeh 2007). [16] It was re-endorsed at the Riyadh Summit in 2007 (Macleod 2009). [17] The API seeks to end the Arab-Israeli conflict, normalising relations between the entire Arab region and Israel, in exchange for a complete withdrawal from the Occupied Territories (including East Jerusalem) and a 'just settlement' of the Palestinian refugee issue based on UN resolution 194 (which calls for a diplomatic resolution to the conflict and directs that any refugees 'wishing to return to their homes and live at peace with their neighbours' should be allowed to do so or, if they otherwise wish, should be provided with compensation) (Beirut 2002). [18] The response to the API has been varied with Israeli leaders generally expressing cynicism about the Plan, saying it was a 'non-starter (*BBC* 2002)'. [19] The then Premier Ariel Sharon opined that the new plan could not be accepted as it sought to replace UN resolutions 242 and 338, which call for negotiations between the two parties concerned in the conflict (Hoffman 2002). [20]

The relevant portions of the API state that:

1. Complete withdrawal from the occupied Arab territories, including the Syrian Golan Heights, to the 4 June 1967 line and the territories still occupied in southern Lebanon;
2. Attain a just solution to the problem of Palestinian refugees to be agreed upon in accordance with the UN General Assembly Resolution No. 194.
3. Accept the establishment of an independent and sovereign Palestinian state on the Palestinian territories occupied since 4th June, 1967, in the West Bank and Gaza Strip

with East Jerusalem as its capital. In return the Arab states will do the following: (a) Consider the Arab-Israeli conflict over, sign a peace agreement with Israel, and achieve peace for all states in the region; and (b) Establish normal relations with Israel within the framework of this comprehensive peace (Beirut 2002).

Like most peace plans since 1967, the API was also based on the UNSC 242, which called for the Arab states to normalise relations with Israel in exchange for an Israeli withdrawal to the June 4, 1967 armistice lines. The API was strongly supported by the Bush Administration if not in so many words, but by actions in trying in the fall of 2002 to push for a temporary ceasefire in the Al-Aqsa Intifada so as to give some breathing space to the Beirut Summit meeting of the Arab heads of states. Crown Prince Abdullah made a speech to the assembled delegates and heads of states of the Arab League on the day of the adoption of the API stating that:

In spite of all that has happened and what still may happen, the primary issue in the heart and mind of every person in our Arab Islamic nation is the restoration of legitimate rights in Palestine, Syria and Lebanon...We believe in taking up arms in self-defence and to deter aggression. But we also believe in peace when it is based on justice and equity, and when it brings an end to conflict. Only within the context of true peace can normal relations flourish between the people of the region and allow the region to pursue development rather than war.

In light of the above, and with your backing and that of the Almighty, I propose that the Arab summit put forward a clear and unanimous initiative addressed to the United Nations security council based on two basic issues: normal relations and security for Israel in exchange for full withdrawal from all occupied Arab territories, recognition of an independent Palestinian state with al-Quds al-Sharif as its capital, and the return of refugees (*NYT* 2002). [21]

Road Map for Palestinian-Israeli Peace

The Road Map for peace was a plan devised by the Americans under President George W. Bush to resolve the Israeli-Palestinian conflict, and proposed by the Quartet on the Middle East. The principle of the plan, originally drafted by US Foreign Service Officer Donald Blome, was first outlined by President Bush in a speech on 24th June, 2002, in which he called for an independent Palestinian state situated next to the Jewish state of Israel and living in peace with each other [*JPS*-32(4) 2003: 84]. The final text of the Plan was released on 30th April, 2003 [*JPS*-32(4) 2003: 87]. As was the case with most Israel-Palestine Peace Plans, this plan also did not proceed beyond the first stage with the two sides deadlocked in their respective positions.

The Road Map was defined as a 'performance-driven and goal-oriented peace plan' [*JPS*-32(4) 2003: 88]. It was built on goals without going into details. It could be summarized as: (a) end the violence; (b) halt settlement activity; (c) reform Palestinian institutions; (d) accept Israel's right to exist; (e) establish a viable, sovereign Palestinian state; and (f) reach a final settlement on all issues by 2005 [*JPS*-32(4) 2003: 85]. However, as a performance-based plan, progress would depend upon the good efforts of the parties concerned and their compliance with each of the obligations that the Quartet had put into the plan.

The Road Map composed of three phases:

1. Satisfy the preconditions for a Palestinian state.
2. Creating an independent Palestinian state with provisional borders.
3. Negotiations on permanent status agreement, recognition of a Palestinian state with permanent borders and an end to the conflict (*JPS* 2003: 89-94).

Phase I, the details of which were supposed to have been fulfilled by May 2003 included mutual recognition; an end to Palestinian violence and terrorism; Palestinian political-institutional reform; Palestinian elections; Israeli withdrawal to the positions of 28th September, 2000 (the date denoted the start of the Al-Aqsa Second Intifada); Israelis should refrain from deportations, attacks on Palestinian civilians, demolitions, destructions, etc.; allow the reopening of Palestinian institutions in East Jerusalem; again allow an improvement in the humanitarian situation for the Palestinians; allow free movement of people; put a freeze on settlement expansion and dismantling of settlement outposts built since 2001 [*JPS*-32(4) 2003: 89-92].

Phase II, which was scheduled between June-December 2003, included an International Conference to support Palestinian economic recovery and launch a process, leading to the establishment of an independent Palestinian state with provisional borders; revival of multilateral engagement on issues including regional water resources, the environment, economic development, the refugees and arms control issues; the Arab states, particularly those in the Gulf, were exhorted to restore pre-Intifada links with Israel such as Trade Offices, etc. [*JPS*-32(4) 2003: 92-93].

Phase III which was envisioned to include the period between 2004-2005 was supposed to include a Second International Conference; Permanent Status Agreement and the end of the conflict; agreement on final borders; decisions on the highly controversial question of the fate of Jerusalem, refugees and Israeli settlements in the West Bank and Gaza; individual Arab states were supposed to agree to peace deals with Israel [*JPS*-32(4) 2003: 93-94].

Acceptance of the Road Map by the Parties Concerned

While the Palestinians accepted the Road Map without any major conditions or objections attached, the right wing Liqud-led Israeli government of Ariel Sharon opposed outright acceptance of the Plan. They instead accepted 'the steps set out in the road map, rather than the road map itself' (*JPS*-32(4) 2003: 96).

On 25th May, 2003, the Israeli Prime Minister's Cabinet

approved the Road Map with 14 main reservations:

1. The Palestinians will dismantle the Palestinian Authority's (PA's) security organisations and reform the structures; the Palestinian must cease violence and incitement and educate for peace; the Palestinians must complete the dismantling of Hamas and other militant groups and their infrastructure, and collect and destroy all illegal weapons; there can be no progress to Phase II before all the above-mentioned conditions are fulfilled; Israel is not obliged to cease violence and incitement against the other party, pursuant to the road map.
2. There could be no progress to the next Phase II without a complete cessation of terror, violence and incitement by the Palestinians, of all political and militant affiliations. Israel could also not accept any timelines for carrying out the Road Map.
3. There should be replacement and reform of the current (then) leadership of the Palestinian Authority (PA). In short, the influence and authority of Chairman Arafat must be curtailed, or else there could be no progress to Phase II.
4. The process of monitoring the implementation of the Road Map should fall to the United States of America and not to the Quartet.
5. The status of the provisional Palestinian state will be determined through negotiations. The provisional state must be demilitarised, with provisional borders and only 'certain aspects of sovereignty', and subject to Israeli control of the entry and exit of all persons and cargo, plus its airspace and electromagnetic spectrum (radio, television, internet, radar, etc.).
6. Acknowledgement of the declaration of Israel's right to exist as a Jewish state and the waiver of any right to return of refugees to Israel.
7. End of the Peace Process will be the end of all claims and not only the end of the conflict.
8. The future settlement between the Israelis and the

Palestinians will be reached through agreement and direct negotiations between the two parties, in accordance with the vision outlined by President Bush in his June 24 speech (text of relevant speech attached in appendices).

9. Issues related to the final settlement will not be discussed at present. Issues not to be discussed include: settlement in Judea, Samaria and Gaza (excluding a settlement freeze and illegal outposts); the status of the Palestinian Authority and its institutions in Jerusalem and all other matters related to the final settlement.
10. The removal of references other than UNSC resolutions 242 and 338, such as UNSC 1397, the Saudi Initiative and the Arab Peace Initiative (API) adopted in Beirut. A settlement based on the Road Map will be an autonomous settlement that derives its validity there from. The only Possible references should be to UNSC resolutions 242 and 338, and then only as an outline for the conduct of future negotiations on a permanent settlement.
11. The Palestinian Authority must be subject to reform. A transitional Palestinian constitution must be composed, a Palestinian legal infrastructure must be constructed and cooperation with Israel in this field should be renewed. In the economic sphere, international efforts to rehabilitate the Palestinian economy must be continued and in the financial sphere, the American-Israeli-Palestinian agreement must be implemented in full as a condition for the continued transfer of tax revenues.
12. The redeployment of the IDF forces along the September 2000 line will be subject to the stipulation of Article 4 (previously stated with reference to absolute quiet) and will be carried out in keeping with changes to be required by the nature of the new circumstances and needs created thereby. Emphasis will be placed on the division of responsibilities and civilian authority as on September 2000 and not on the position of ground forces at that time.
13. Subject to security conditions, Israel will work to restore

Palestinian life to normal; promote the economic situation, cultivation of commercial connections, encouragement and assistance for the activities of recognised humanitarian agencies. No reference will be made to the Bertini report as a binding source document within the framework of the humanitarian issue.

14. Arab states will assist the process through the condemnation of terrorist activity. No link will be established between the Palestinian track and other tracks [Syrian, Lebanese, etc.] [*JPS*-32(4) 2003: 97-99].

Post-Road Map Developments

After the Road Map was published, President Bush visited the region from June 2-4, 2003 for two summit meetings in an attempt to gain acceptance for his Peace Plan across the region and abroad as well. Bush met with leaders of Egypt, Saudi Arabia, Jordan and Bahrain and with Prime Minister Abbas. The Arab leaders declared their support for the Road Map and promised to work on cutting the sources of funding for terrorist groups. Later Bush also met Ariel Sharon and Mahmoud Abbas to encourage them to carry forward the Road Map and to meet the stipulated deadlines given in the Peace Process (Migdalovitz 2010: 10).

The first step on the Road Map was the appointment of Mahmud Abbas as the first ever Palestinian Prime Minister. The US and Israel had demanded that Arafat yield at least some of his power to a Prime Minister who would also be his designated successor, should anything untoward happen to him. The US and the Israelis also demanded that Arafat be neutralised or sidelined in the Road Map, as they had serious doubts about his trustworthiness and ability to manage the complicated negotiations and necessary practical decisions that would of necessity have to take place between Israel and the Palestinian Authority as a result of the Road Map to Peace in the region. In fact the US refused to release and officially declare the Road Map peace process open until a Prime

Minister was appointed by Arafat for the Palestinian Authority. Mahmud Abbas was appointed on 19th March, 2003, thereby clearing the way for the release of the Road Map on 30th April, 2003 (Migdalovitz 2010: 10).

On 1st July, 2003, Israeli Premier Ariel Sharon and Palestinian Premier Mahmud Abbas both held a first-ever bilateral discussion in Jerusalem to declare their support for the Road Map Peace process (Freedman 2011: 18). In November 2003, the United Nations Security Council endorsed the Road Map through UNSC Resolution 1515 (document attached in the appendices) which called for an end to all violence including 'terrorism, provocation, incitement and destruction (UNSC 2003)'. [22] By the end of 2003, the Palestinian Authority had not succeeded in preventing terrorism and Israel had neither withdrawn from areas occupied since September 2000, nor worked to stop settlement expansion (Migdalovitz 2010: 10). As a result the requirements of Phase I of the Road Map were not fulfilled and the Road Map was not continued further. There was deadlock in the so-called Peace Process.

It was during this process of deadlock in the Road Map that the Palestinian Authority President and PLO Chairman Yasser Arafat died in a French hospital at the age of 75 (Hockstader 2004). [23] Mahmud Abbas was thus elevated to the presidency of the Palestinian National Authority (PNA). On 8th February, 2005, the leaders of Israel, Egypt, Jordan and the Palestinian Authority together held a summit meeting at Sharm el-Sheikh, known as the Sharm el-Sheikh Summit of 2005, where they all declared their ongoing commitment to the Road Map for peace in the region (Oliver 2005). [24] The Sharm el-Sheikh summit also meant the formal end of the four-year long Al-Aqsa Intifada between the Israelis and the Palestinians (Oliver 2005). The death of Arafat itself had meant the end of the Intifada that had caused something like 5000 Palestinian and Israeli casualties, the overwhelming majority of whom were Palestinians (Oliver 2005).

In August 2005, the Israelis under Sharon went ahead with what they termed the unilateral disengagement plan in the Gaza Strip (Ayalon 2005). [25] They forcibly evacuated the Gaza settlers, destroyed the settlements and also a few unauthorised ones in the West Bank (Ayalon 2005). Roughly six months after this process was completed, in early January 2006, Ariel Sharon suffered a debilitating stroke from which he never recovered (Urquhart 2006). [26] Power was transferred to his deputy, the then Finance Minister Ehud Olmert (Urquhart 2006). Olmert pledged to continue the peace process with the Palestinians through the medium of the Road Map for peace in the region (Benn 2006). [27]

Endnotes

1. Assaf Uni, Barak Ravid and Aluf Benn, 'Israel, PA agree to strive for deal by end of 2008. PM: Reality formed in 1967 will change significantly; Abbas: Israel must end occupation of W. Bank, E. J'lem.' *Ha'aretz*, November 27, 2007. Available at, http://www.haaretz.com/news/israel-pa-agree-to-strive-for-deal-by-end-of-2008-1.234086.
2. Available at, http://www.peacelobby.org/clinton_parameters.htm.
3. Ari Shavit, 'Eyes Wide Shut', [interview with Ehud Barak] *Ha'aretz*, September 6, 2002. Available at, http://www.haaretz.com/eyes-wide-shut-1.35090.
4. Available at, http://www.nad-plo.org/etemplate.php?id=98.
5. Available at, http://www.usembassy-israel.org.il/publish/peace/archives/2001/january/me0103b.html.
6. Available at, http://www.mfa.gov.il/MFA/MFAArchive/2000_2009/2001/1/Israeli-Palestinian%20Joint%20Statement%20-%2027-Jan-2001.
7. Available at, http://www.fmep.org/reports/archive/vol.-11/no.-2/deconstructing-the-taba-talks.
8. 'EU Description of the Outcome of Permanent Status Talks at Taba', *Ha'aretz*, February14, 2002. Available at, http://www.haaretz.com/news/eu-description-of-the-outcome-of-

permanent-status-talks-at-taba-1.52973.

9. Available at, http://www.mfa.gov.il/MFA/MFAArchive/2000_2009/2001/2/Barak%20to%20Bush-%20Sharon%20is%20not%20bound%20by%20negotiating.
10. Joel Greenberg, 'Unapologetic, Sharon Rejects Blame for Igniting Violence', *The New York Times*, October 5, 2000. Available at, http://www.nytimes.com/2000/10/05/world/unapologetic-sharon-rejects-blame-for-igniting-violence.html?pagewanted=print&src=pm.
11. Available at, http://eeas.europa.eu/mepp/docs/mitchell_report_2001_en.pdf.
12. "Or Panel" Finds Decades Israeli Discrimination', *Press Release: Palestine Media Centre–PMC*, Thursday, September 4, 2003. Available at, http://www.scoop.co.nz/stories/WO0309/S00048.htm.
13. Brian Whitaker, 'Middle East Dispatch: Sharon has a Mountain to Climb', *The Guardian* (London), Wednesday, February 7, 2001. Available at, http://www.theguardian.com/world/2001/feb/07/worlddispatch.brianwhitaker/print.
14. Steven R. Weisman, 'U.S. Says Sharon Is Set To Endorse Bush's Peace Plan', *The New York Times*, May 23, 2003. Available at, http://www.nytimes.com/2003/05/23/world/us-says-sharon-is-set-to-endorse-bush-s-peace-plan.html.
15. Simon Jeffery, 'Sharon Endorses Palestinian State', *The Guardian* (London), Wednesday, June 4, 2003. Available at, http://www.theguardian.com/world/2003/jun/04/usa.israel2/print
16. Elie Podeh (2007), 'The Arab Peace Initiative: A Missed Opportunity?', *Palestine-Israel Journal of Politics, Economics and Culture*, 14 (4), available at, http://www.pij.org/details.php?id=1126.
17. Scott MacLeod, 'Time to Test the Arab Peace Offer', *Time,* January 8, 2009. Available at, http://content.time.com/time/magazine/article/0,9171,1533444,0.
18. 'Excerpts from text of "Beirut Declaration" issued on the closing day of the Arab League summit', *BBC News*. March 28, 2002. Available at, http://news.bbc.co.uk/2/world/monitoring/reports/1899395.htm.

19. Arabs Offer Israel Peace Plan', *BBC News*, March 22, 2002. Available at, http://news.bbc.co.uk/2/hi/middle_east/1898736.stm.
20. Gil Hoffman, 'Sharon Warns Saudi Plan May be Arab Plot', *The Jerusalem Post*, March 4, 2002. Available at, http://www.jpost.com/Editions/2002/03/04/News/News.44486.html.
21. "Mid-east Turmoil; In Words of Saudi Prince, Peace Requires 'Two Equal Parties', The Saudi Peace Plan: Excerpts From Speech by Crown Prince of Saudi Arabia", *The New York Times*, March 27, 2002. Available at, http://www.nytimes.com/2002/03/28/world/mideast-turmoil-in-words-of-saudi-prince-peace-requires-two-equal-parties.html.
22. Available at, http://www.un.org/News/Press/docs/2003/sc7924.doc.htm.
23. Lee Hockstader, 'A Dreamer Who Forced His Cause Onto World Stage Goal of Palestinian State Proved Elusive', *Washington Post* Foreign Service, Thursday, November 11, 2004. Available at, http://www.washingtonpost.com/wp-dyn/articles/A41509-2004Nov10.html.
24. Mark Oliver, 'Sharon and Abbas Agree Ceasefire: Pledge to End Four Years of Violence', *The Guardian* (London), February 8, 2005. Available at, http://www.theguardian.com/world/2005/feb/08/israel4.
25. Daniel Ayalon, 'In Gaza, a Test Case for Peace', *The Washington Post*, July 20, 2005. Available at, http://www.washingtonpost.com/wp-dyn/content/article/2005/07/19/AR2005071901552.html.
26. Conal Urquhart, 'Israel plunged into *crisis* as Sharon suffers massive stroke Claims that prime minister's career could be at an end after haemorrhage', *The Guardian*, Thursday, January 5, 2006. Available at, http://www.theguardian.com/world/2006/jan/05/israel1.
27. Aluf Benn, 'PM Tells Blair: Road Map is Key to Progress/ Olmert Willing to Meet Abbas with no Preconditions', *Ha'aretz* (Israel), September 10, 2006. Available at, http://www.haaretz.com/print-edition/news/pm-tells-blair-road-map-is-key-to-progress-olmert-willing-to-meet-abbas-with-no-preconditions-1.196895.

8

Annapolis Conference and the Obama Era

Post-Sharon Situation

Sharon's deputy and then Finance Minister Ehud Olmert won the national elections that were held in March 2006 after the incapacitation of Sharon due to a major stroke. Olmert became Prime Minister in his own right on May 4, 2006 (Olmert 2013). [1] On June 4, he announced that he would be meeting with PNA President Mahmud Abbas to revive the Peace Process through the medium of the Road Map. The first met along with King Abdullah of Jordan on June 22, 2006 at Petra in the Hashemite Kingdom of Jordan (*IHT* 2006). [2] In January 2006, Hamas surprised all people including itself by winning the much-delayed elections to the Palestinian Legislative Council (PLC), the Palestinian Parliament (Wilson 2006). [3] Both Israel and the United States reacted in predictable ways by declaring that they would have no exchange with a terrorist group, or in short, that they would not recognise a Palestinian Government led by Hamas (Wilson 2006). US President George Bush said that the US would not deal with Hamas until it renounced the call, implicit in the Hamas Constitution for the destruction of the state of Israel. Hamas refused to do so (Goldenberg and MacAskill 2006). [4]

Meanwhile, 2006 saw two major conflicts in the region, the 2006 Israel-Gaza Conflict, also known as Operation Summer Rains, which was fought mainly in reaction to the kidnapping of the Israeli reservist Gilad Shalit by Hamas militants on June 25, 2006. [5] The war was fought between June 28 and November 26, 2006 and resulted in the death of over 400 people, soldiers and civilians and mainly Palestinians (OCHA 2006). [6] The 2006 Lebanon War was also known as the 2006 Israel-Hezbollah war and in known in Lebanon as the

July War and in Israel as Second Lebanon War. The war was fought between July 12 and August 14, 2006. Casualties stood in the range of 1,500-2,000 dead, including soldiers and civilians on both sides (Boot and Kirkpatrick 2006). [7]

Again in 2007, there was further conflict in the region, this time of an intra-Palestinian fratricidal kind, between Fatah and Hamas, fought primarily in the Gaza Strip (Erlanger, Kershner 2007). [8] The Fatah-Hamas conflict was also referred to as the Palestinian Civil War and the Conflict of Brothers (Erlanger and Kershner 2007). This conflict resulted in Hamas taking control of the Gaza Strip and simultaneously Fatah controlling most of the West Bank, coupled with each group trying to drive the other out of the areas that they occupied. Palestinian internal politics since then has been characterised by a fractured polity, with Hamas's control of the Gaza Strip meaning almost total isolation for the people of the Strip from the outside world, as Israel has enforced a strict blockade of the area from both land as well as sea to put pressure on the radical Islamist grouping, thereby putting the people of the Strip under incredible economic and social hardship and suffering (OCHA 2009). [9]

Hamas's control over the Gaza Strip and virtually half of the Palestinian political spectrum has also given the Israelis a good excuse to desist from serious or meaningful peace negotiations with the Palestinians on the pretext of not having a suitable partner for peace in the region, Hamas being ideologically committed to the establishment of an Islamic state on all of the historic territories of Palestine, much of which is now the state of Israel. The founding Charter of Hamas mentions that the state of Israel would be eventually destroyed by Islam (Hamas 1998).

Hamas has never to date formally repudiated this founding Charter of principles that seek to guide the Palestinian Islamic Movement (Hamas 1998). Hamas and Fatah have periodically sought to bury their differences and come together in a show of unity to form a pan-Palestinian national government of unity, but these efforts have also been stoutly opposed by Israel and also by the US under the pretext of having nothing whatsoever to do with a 'fundamentalist' Islamist grouping such as Hamas (Baconi 2011). [10] It remains to be seen whether Hamas and Fatah will really be able to cooperate together in forming a national government as being envisaged in the present-future as the two parties have never had a history of collaborating effectively with each other and indeed have only had an experience of intense political and sometimes fratricidal rivalry and conflict. For all practical purposes, the Palestinian polity remains split into two with Fatah-led and Ramallah-based Palestinian National Authority and the Hamas Government in Gaza, both seeing themselves as the true representatives of the Palestinian people.

Annapolis Conference

The Annapolis conference was a Middle East Peace Conference that was held at the United States Naval Academy in Annapolis, Maryland on November 27, 2007 (McCormack 2007). [11] The Conference was the first time that a two-state solution was announced as the ultimate procedural devise by which peace could be assured in the Palestinian-Israeli situation. The then US Secretary of State Condoleezza Rice organised the conference which was attended by Palestinian President Mahmud Abbas, Israeli Premier Ehud Olmert and then US President George W. Bush. The purpose of the conference was to produce a document that would address most of the issues that needed to be solved to end the Palestinian-Israeli conflict. The conference was also a last-ditch attempt to resuscitate the, by then, largely moribund Road Map for Peace in the region that George Bush had invested so much political and diplomatic capital in, during his first term in office. The aim was the eventual establishment of a Palestinian state.

For the Palestinians, Mahmud Abbas categorically stated that only a Palestinian state comprising of the West Bank and

Gaza Strip in its entirety would be acceptable to them, with any Israeli desire to annex portions of the West Bank (which were occupied by the Settlers) subject to discussions between the Palestinians and the Israelis on a one to one basis. Abbas also demanded that all six central issues to the conflict be debated at the conference including Jerusalem, the Refugees and Right to Return, Borders, Settlements, Water and Security (*JPS* 2008: 80-82).

Given the impression that the then Premier Ehud Olmert was not so much a hawk and hardliner as his predecessor Ariel Sharon or his contemporary *Liqud* leader and rival Benjamin Netanyahu, there were hopes particularly among the Palestinians that it would be possible to come to a final agreement with him in resolving the conflict. Abbas is reported to have gone on record as stating that he hoped to reach an agreement with Israel by the end of November 2007, that is, by the time of the conference which he then intended to put to popular agreement through the medium of a referendum (Abbas 2007). [12] He also expressed the hope that a final agreement with Israel might be possible within six months of the conference. Hamas was staunchly against the conference and organised protests in opposition to Palestinian participation in the Annapolis process (MacLeod 2007). [13]

On the Israeli side, there were problems for Ehud Olmert when he indicate din October 2007 that he might be willing to give up some parts of East Jerusalem to the Palestinians as part of a peace deal with them. This proposal of his drew heavy flak from right wing Israelis and Jewish organisations outside Israel as well as the strong Christian Zionist lobby in the United States. The joint statement that was provided by President Bush just prior to the conference was signed by both parties to the conflict and called for the launch of 'good faith, bilateral negotiations in order to conclude a peace treaty resolving all outstanding issues, including core issues, without exception. The final peace settlement will establish Palestine as a homeland for the Palestinian people just as Israel is the homeland for the Jewish people' (*JPS* 2008: 77-80).

The Annapolis Conference differed from other previous Middle Eastern peace conferences in many respects. This was the first time that both Israelis and Palestinians started talks at a major international conference on the basis of a two-state solution as the ultimate harbinger of peace in the region. This was also the first time in many decades that the context of the conference did not include adversarial positions from either the UN or the EU against the Israelis. This time round, the UN and the EU were both largely behind the US effort. Another fact that would have been pleasing to the Israelis was that the importance of the Quartet had reduced since it was first formed. At Annapolis, the US as host played the role of the major mediator while the other three members of the Quartet had to be content with reduced and supporting roles (*JPS* 2008: 74-75).

Jewish organisations that were staunchly against any form of concessions to the Palestinians as part of any peace deal actively protested against the Olmert government's participation in the Annapolis Summit, on the basis of territorial concessions to the Palestinians. There were protests organised in front of Israeli embassies in New York and Washington D.C. There were also protests against any move to alter the status of Jerusalem (Morrison 2007). [14]

2008 Gaza War

After the Hamas consolidation of power in the Gaza Strip, Hamas fought a brief war with Israel in December-January 2008, the so-called Operation Cast Lead as it was termed by the IDF (Ibish 2012). [15] The Gaza War was known by the Palestinians as the Gaza Massacre or the Battle of al-Furqan (the Criterion) (Wiegand 2010: 131; Al-Kayyali 2009). [16] It was a three-week long conflict that began on December 27, 2008 and ended on January 18, 2009, with both sides declaring a unilateral ceasefire. This was a conflict that was fought in terms of the recurrent rocket attacks that were launched from

Gaza in to southern Israel and the resultant retaliatory bombings and missile attacks that the Israelis launched against the Palestinian militants in Gaza. The Israelis also wanted to stop weapons smuggling into the Gaza Strip through the tunnels dug across the Egyptian border in and around Rafah in the Gaza Strip (*CSM* 2008). [17]

This conflict resulted in well over a thousand Palestinians and Israelis dead with Palestinian civilians being the overwhelming majority of those killed. In September 2009, the controversial Goldstone Report was published by the UN special commission that was set up to investigate human rights abuses during the Gaza War (Goldstone 2009). [18] The report concluded that there had been large-scale violations of human rights (as could be expected), war crimes and crimes against humanity by both parties; the Israelis and Palestinians during the war and recommended bringing the guilty form both sides to justice (Goldstone 2009).

On September 24, 2009, Israel released a report rejecting the findings of the UN-sponsored Goldstone Report and disputing its findings (MFA 2009). [19] The strong Israeli rejection of the Goldstone Report eventually forced Justice Goldstone to issue a reversal of his earlier conclusion, making a statement in 2011, in which he concluded that he no longer believed that Israeli forces had deliberately targeted Palestinian civilians (Goldstone 2011). [20]

In January 2009, before the February 2009 Israeli elections, Benjamin Netanyahu who was the election front-runner and the Liqud Party leader informed Tony Blair, the Middle East Envoy of the Quartet that he would continue the policy of Ariel Sharon and Ehud Olmert in allowing the 'natural' growth of the settlements, while not building new ones, thereby both contravening as well as complying with the stipulations of the Road Map for peace in the region (Netanyahu 2009). [21]

Obama Era

When President Barack Obama took office in January

2009, he made peaceful settlement of the Palestinian-Israeli issue a top commitment of his foreign policy agenda (Black 2009). [22] He made this clear by appointing former Senator George Mitchell as his special peace envoy to the Israel-Palestine region (Black 2009). When Mitchell reached the region, Netanyahu stated that he would be only willing to resume negotiations with the Palestinians if they recognised Israel as a Jewish state (Harel, Issacharoff and Eldar 2009). [23] This proposal by Netanyahu eventually got US-backing, but it was rejected by the Palestinians with good reason, the proposal being something entirely new and not something that the Israelis had previously sounded the Palestinians about (Khatib 2009). [24]

Meanwhile in Obama's June 4, 2009 speech at Cairo University, where he took the opportunity to address the Muslim world in general, he stated with respect to the Palestinian-Israeli conflict that 'the only solution is for the aspirations of both sides to be met through two states' (Obama 2009). [25] Obama also called upon both the Israelis and the Palestinians to resume negotiations. With regard to the Settlements in what was Palestinian land, Obama stated that, 'The United States does not accept the legitimacy of continued Israeli settlements, as they undermine efforts to achieve peace. It is time for these settlements to stop (Obama 2009)'. [26]

Netanyahu 'Peace Process'

In what was billed as a response to Obama's Cairo speech, Netanyahu gave a speech at Bar-Ilan University in Israel where for the first time; he acknowledged that a demilitarised Palestinian state might be possible if the Palestinians agreed to the whole of Jerusalem, East and West, being the unified capital of Israel, but kept open as a city of all religions. He also stated that the Palestinians would have to accept an existence without a military and should also give up their refugee population's right of return. He also insisted that the Palestinians must accept the right for a natural growth in the settlements, especially when their permanent status is up for further negotiation. [27]

Again in response to this speech, Mahmoud Abbas on July 12, 2009 gave a press conference where he categorically stated that the Palestinians would never agree to cede any part of the West Bank to Israel, that he would demand territorial contiguity between Gaza and the West Bank, and that he would never agree to waive the Palestinian right of return (Waked 2009). [28] In a later letter to President Obama, Abbas demanded that any peace deal be strictly based on the 1967 borders and the Arab Peace Initiative (API) (Waked 2009). Saeb Erekat, one of the lead Palestinian negotiators' also stated that the Palestinians would not accept any 'mid-way' solutions, maintaining that the Palestinians would reject any deal between the US and Israel that would allow Israel to continue with settlement construction, while at the same time pursuing a so-called 'peace deal' with the Palestinians (Waked 2009).

Meanwhile on September 20, 2009, the White House announced that they would host a three-way meeting between Obama, Netanyahu and Abbas, within the framework of the UN General assembly, with the aim being to restart the negotiations on Middle East Peace. This proposed meeting took place on September 22, 2009 in New York (Ravid 2009). [29] After this meeting, Netanyahu stated that he had agreed with Abbas that peace talks should be restarted as soon as possible (*Xinhua* 2009). [30]

In November 2009, the Israelis under Netanyahu announced a ten-month settlement-building freeze that excluded East Jerusalem, public buildings within the settlements and projects already underway (Ravid 2009). [31] Netanyahu for the first time also reaffirmed Israel's commitment to the Road Map, during the first US Presidential term of Barack Obama (Ravid 2009). In September 2010, Netanyahu further confirmed that the partial settlement freeze would not be extended beyond November 2010, reverting to

Israel's previous and preferred stand that there would be no settlement freeze until the Palestinians also fulfilled their obligations under the Road Map of forsaking violence in the West Bank and the Gaza Strip (Sherwood 2010). [32]

President Obama in his maiden speech before the UN in September 2010, made the statement that he was hopeful of a success in Israel-Palestinian peace talks within one year (Obama 2010). [33] Throughout 2010, there was pressure from the Obama administration on both the Palestinians and the Israelis to restart peace talks (Sherwood 2010). [34] The Americans got the support of both the Egyptians and the Jordanians to put pressure on the Palestinians to enter into peace negotiations with the Israelis. The main purpose was to get the Palestinians to accept the Israeli settlement freeze and enter into the negotiations process with them. The aim of the talks was to forge the framework of a final agreement within one year on a two-state solution (Benn 2010). [35] Expectations of a breakthrough were not very high given the history of Israeli-Palestinian negotiations over a long period.

The talks that started in Washington D.C. in September 2010, after ten months and seven rounds of indirect talks that began in November 2009, continued into a second round at Sharm el-Sheikh from September 14 onwards (*Guardian* 2010). [36] The main agreement that was reached during these talks was on the principle of a land swap, with Israel exchanging small parts of its territory for border settlement areas in the West Bank. An issue of dispute arose with the Palestinians demanding that the land annexed should be on the basis of a 1:1 exchange of territory and the Israelis arguing for something less from their side (Migdalovitz 2010: 2). Direct talks however broke down in late September 2010 over the refusal by Netanyahu to extend a partial freeze on settlement construction in the West Bank (Migdalovitz 2010: 34-35).

On October 2, 2010, Palestinian President Mahmud Abbas made it clear that the Palestinians would abandon the negotiations process if settlement construction was restarted

(Greenberg 2010). [37] In short, he expected the Netanyahu government to extend the moratorium that they had declared on the construction of new settlements in the West Bank. The Palestinians were asking for an extension of the settlement freeze for just a couple of months more. They believed that would be sufficient time for peace negotiations with the Israelis to be concluded and a peace treaty signed. In the view of the Palestinian Authority, Israeli construction of settlements constituted an imposition of 'facts on the ground' in the West Bank and was a violation of international law. By refusing to extend the moratorium on settlement construction, Palestinian President Mahmud Abbas stated that 'Netanyahu could not be trusted as a genuine peace negotiator if the settlement freeze was not extended' (Greenberg 2010).

Meanwhile on October 11, 2010, Netanyahu during a speech at the opening of the third session of the 18th Knesset linked the extension of the moratorium on settlement construction to the Israeli demand that the Palestinian Authority recognise the state of Israel as the state of the Jewish people (*Ha'aretz* 2010). [38] This proposal was rejected by the Palestinian leadership that stressed that the recognition of Israel as a Jewish state had nothing whatsoever to do with the settlement freeze (*Ha'aretz* 2010). European countries and the US were quite critical of the refusal by the Israelis to continue with the settlement freeze. Palestinian President Abbas stated that 'We will never sign an agreement recognising Israel as a Jewish state' (Khoury 2010). [39] Palestinian negotiators confirmed that their hypothetical recognition of Israel as a Jewish state would undermine the rights of the million plus Israeli Arabs while at the same time degrade the right to return of millions of Palestinian refugees to their former homes in Israel proper (Khoury 2010).

Palestinian Counter Steps

Given the freeze in the negotiations process, the Palestinians began to think of other means by which to achieve their critical needs vis-à-vis a state of their own next to the state of Israel. Their new strategy was to unilaterally declare an independent state of Palestine and get it recognized by a majority of states in the United Nations. The initial step in this strategy was to ask the international community to recognize an independent Palestine along 1967 borders. During the period from late 2010 and early 2011, a number of Latin American countries such as Brazil, Argentina, Chile, Ecuador, Bolivia, Venezuela, and Uruguay recognised the State of Palestine (*Ha'aretz* 2010). [40] The Israelis were decidedly opposed to this process as they claimed that it was in opposition to the now 'practically defunct' Bush-era Road Map for peace in the region (Bronner and Hauser 2012). [41]

New Israeli Peace Offers

In January 2011, Israeli Foreign Minister Avigdor Lieberman proposed a peace plan that would see a Palestinian state being established on around 50 percent of the West Bank and the whole of Gaza, with the final borders to be negotiated later on (Ravid 2011). [42] This was a proposal that had initially found favour with present Israeli Premier Benjamin Netanyahu as well as with many of other right-wing Israelis as this plan would mean that the Israelis would get to keep almost 50 percent of the West Bank and could go ahead with their settlement construction activities and other military activities on this land. This plan was rejected outright by the Palestinians (*Hindu* 2011). [43]

In February 2011, the Israelis offered further concessions that included easing economic and security restrictions against the Palestinians, allowing additional Arab construction to take place in East Jerusalem, giving the Palestinian Authority security control in several West Bank cities and discussing a proposed Palestinian gas field alongside an Israeli one in the sea off the coast of Gaza (Antreasyan 2013: 34). Their only condition was that the Palestinians resume direct negotiations. The proposal was agreed to by the Middle East Quartet Chief

Tony Blair and rejected by the Palestinians who characterised the proposal as hyperbole intended to divert attention from the real issue which was the refusal by the Israelis to stop settlement construction in the West Bank and East Jerusalem (Antreasyan 2013: 34).

On February 12, 2011, the chief Palestinian Negotiator Saeb Erekat announced his resignation from the post over the revelations of the Wiki Leaks inspired Palestine Papers that portrayed him as being willing to agree to wide-ranging concessions on the issues of primary importance to the Palestinians such as Jerusalem, Refugees, Borders and Israeli Security. He however maintained that the documents were concocted and false (*Ha'aretz* 2011). [44]

Meanwhile on February 18, 2011, the United States vetoed a United Nations Security Council Resolution condemning Israeli settlement activity (Pilkington 2011). [45] The purpose of the US veto was indicated by US Ambassador to the UN as being the only way to demonstrate the Obama administration's commitment that the goal of peace in the Israel-Palestine conflict could be only reached through direct negotiations (Pilkington 2011). This act by the Obama government was met by mixed reactions from both the Israelis and the Palestinians with the Israeli Premier Netanyahu expressing his appreciation of the US veto while the Palestinians accused the US of bias (Pilkington 2011).

In March 2011, Israeli Premier Netanyahu reportedly made reference to a consideration of a temporary peace deal that would see a Palestinian state established with provisional borders with the final borders to be left to negotiations at a later stage, due to the present Palestinian refusal to negotiate (Ravid 2011). [46] The Palestinians rejected this idea as they had done with the Lieberman Proposals in January 2011 (Teibel 2011). [47]

Palestinian Responses

The Palestinians meanwhile announced that unless a deal

was done by September 2011, they would unilaterally declare independence and would seek recognition from the United Nations and also apply for membership in that organisation (Bronner and Kershner 2011). [48] Palestinian President Mahmoud Abbas claimed that the new state that was envisaged to be formed by the Palestinians through UN recognition would be ready to negotiate all core issues with the Israelis and a key focus would be finding a 'just solution' for the Palestinian refugees in accordance with UNGA resolution 194 (Bronner and Kershner 2011). [49] The Palestinians declared that they would be unwilling to re-enter negotiations or reconsider plans for a unilateral declaration of statehood until Israel froze all settlement building activities and agreed to a negotiated solution based on the 1967 borders (Bronner and Kershner 2011).

In April 2011, Fatah and Hamas signed a unity agreement, the first of many that would never really take off, because of the fundamental differences in the ideological make-up of both these parties (Levy 2011). [50] There were also plans by both parties to form a unity government. Israel showed displeasure at this proposed 'national unity' government by deciding to withhold funds that they collected through taxes on behalf of the Palestinian Authority. The funds were later released when the PA promised that the funds would not be made accessible to Hamas (Sanders 2011). [51] Israeli PM Netanyahu went so far as to warn the PA that they would have to choose between peace with Israel or peace with Hamas, showing that there would be no compromise on the Israeli-side with the Islamist-militant movement based in Gaza (Toameh 2013). [52]

In September 2011, the Palestinian Authority conducted a diplomatic campaign at the United Nations General Assembly to get recognition for the State of Palestine within the 1967 borders with Jerusalem as its capital (Abbas 2011). [53] On September 23, President Mahmoud Abbas presented a request to recognize the State of Palestine as the 194th member state of the UN. No decision has yet been taken on this step by the present UN Secretary-General Ban Ki-moon (UNNC 2011). [54] This action was understandably condemned by Israel as a unilateral step on the part of the Palestinians that would have no beneficial impact whatsoever on the peace process (*Economist* 2011). [55]

In April 2012, Palestinian Authority (PA) President Mahmud Abbas sent a letter to Israeli PM Netanyahu in which he emphasized that for peace talks to resume, Israel must stop settlement building activity in the West Bank and East Jerusalem as well as recognize the 1967 borders as the basis of a two-state solution (Brulliard 2012). [56] Netanyahu in his reply to Abbas's letter, recognised for the first time the right of the Palestinian people to have a state of their own, but as he had done earlier, emphasized that such a state must be demilitarised. He expressed hope that his new national unity government in Israel would provide a new opportunity for negotiations to take place (*Dawn* 2012). [57]

It was in 2012 that the Palestinian Authority requested the UN for admission as a UN non-member state, a move that only required the vote of the UN General Assembly. Hamas also supported this move (Bronner and Hauser 2012). It was over a year after the Palestinian attempt for recognition at the UN, that the UN General Assembly on November 29, 2012 passed a motion that bestowed non-member observer status on the Palestinians, a move that was enough to incur the censure and displeasure of the Israelis and the Americans (Bronner and Hauser 2012).

In November 2012, the Israelis and Palestinians based in Gaza fought another limited war known by the Israelis as Operation Pillar of Defence (in Hebrew, Pillar of Cloud) (Ha'aretz 2012). [58] The war started with the killing of Ahmed Jabari, chief of the military wing of Hamas in Gaza (Meo 2012). [59] The war ended with an Egyptian-mediated ceasefire on November 21, 2012. This represented a major diplomatic victory for the post-Mubarak Islamic Brotherhood-led Egyptian government (Aneja 2012). [60] Well over a hundred Palestinians, both civilians and militants were killed in this war (Aneja 2012).

Secretary of State John Kerry's Initiatives

President Obama appointed Senator John Kerry as his new Secretary of State succeeding Hillary Clinton who resigned her post at the end of Obama's first term (Kerry 2013). [61] Ever since taking office in February 2013, Kerry dedicated much of his time towards restarting the peace talks between the Israelis and the Palestinians that were frozen in September 2010 (Khouri 2013). [62] Under intense pressure from the US administration, both sides resumed peace negotiations in July 2013. The Kerry peace moves also gained the acceptance and sanction of the Arab League (Sheinman 2013). [63]

Hamas as expected rejected the Kerry initiative stating that Mahmud Abbas had no legitimacy to negotiate in the name of the Palestinian people (Hamas 2013). [64] The talks were held under extreme secrecy, the whole point being that learning from previous experiences of Israeli-Palestinian peace negotiations, publicity was felt to be one of the main stumbling blocks to the successful pursuit of the deliberations (Weiss 2013). [65] The talks were to be held on the basis of a return to the 1967 borders (to please the Palestinians) and on the premise that Israel would be recognised as a Jewish state by the Palestinians (to please the Israelis), while giving both sides the option to differ with these conditions whilst themselves engaging in the deliberations (Weiss 2013).

After several rounds of talks, the Israelis, Palestinians and the Americans agreed that sufficient progress had been achieved in the negotiations to warrant an intensification of the deliberations with an increased US participation (Kerry 2013). [66] This was made clear by Kerry while speaking at a meeting that was held on the sidelines of the yearly UN General Assembly in September 2013 (Kerry 2013). Kerry also made it clear that there was a two track negotiations system in progress. The first track included the four main

Israeli and Palestinian negotiators, namely Tzipi Livni, Yitzhak Molcho, Saeb Erekat, and Muhammad Shtayyeh (Kerry 2013).

The second track included the top bosses of Israeli premier Binyamin Netanyahu, Palestinian President Mahmud Abbas and US President Barack Obama (Kerry 2013). Kerry also stressed that he was the only person mandated to make any comments on the peace talks. All the final status issues were on the table including Territory, Security, Refugees and Jerusalem (Kerry 2013). And the negotiators were working towards the final accords and not any interim agreements. A total of 13 meetings had been held by the negotiators since July and there was a provisional deadline of nine months in which to finalise an accord. A final accord was provisionally forecast for the middle of 2014 (Kaufman 2013). [67]

Deadlock in the Peace Process

A common problem with all the peace plans attempted by the Palestinians and the Israelis was that, very often, the parties concerned failed to carry out, to a sufficient extent the minimum of goodwill measures necessary for the peace process to go forward. Negotiations that were attempted to deal with the 'final status' issues always collapsed due to an outbreak of hostilities that inevitably involved both sides (Ward 2013). [68]

The understandable result was that both Palestinians and Israelis have got tired of the so-called 'Peace Process' that does not adequately reflect the realities on the ground. The further division of the Palestinian territories since 2007, with the West Bank under the control of the Fatah movement and the Gaza Strip under the control of Hamas has made any attempts at all-inclusive peace talks all the more complicated. Israelis doubt the attitude of Hamas towards a negotiated peace with Israel. They also have serious doubts about the ability of the Palestinians to make peace with each other and with the Israelis and to make that 'peace' durable over the long-term.

The Israelis also fear a worst-case scenario where the Hamas movement might try to seize control of the West Bank given the unstable nature of Palestinian politics and the rivalry among the various factions within and without the nationalist Fatah movement (Mahnaimi 2012). [69]

The Israelis also do not trust many Palestinian high-ranking members of Fatah whom they say promise their people in the Arabic language a full and complete return of every refugee into the original Palestine (mainly today's Israel), a position totally unacceptable to the Israelis as this would change the Jewish character of the state of Israel (Ibish 2011). [70] On the Palestinian side, there is the ever present issue of the extensive and expanding Israeli settlements in the West Bank that make peace talks with the Israelis all but impossible as well as continually reduce the land that is available for the Palestinians to build, live and establish their state on.

Endnotes

1. 'Ehud Olmert: Biography', *Ha'aretz* (Israel), Thursday, November 14, 2013. Available at, http://www.haaretz.com/misc/tags/Ehud%20Olmert-1.476763.
2. 'Olmert and Abbas Meet in Jordan': Africa and Middle East, *International Herald Tribune*, June 22, 2006. Available at, http://www.nytimes.com/2006/06/22/world/africa/22iht-web.0622israel.2027161.html?_r=0.
3. Scott Wilson, 'Hamas Sweeps Palestinian Elections, Complicating Peace Efforts in Mideast', *The Washington Post Foreign Service*, Friday, January 27, 2006, available at, http://www.washingtonpost.com/wp-dyn/content/article/2006/01/26/AR2006012600372_pf.html.
4. Suzanne Goldenberg and Ewen MacAskill, 'Bush Demands Renunciation of Violence and Recognition of Israel', *The Guardian*, Washington, Friday, January 27, 2006. Available at, http://www.theguardian.com/world/2006/jan/27/usa.israel.
5. Refer 'Operation Summer Rains,' *GlobalSecurity.org*. Available at, http://www.globalsecurity.org/military/world/war/intifada2_summer-rains.htm.

6. Available at, http://www.ochaopt.org/documents/GazaStrip_10Oct06.pdf.
7. Max Boot, Jeane J. Kirkpatrick, 'The Second Lebanon War', *The Weekly Standard*, Washington D.C., 11 (47), September 4, 2006. Available at, http://www.weeklystandard.com/Content/Public/Articles/000/000/012/621hdtho.asp.
8. Steven Erlanger, Isabel Kershner, 'Attacks Escalate as Palestinians Fight for Power', *The New York Times*, June 13, 2007. Available at, http://www.nytimes.com/2007/06/13/world/middleeast/13mideast.html?_r=1&oref=slogin.
9. Available at, http://www.ochaopt.org/documents/Ocha_opt_Gaza_impact_of_two_years_of_blockade_August_2009_english.pdf.
10. Tareq Baconi, 'Hamas and Fatah Can Work Together', Comment is free, *The Guardian* (London), Tuesday, May 17, 2011. Available at, http://www.theguardian.com/commentisfree/2011/may/17/hamas-fatah-palestinians-eu-us-israel.
11. Sean McCormack, 'Announcement of Annapolis Conference', U.S. State Department, Washington, DC, November 20, 2007. Available at, http://2001-2009.state.gov/r/pa/prs/ps/2007/nov/95458.htm.
12. Abbas to call for referendum in case deal reached with Israel: official", *People's Daily Online* (China), October 3, 2007. Available at, http://english.people.com.cn/90001/90777/6276123.html.
13. Scott MacLeod, 'Can Iran and Hamas Sink Annapolis?' *Time*, Nov. 28, 2007. Available at, http://content.time.com/time/world/article/0,8599,1688472,00.html.
14. James Morrison, 'Not an Inch', *The Washington Times*, November 26, 2007. Available at, http://www.highbeam.com/doc/1G1-171785170.html" title="Not an Inch | HighBeam Research">Not an Inch</a.
15. Hussein Ibish, 'Operation Cast Lead 2.0: Israel and Hamas are Battling it Out in the Gaza Strip in a Conflict No One Can Win', *Foreign Policy*, November 14, 2012. Available at, http://www.foreignpolicy.com/articles/2012/11/14/operation_cas

t_lead_20?print=yes&hidecomments=yes&page=full.

16. Available at, http://www.alzaytouna.net/index.php?c=137&a=99677.
17. "Report: Israel Set to Launch 'limited operation' in Gaza: But Israel Also Reopens Border to Allow Humanitarian Supplies into Palestinian Territory", *The Christian Science Monitor-CSMonitor.com*, December 26, 2008. Available at, http://www.csmonitor.com/World/terrorism-security/2008/1226/p99s01-duts.html.
18. Available at, http://www.theguardian.com/world/2009/sep/16/israel-rejects-war-crimes-gaza.
19. Available at, http://mfa.gov.il/MFA/ForeignPolicy/Terrorism/Pages/Initial-response-goldstone-report-24-Sep-2009.aspx.
20. Richard Goldstone, 'Reconsidering the Goldstone Report on Israel and War Crimes', Washington Post Opinions, *The Washington Post*, April 1, 2011. Available at, http://articles.washingtonpost.com/2011-04-01/opinions/35207016_1_drone-image-goldstone report-israeli-evidence.
21. 'Netanyahu Wants to Let West Bank Settlements Grow', *The Washington Times*, Tuesday, January 27, 2009. Available at, http://www.washingtontimes.com/news/2009/jan/27/netanyahu-wants-to-let-west-bank-settlements-grow/?page=all#pagebreak.
22. Ian Black, 'Arab World Fears Barack Obama's Stance on the Israeli-Palestinian Conflict is Just More of the Same', *The Guardian* (London), Friday, March 20, 2009. Available at, http://www.theguardian.com/world/2009/mar/20/ian-black-middle-east.
23. Amos Harel, Avi Issacharoff and Akiva Eldar, 'Netanyahu Demands Palestinians Recognize Jewish State', PM to U.S. envoy George Mitchell: No talks on Palestinian statehood without this recognition', *Ha'aretz* (Israel), April 16, 2009. Available at, http://www.haaretz.com/news/netanyahu-demands-palestinians-recognize-jewish-state-1.274207.
24. Ghassan Khatib, 'Netanyahu is Throwing Obstacles in the Way of Peace', Palestinian-Israeli crossfire, *bitterlemons.org*, Edition 17, May 4, 2009. Available at,

http://www.bitterlemons.org/previous/bl040509ed17.html.

25. Refer Document IX in Appendices.
26. Ibid.
27. Refer Document X in Appendices.
28. Ali Waked, 'Abbas: We Won't Waive Right of Return', *Ynet news/Reuters*, July 12, 2009. Available at, http://www.ynetnews.com/articles/0,7340,L-3745068,00.html.
29. Barak Ravid (The Associated Press), 'Obama to Host Abbas, Netanyahu at Summit Tuesday, *Ha'aretz* (Israel), September 20, 2009. Available at, http://www.haaretz.com/news/obama-to-host-abbas-netanyahu-at-summit-tuesday-1.7578.
30. 'Obama, Netanyahu, Abbas Agree to Resume Negotiations', *Xinhua* News Agency, September 23, 2009. Available at, http://www.china.org.cn/international/2009-09/23/content_18581227.htm.
31. Barak Ravid, 'Netanyahu Declares 10-month Settlement Freeze to Restart Peace Talks', *Ha'aretz* (Israel), November 25, 2009. Available at, http://www.haaretz.com/news/netanyahu-declares-10-month-settlement-freeze-to-restart-peace-talks-1.3435.
32. Harriet Sherwood, 'Netanyahu Urges Restraint as West Bank Settlement Building Freeze is Lifted', *The Guardian* (London), Sunday, September 26, 2010. Available at, http://www.theguardian.com/world/2010/sep/26/settlements-freeze-israel-palestine-netanyahu.
33. 'Obama's Remarks at the United Nations', *The New York Times*, September 23, 2010. Available at, http://www.nytimes.com/2010/09/24/us/politics/24obama-text.html?pagewanted=all.
34. Harriet Sherwood, 'Netanyahu Urges Restraint as West Bank Settlement Building Freeze is Lifted'.
35. Aluf Benn, 'At the Mideast Peace Talks, a Changed Netanyahu', Opinions, *The Washington Post*, Sunday, September 5, 2010. Available at, http://www.washingtonpost.com/wp-dyn/content/article/2010/09/03/AR2010090302209.html.
36. 'Middle East Peace Talks Set to Resume: Clinton to Meet Binyamin Netanyahu and Mahmoud Abbas in Egypt for Talks Amid Tensions Over Settlements', *theguardian.com,* Monday 13

September 2010. Available at, http://www.theguardian.com/world/2010/sep/13/middle-east-clinton-peace-talks.

37. Joel Greenberg, 'Palestinians: Peace Talks Hinge on Israeli Settlement Construction', *The Washington Post*, Sunday, October 3, 2010. Available at, http://www.washingtonpost.com/wp-dyn/content/article/2010/10/02/AR2010100200797.html.
38. 'Netanyahu Offers Settlement Freeze in Return for Recognition as Jewish State, Palestinians Say No', *Haaretz* Service and News Agencies, October 11, 2010. Available at, http://www.haaretz.com/news/national/netanyahu-offers-settlement-freeze-in-return-for-recognition-as-jewish-state-palestinians-say-no-1.318447.
39. Jack Khoury, 'Abbas: We'll Never Sign Deal Demanding Recognition of Israel as Jewish State', *Ha'aretz* (Israel), October 15, 2010. Available at, http://www.haaretz.com/news/diplomacy-defense/abbas-we-ll-never-sign-deal-demanding-recognition-of-israel-as-jewish-state-1.319329.
40. 'Ecuador Becomes Fifth Latin American Country to Recognize Palestinian State', *Haaretz* News Service, December 25, 2010. Available at, http://www.haaretz.com/news/diplomacy-defense/ecuador-becomes-fifth-latin-american-country-to-recognize-palestinian-state-1.332845.
41. Ethan Bronner, Christine Hauser, 'U.N. Assembly, in Blow to U.S., Elevates Status of Palestine', *The New York Times*, November 29, 2012. Available at, http://www.nytimes.com/2012/11/30/world/middleeast/Palestinian-Authority-United-Nations-Israel.html.
42. Barak Ravid, 'Lieberman Drafts Own Map of Future Palestinian Borders', *Ha'aretz*, January 23, 2011. Available at, http://www.haaretz.com/print-edition/news/lieberman-drafts-own-map-of-future-palestinian-borders-1.338583.
43. 'Israel Drafting Interim Peace Plan', *The Hindu, (Associated Press)* Jerusalem, January 24, 2011 Available at, http://www.thehindu.com/todays-paper/tp-international/israel-drafting-interim-peace-plan/article1119771.ece.
44. 'Palestinians Announce September Elections as Top Negotiator

Resigns', *Ha'aretz* (Israel), February 12, 2011. Available at, http://www.haaretz.com/news/diplomacy-defense/palestinians-announce-september-elections-as-top-negotiator-resigns-1.342922.

45. Ed Pilkington, 'US Vetoes UN Condemnation of Israeli Settlements', *The Guardian*, Saturday, February 19, 2011. Available at, http://www.theguardian.com/world/2011/feb/19/us-veto-israel-settlement.
46. Barak Ravid, 'Netanyahu Mulls Palestinian State with Temporary Borders as Part of Interim Peace Deal, *Ha'aretz*, March 2, 2011. Available at, http://www.haaretz.com/print-edition/news/netanyahu-mulls-palestinian-state-with-temporary-borders-as-part-of-interim-peace-deal-1.346555.
47. Amy Teibel, 'Israel: No Palestinian Peace Deal Possible Now', *The Associated Press, The Washington Post*, Thursday, March 3, 2011. Available at, http://www.washingtonpost.com/wp-dyn/content/article/2011/03/03/AR2011030302343.html.
48. Ethan Bronner, Isabel Kershner, 'Palestinians Set Bid for U.N. Seat, Clashing With U.S.', *The New York Times*, September 16, 2011. Available at, http://www.nytimes.com/2011/09/17/world/middleeast/Abbas-Security-Council-United-Nations-Vote.html?pagewanted=all&_r=0.
49. Also refer to Document II in Appendices.
50. Daniel Levy, 'How Hamas-Fatah Unity Could Break Middle East Deadlock', *theguardian.com*, Thursday April 28, 2011. Available at, http://www.theguardian.com/commentisfree/2011/apr/28/palestinian-territories-hamas.
51. Edmund Sanders, 'Israel Halts Tax Funds to Palestinians', *Los Angeles Times*, May 2, 2011. Available at, http://articles.latimes.com/2011/may/02/world/la-fg-israel-palestinian-taxes-20110502.
52. Khaled Abu Toameh, 'Fatah: Palestinian Unity is Best Weapon Against Occupation', *The Jerusalem Post*, Monday, November 18, 2013. Available at, http://www.jpost.com/Middle-East/Fatah-Palestinian-unity-is-

best-weapon-against-occupation.

53. Available at, http://www.haaretz.com/news/diplomacy-defense/full-transcript-of-abbas-speech-at-un-general-assembly-1.386385.
54. 'Ban Sends Palestinian Application for UN Membership to Security Council', *UN News Centre,* September 23, 2011. Available at, http://www.un.org/apps/news/story.asp/html/realfile/story.asp?NewsID=39722&Cr=palestin&Cr1=#.
55. 'Israel, Palestine and the UN: The War Over Statehood', *The Economist* (London), September 24, 2011, Jerusalem and Ramallah (From the print edition). Available at, http://www.economist.com/node/21530174.
56. Karin Brulliard, 'Palestinians Deliver Letter from Abbas to Israel's Netanyahu', *The Washington Post,* April 17, 2012. Available at, http://articles.washingtonpost.com/2012-04-17/world/35454540_1_palestinian-statehood-bid-saeb-erekat-yitzhak-molcho.
57. 'Israel PM Replies to Abbas Letter on Peace Process', (AFP), *The Dawn* (Karachi), May 13, 2012. Available at, http://dawn.com/news/718026/israel-pm-replies-to-abbas-letter-on-peace-process.
58. 'Timeline: Israel Launches Operation Pillar of Defense Amid Gaza Escalation', *Ha'aretz*, Wednesday, November 20, 2012. Available at, http://www.haaretz.com/news/diplomacy-defense/timeline-israel-launches-operation-pillar-of-defense-amid-gaza-escalation.premium-1.479284.
59. Nick Meo, 'How Israel killed Ahmed Jabari, Its Toughest Enemy in Gaza', *The Telegraph* (London), November 17, 2012. Available at, http://www.telegraph.co.uk/news/worldnews/middleeast/israel/9685598/How-Israel-killed-Ahmed-Jabari-its-toughest-enemy-in-Gaza.html.
60. Atul Aneja, 'Egypt-mediated Ceasefire Talks in Progress', *The Hindu*, November 20, 2012. Available at, http://www.thehindu.com/news/international/egyptmediated-ceasefire-talks-in-progress/article4110661.ece.
61. 'Kerry Sails Through the Senate as Secretary of State', *The New*

York Times, January 29, 2013. Available at, http://www.nytimes.com/2013/01/30/us/politics/senate-panel-approves-kerry-for-secretary-of-state.html.

62. Rami G. Khouri, 'Kerry Merits Support, and a New Strategy', *The Daily Star* (Lebanon), July 20, 2013. Available at, http://dailystar.com.lb/Article.aspx?id=224340.
63. Anna Sheinman, 'Kerry Wins Arab League Support for Peace Talks', *The Jewish Chronicle Online*, July 17, 2013. Available at, http://www.thejc.com/news/world-news/109558/kerry-wins-arab-league-support-peace-talks.
64. 'Hamas Rejects Arab League Initiative for Israeli-Palestinian Peace', *Reuters*, May 3, 2013. Available at, http://www.haaretz.com/news/diplomacy-defense/hamas-rejects-arab-league-initiative-for-israeli-palestinian-peace-1.519109.
65. Mark Weiss, 'Kerry Visits Israel to Try to Invigorate Peace Talks', *The Irish Times*, Monday, November 4, 2013, Available at, http://www.irishtimes.com/news/world/middle-east/kerry-visits-israel-to-try-to-invigorate-peace-talks-1.1583761.
66. 'Kerry: Israel, Palestinians Agree to Intensify Talks, Greater U.S. Role', *Reuters and Haaretz*, September 25, 2013. Available at, http://www.haaretz.com/news/diplomacy-defense/1.549061.
67. Stephen Kaufman, 'Israel, Palestinians Set Goal of Final Peace Agreement in 2014,' *International Information Program (IIP-Digital)*, US Department of State, July 30, 2013. Available at, http://iipdigital.usembassy.gov/st/english/article/2013/07/20130730279720.html#axzz2l1JIbAYl.
68. Lauren Ward, 'Explorer's Analysis: Inside Key Issues of Israeli-Palestinian Peace Talks', *Explorers Journal (National Geographic)*, August 13, 2013. Available at, http://newswatch.nationalgeographic.com/2013/08/13/israeli-settlement-expansion-casts-shadow-over-renewed-peace-talks.
69. Uzi Mahnaimi, 'Israel Fears Plot by Hamas to Seize West Bank,' *The Sunday Times* (London), Tel Aviv, December 23, 2012. Available at, http://www.thesundaytimes.co.uk/sto/news/world_news/Middle_East/article1182012.ece#.
70. Hussein Ibish, Should the Palestinians Recognize Israel as a Jewish State?, *Foreign Policy*, May 25, 2011. Available at, http://www.foreignpolicy.com/articles/2011/05/25/should_the_palestinians_recognize_israel_as_a_jewish_state.

9

US Presidency, Obama and Israel-Palestine Peace Process

When Barack Hussein Obama assumed office as the 44th President of the United States of America in January 2009, the world truly assumed that the US was poised for the change that the new President had so eloquently campaigned for during the hard-fought Presidential race. Particularly for the Arab and Islamic worlds, there was a special interest in the election of a new US President with such an interesting pedigree. It was hoped that Obama with his unique part-Muslim heritage would be able to make a suitable contribution towards overcoming the historical animosity in the US and the Western world in general towards the Islamic-Arab worlds.

In June 2009, six months after his inauguration, Obama made his famous Cairo speech in which he sought to enunciate his administration's new approach towards the Arab and Islamic worlds and indeed the whole non-Western world. To quote him, "America respects the right of all peaceful and law-abiding voices to be heard around the world, even if we disagree with them. And we will welcome all elected, peaceful governments, provided they govern with respect for all their people" (Ignatius 2012). [1]

This statement was at odds with what has often been the US historical praxis in the region and the rest of the 'developing' world at large, where elected governments led by parties whose ideological moorings were perceived to be anti-Western (such as the Communists during the Cold War or the Islamists later on), have been discouraged from taking office or even continuing in office. A classic case in this context is the US effort, along with that of Israel, to sideline, boycott and deny Hamas its electoral victory in the January 2006 elections and the right to form the Palestinian government (Karon 2009). [2]

Fatah, the main Palestinian Liberation Organisation grouping, too contributed to this effort and the resulting clash between the two rival Palestinian factions led to Hamas taking over the Gaza Strip in June 2007 (Erlanger 2007). [3] Palestinian internal politics since then has been characterised by a fractured polity, with Hamas's control of the Gaza Strip meaning almost total isolation for the people of the Strip from the outside world, as Israel has enforced a strict blockade of the area from both land as well as sea to put pressure on the radical Islamist grouping, thereby putting the people of the Strip under incredible economic and social hardship and suffering (*AFP* 2013). [4]

Most 'visionary' Presidents in Washington have run into rough weather as far as the Israeli-Palestinian peace process is concerned and Obama was no exception to this phenomenon. His first Presidency did not come at the right time for the solution of the conflict unlike former President Bill Clinton's first and the end of his second presidency that saw positive movement towards a possible resolution of this long-standing sore in Arab West Asia. Obama from day-one of his Presidency had to deal with the hawkish Israeli Premier Binyamin Netanyahu who was always known to be against making a negotiated peace with the Palestinians, having played a major role in delaying and eventually all but wrecking the Oslo process in the late 1990s (Shlaim 2013). [5]

Diplomatic interactions between the Israelis and Palestinians started with the Madrid Peace Conference in October 1991 and the substance of negotiations has since meandered from 'self-rule' (as in the Oslo Agreement, September 1993) and the 'final settlement' negotiations at Washington (Camp David, July 2000) to the so-called 'road-map' for peace touted by the Bush administration and the present Obama administration's insistence on preventing the Palestinians from seeking recognition for their state-building efforts on the multilateral level (such as at the UN), in the absence of a bilateral negotiated settlement with the Israelis, under the tutelage and patronage of active US mediation (Cooper 2011). [6] But none of these efforts have so far been successful in ending the hostilities and resolving the conflict.

The Oslo Process collapsed over mutual distrust and acrimony on the part of both the Israelis and the Palestinians, with both sides accusing the other of having reneged on aspects of the Contract mainly relating to adequate and timely Israeli withdrawals from the occupied Palestinian Territories and the Israelis equally if not more concerned about the rise of terrorist activities in the Territories targeting Israeli civilians (Shlaim 2005). [7] Coupled with this were the intense differences in perceptions over critical areas of the dispute regarding the future status of Jerusalem and the potential return of hundreds of thousands of refugees as well as the descendents of refugees who fled the region after 1948, when the state of Israel was established (Shlaim 2005).

It is generally accepted that the Camp David II Summit Process in July 2000 broke down over differences in perceptions on the status and ownership of the 'holy' city of Jerusalem and its suburbs as well as the whole vexed issue of the Palestinian refugees and their purported 'right of return' to the territories that now form part of the state of Israel or Palestine (Malley and Agha 2001). [8] Following the failure of the Camp David Process and the electoral failure of Ehud Barak to secure a second term as Israeli premier, Ariel Sharon took office in 2001 roughly coinciding with the arrival of George H. W. Bush as President of the United States (Kaiser 2003). [9]

Bush was initially hesitant to enter into the turbulent world of the Palestinian-Israeli Peace Process and Sharon capitalised on this hesitation as well as the extreme frustration being felt among the Palestinian populace at the state of the 'no-peace' process. He provoked an intense backlash known as the *Al-Aqsa Intifada* by making a trip to the Temple Mount/*Al-Aqsa*

Esplanade above the Wailing Wall plaza right in the burning heart of the Old 'Holy' City of Jerusalem (Cassel 2008). [10] In 2002, Sharon sent the Israeli army back into all the Territories that they had withdrawn from in the previous decade under the Oslo Accords and managed to cause serious damage to the Palestinian Authority and all the infrastructure that they had built up over the previous decade or so since the Palestinian Liberation Organisation had returned to the Occupied Territories from exile abroad (Gilmore and Wastell 2002). [11]

Finally, Bush got involved with the so-called 'Road Map to Peace' in the region that sought to set out a point-by-point formula for achieving lasting peace and a Palestinian state into the bargain in the region (Kuruvilla 2012). [12] The onus in the Road Map was mainly on the Palestinians to develop responsible institutions that would last the test of statehood and to desist from violent activities like terrorism while the Israelis were asked to desist from or freeze activities such as settlement-building in the Occupied Territories that would add fat to the furnace as far as Israeli-Palestinian relations was concerned (Kuruvilla 2012). The problem with the Road Map as with the Oslo Accords before it was that they both sought to postpone the resolution of contentious issues like the return of refugees and the status of Jerusalem until later on in the process (Kuruvilla 2012).

This approach ultimately undermined the peace process as invariably the in-built tensions burst out well before any suitable resolution or progress had been achieved on the main question, namely, the now 45-year long Israeli occupation of the West Bank and the presently five-year long blockade of Gaza after the Israeli withdrawal from the Strip in 2005.

Obama initially opted to go along with the Road Map which had been drawn up as part of his predecessor's plan for the region in 2003 (Kuruvilla 2012). However, he ended up losing his commitment to this process in the face of the roadblocks that he had to encounter along the way. The roadblocks included intense suspicion on the Israeli side towards Obama's actual motives and sympathies.

However, it is on record that during the ongoing first Obama administration, military to military relations between the US and Israel showed considerable upward growth on all fronts, including military aid (Kuruvilla 2012). Israel was and still is the largest recipient of US military and non-military aid in the world (Levinson 2010). [13] The Obama administration had also consistently stood with the Israelis in ensuring that nothing inimical to their interests is passed at multilateral fora, such as the UN (Knickerbocker 2011). [14] For example on February 18, 2011, the US vetoed a United Nations Security Council resolution which demanded that "Israel, as the occupying power, immediately and completely ceases all settlement activities in the occupied Palestinian territory, including East Jerusalem and that it fully respect its legal obligations in this regard" (UNNC 2011). [15]

President Obama has also gone on record stating that 'a lasting peace will involve two states for two peoples. Israel as a Jewish state and the homeland for the Jewish people, and the state of Palestine as the homeland for the Palestinian people' (Obama 2011). [16] As regards the borders of a future state of Palestine, Obama has been clear that "The borders of Israel and Palestine should be based on the 1967 lines with mutually agreed swaps, so that secure and recognized borders are established for both states" (Levy 2011). [17]

Prime Minister Netanyahu, in particular, had led the pack of Israeli ministers in being especially critical of the Obama administration at a time when the conservative Republican Party as well as the ultra-conservative Tea Party Movement had become ascendant in US domestic politics (Yakabuski and Martin 2011). [18] Obama's main problem with the administration of Binyamin Netanyahu was the latter's unwillingness to sanction a total settlement construction freeze which had been one of the original commitments under the Bush Road Map of 2003 (Eldar 2013). [19] The Palestinians, on their part, walked out of the peace process in September 2010 over the question of Israel's continued building of settlements in the Occupied Territories, thus stalling the negotiations (Ravid 2010). [20]

Hamas's control over the Gaza Strip and virtually half of the Palestinian political spectrum has also given the Israelis a good excuse to desist from serious or meaningful peace negotiations with the Palestinians on the pretext of not having a suitable partner for peace in the region, Hamas being ideologically committed to the establishment of an Islamic state on all of the historic territories of Palestine, much of which is now the state of Israel (Somfalvi 2011). [21] The founding Charter of Hamas mentions that the state of Israel would be eventually destroyed by Islam (Hamas 1988).

Hamas has never to date formally repudiated this founding Charter of principles that seek to guide the Palestinian Islamic Movement. Hamas and Fatah have periodically sought to bury their differences and come together in a show of unity to form a pan-Palestinian national government of unity, but these efforts have also been stoutly opposed by Israel and also by the US under the pretext of having nothing whatsoever to do with a 'fundamentalist' Islamist grouping such as Hamas. It remains to be seen whether Hamas and Fatah will really be able to cooperate together in forming a national government as being envisaged in the present-future as the two parties have never had a history of collaborating effectively with each other and indeed have only had an experience of intense political and sometimes fratricidal rivalry and conflict.

The second Obama administration will need to be deft and adroit enough to project itself as an impartial mediator between Palestinians and Israelis while taking into consideration the vast differences in both the Palestinian and Israeli view of the conflict and will also need to be able to mediate between opposing Palestinian views such as that being held by the two main Palestinian political parties Fatah and Hamas. The appointment of Senator John Kerry as Secretary of State replacing Hillary Clinton was a major step in ensuring that somebody with more credibility in the Arab world was at the helm of foreign policy in the US.

In this context, Obama was proceeding diplomatically down the same road that President Bill Clinton went during his second term in 1997-2001. The only difference being that Clinton's interest in the Israeli-Palestinian dispute was that of a hands-on deeply involved practitioner as has being previously discussed in a number of chapters in this volume. Given the experiences gained by Obama in his first term, particularly with reference to the sensitivities that surround his own origins and perceptions in the Jewish community both in the US as well as in Israel, he has very wisely opted for a much more behind-the-scenes approach to dealing with deeply complicated conflict.

The question of where Obama's loyalties really lie has been a sorely discussed topic of debate both in his home country and abroad ever since he appeared on the international scene over four years ago. Suspicions and speculation that he was biased towards Jews because of his origins and more partial towards Arabs and Muslims were widespread among both right wing Jews and Israelis as well as fundamentalist Christians worldwide and particularly in the West.

The actual reality was however quite the opposite and the Obama presidency has gone out of his way to court Israel and the American Jewish community as two of the most influential foreign and domestic policy players in the US today. It remains to be seen what the ultimate result of this latest peace effort will be. One can only hope that a negotiated end to the conflict will be arrived at that within the time prescribed, one that will satisfy both the Israelis with all their apprehensions about security and the Palestinians who have lost so much over the last couple of decades and will need to build up a state from virtually nothing on less than 20 percent of the original territory of Palestine.

Endnotes

1. David Ignatius, 'Obama Wagers Heavily on the Muslim Brotherhood', *The Daily star*, (Lebanon), February 16, 2012.

Available at, http://www.google.co.uk/url?sa=t&rct=j&q=&esrc=s&frm=1&source=web&cd=1&ved=0CC4QFjAA&url=http%3A%2F%2Fwww.dailystar.com.lb%2FOpinion%2FColumnist%2F2012%2FFeb-16%2F163426-obama-wagers-heavily-on-the-muslim-brotherhood.ashx.

2. Tony Karon, 'Dealing with Hamas: Can the U.S. Avoid It?, *Time* Magazine (New York), March 5, 2009.Available at, http://content.time.com/time/world/article/0,8599,1883382,00.ht
3. Steven Erlanger 'Hamas Seizes Broad Control in Gaza Strip', *The New York Times*, June 14, 2007. Available at, http://www.nytimes.com/2007/06/14/world/middleeast/14mideast.html?_r=0.
4. 'Key Facts About Israel's Blockade on Gaza', (Agence France-Presse- AFP), *The Global Post*, May 6, 2013. Available at, http://www.globalpost.com/dispatch/news/afp/130506/key-facts-about-israels-blockade-gaza.
5. Avi Shlaim, 'It's Now Clear: The Oslo Peace Accords Were Wrecked by Netanyahu's Bad Faith', *The Guardian* (London), Thursday 12 September 2013. Available at, http://www.theguardian.com/commentisfree/2013/sep/12/oslo-israel-reneged-colonial-palestine.
6. Helene Cooper, 'Obama Says Palestinians Are Using Wrong Forum', *The New York Times*, September 21, 2011. Available at, http://www.nytimes.com/2011/09/22/world/obama-united-nations-speech.html?_r=0.
7. Available at, http://users.ox.ac.uk/~ssfc0005%20/The%20Rise%20and%20Fall%20of%20the%20Oslo%20Peace%20Process.html.
8. Robert Malley and Hussein Agha, 'Camp David: The Tragedy of Errors', *The New York Review of Books (NYRB)*, August 9, 2001 (from the print issue). Available at, http://www.nybooks.com/articles/archives/2001/aug/09/camp-david-the-tragedy-of-errors.
9. Robert G. Kaiser, 'Bush and Sharon Nearly Identical on Mideast Policy', *The Washington Post*, February 9, 2003. Available at, the *Electronic Intifada* website at http://electronicintifada.net/content/bush-and-sharon-nearly-identical-mideast-policy/4394.
10. Matthew Cassel, 'The Weapon of the Occupied',

Opinion/Editorial, *The Electronic Intifada*, December 16, 2008. Available at, http://electronicintifada.net/content/weapon-occupied/7861.

11. Inigo Gilmore and David Wastell, 'Sharon Plans to Annex Half the West Bank, says Coalition Ally', Jerusalem/ Washington, *The Telegraph* (London), April 21, 2002. Available at, http://www.telegraph.co.uk/news/worldnews/middleeast/israel/1391714/Sharon-plans-to-annex-half-the-West-Bank-says-coalition-ally.html.
12. Samuel J. Kuruvilla, 'Obama and the Israel-Palestine Peace Process', *IDSA Comment*, Institute for Defence Studies and Analyses (IDSA), New Delhi, February 27, 2012. Available at, http://www.idsa.in/idsacomments/ObamaandtheIsraelPalestinePeaceProcess_skuruvilla_270212.
13. Charles Levinson, 'U.S., Israel Build Military Cooperation', *Wall Street Journal*, August 14, 2010. Available at, http://online.wsj.com/news/articles/SB10001424052748703321004575427272550050504.
14. Brad Knickerbocker, 'If Obama Opposes Israeli Settlement Activity, Why Did US Veto UN vote?, *The Christian Science Monitor-CSMonitor.com*, February 18, 2011. Available at, http://www.csmonitor.com/USA/Foreign-Policy/2011/0218/If-Obama-opposes-Israeli-settlement-activity-why-did-US-veto-UN-vote.
15. 'United States Vetoes Security Council Resolution on Israeli Settlements', *United Nations News Centre*, February 18, 2011. Available at, www.un.org/apps/news/story.asp?NewsID=37572.
16. Available at, www.whitehouse.gov/.../remarks-president-middle-east-and-north-africa.
17. Elior Levy, 'PA Challenges Netanyahu to Accept 1967 Lines', *Ynetnews*, May 22, 2011. Available at, http://www.ynetnews.com/articles/0,7340,L-4072210,00.html.
18. Konrad Yakabuski and Patrick Martin, '1967: A Critical Year for Obama's Presidency', *The Globe and Mail* (Toronto), May 20, 2011. Available at, http://www.theglobeandmail.com/news/world/1967-a-critical-year-for-obamas-presidency/article624830/?page=all.
19. Akiva Eldar, 'Why Is Obama Giving Up on Bush's Peace Road

Map?,' *Al-Monitor* (Israel Pulse), April 29, 2013. Available at, http://www.al-monitor.com/pulse/originals/2013/04/why-is-obama-giving-up-on-bushs-road-map-to-peace.html##ixzz2l7BUOvCI.

20. Barak Ravid, 'Lieberman: Palestinians Use Settlement Freeze as an Excuse to Undermine Peace Talks', *Ha'aretz*, September 18, 2010. Available at, http://www.haaretz.com/news/diplomacy-defense/lieberman-palestinians-use-settlement-freeze-as-an-excuse-to-undermine-peace-talks-1.314508.
21. Attila Somfalvi, 'The Good, the Bad and the PA-Hamas Pact', *Ynet News.com (magazine)*, April 28, 2011. Available at, http://www.ynetnews.com/articles/0,7340,L-4061782,00.html.

Appendices Containing Documents

Document I

Text of the United Nations General Assembly Resolution: A/Res/181(II), November 29, 1947 Future Government of Palestine

---

The General Assembly, Having met in special session at the request of the mandatory Power to constitute and instruct a special committee to prepare for the consideration of the question of the future government of Palestine at the second regular session;

Having constituted a Special Committee and instructed it to investigate all questions and issues relevant to the problem of Palestine, and to prepare proposals for the solution of the problem, and

Having received and examined the report of the Special Committee (document A/364) [1/] including a number of unanimous recommendations and a plan of partition with economic union approved by the majority of the Special Committee,

Considers that the present situation in Palestine is one which is likely to impair the general welfare and friendly relations among nations;

Takes note of the declaration by the mandatory Power that it plans to complete its evacuation of Palestine by 1 August 1948;

Recommends to the United Kingdom, as the mandatory Power for Palestine, and to all other Members of the United Nations the adoption and implementation, with regard to the future government of Palestine, of the Plan of Partition with Economic Union set out below;

Requests that

(a) The Security Council take the necessary measures as provided for in the plan for its implementation;

(b) The Security Council consider, if circumstances during the transitional period require such consideration, whether the situation in Palestine constitutes a threat to the peace. If it decides that such a threat exists, and in order to maintain international peace and security, the Security Council should supplement the authorization of the General Assembly by taking measures, under Articles 39 and 41 of the Charter, to empower the United Nations Commission, as provided in this resolution, to exercise in Palestine the functions which are assigned to it by this resolution;

(c) The Security Council determine as a threat to the peace, breach of the peace or act of aggression, in accordance with Article 39 of the Charter, any attempt to alter by force the settlement envisaged by this resolution;

(d) The Trusteeship Council be informed of the responsibilities envisaged for it in this plan;

Calls upon the inhabitants of Palestine to take such steps as may be necessary on their part to put this plan into effect;

Appeals to all Governments and all peoples to refrain from taking action which might hamper or delay the carrying out of these recommendations, and

Authorizes the Secretary-General to reimburse travel and subsistence expenses of the members of the Commission referred to in Part I, Section B, paragraph 1 below, on such basis and in such form as he may determine most appropriate in the circumstances, and to provide the Commission with the necessary staff to assist in carrying out the functions assigned to the Commission by the General Assembly.

The General Assembly

Authorizes the Secretary-General to draw from the Working Capital Fund a sum not to exceed $2,000,000 for the purposes set forth in the last paragraph of the resolution on the future government of Palestine.

Hundred and twenty-eighth plenary meeting on November 29, 1947

[At its hundred and twenty-eighth plenary meeting on 29th

November 1947 the General Assembly, in accordance with the terms of the above resolution [181 A], elected the following members of the United Nations Commission on Palestine: Bolivia, Czechoslovakia, Denmark, Panama and Philippines].

Plan of Partition with Economic Union (Part I)
Future Constitution and Government of Palestine
A. Termination of Mandate, Partition and Independence

1. The Mandate for Palestine shall terminate as soon as possible but in any case not later than 1 August 1948.

2. The armed forces of the mandatory Power shall be progressively withdrawn from Palestine, the withdrawal to be completed as soon as possible but in any case not later than 1 August 1948.

The mandatory Power shall advise the Commission, as far in advance as possible, of its intention to terminate the Mandate and to evacuate each area.

The mandatory Power shall use its best endeavours to ensure than an area situated in the territory of the Jewish State, including a seaport and hinterland adequate to provide facilities for a substantial immigration, shall be evacuated at the earliest possible date and in any event not later than 1 February 1948.

3. Independent Arab and Jewish States and the Special International Regime for the City of Jerusalem, set forth in part III of this plan, shall come into existence in Palestine two months after the evacuation of the armed forces of the mandatory Power has been completed but in any case not later than 1 October 1948. The boundaries of the Arab State, the Jewish State, and the City of Jerusalem shall be as described in parts II and III below.

4. The period between the adoption by the General Assembly of its recommendation on the question of Palestine and the establishment of the independence of the Arab and Jewish States shall be a transitional period.

B. Steps Preparatory to Independence

1. A Commission shall be set up consisting of one representative of each of five Member States. The Members represented on the Commission shall be elected by the General Assembly on as broad a basis, geographically and otherwise, as possible.

2. The administration of Palestine shall, as the mandatory Power withdraws its armed forces, be progressively turned over to the Commission; which shall act in conformity with the recommendations of the General Assembly, under the guidance of the Security Council. The mandatory Power shall to the fullest possible extent co-ordinate its plans for withdrawal with the plans of the Commission to take over and administer areas which have been evacuated.

In the discharge of this administrative responsibility the Commission shall have authority to issue necessary regulations and take other measures as required.

The mandatory Power shall not take any action to prevent, obstruct or delay the implementation by the Commission of the measures recommended by the General Assembly.

3. On its arrival in Palestine the Commission shall proceed to carry out measures for the establishment of the frontiers of the Arab and Jewish States and the City of Jerusalem in accordance with the general lines of the recommendations of the General Assembly on the partition of Palestine. Nevertheless, the boundaries as described in part II of this plan are to be modified in such a way that village areas as a rule will not be divided by state boundaries unless pressing reasons make that necessary.

4. The Commission, after consultation with the democratic parties and other public organizations of The Arab and Jewish States, shall select and establish in each State as rapidly as possible a Provisional Council of Government. The activities of both the Arab and Jewish Provisional Councils of Government shall be carried out under the general direction of the Commission.

If by 1 April 1948, a Provisional Council of Government cannot be selected for either of the States, or, if selected, cannot carry out its functions, the Commission shall communicate that fact to the Security Council for such action with respect to that State as the Security Council may deem proper, and to the Secretary-General for communication to the Members of the United Nations.

5. Subject to the provisions of these recommendations, during the transitional period the Provisional Councils of Government, acting under the Commission, shall have full authority in the areas under their control, including authority over matters of immigration and land regulation.

6. The Provisional Council of Government of each State acting under the Commission, shall progressively receive from the Commission full responsibility for the administration of that State in the period between the termination of the Mandate and the establishment of the State's independence.

7. The Commission shall instruct the Provisional Councils of Government of both the Arab and Jewish States, after their formation, to proceed to the establishment of administrative organs of government, central and local.

8. The Provisional Council of Government of each State shall, within the shortest time possible, recruit an armed militia from the residents of that State, sufficient in number to maintain internal order and to prevent frontier clashes.

This armed militia in each State shall, for operational purposes, be under the command of Jewish or Arab officers resident in that State, but general political and military control, including the choice of the militia's High Command, shall be exercised by the Commission.

9. The Provisional Council of Government of each State shall, not later than two months after the withdrawal of the armed forces of the mandatory Power, hold elections to the Constituent Assembly which shall be conducted on democratic lines.

The election regulations in each State shall be drawn up by

the Provisional Council of Government and approved by the Commission. Qualified voters for each State for this election shall be persons over eighteen years of age who are: (a) Palestinian citizens residing in that State, and (b) Arabs and Jews residing in the State, although not Palestinian citizens, who, before voting, have signed a notice of intention to become citizens of such State.

Arabs and Jews residing in the City of Jerusalem who have signed a notice of intention to become citizens, the Arabs of the Arab State and the Jews of the Jewish State, shall be entitled to vote in the Arab and Jewish States respectively.

Women may vote and be elected to the Constituent Assemblies.

During the transitional period no Jew shall be permitted to establish residence in the area of the proposed Arab State, and no Arab shall be permitted to establish residence in the area of the proposed Jewish State, except by special leave of the Commission.

10. The Constituent Assembly of each State shall draft a democratic constitution for its State and choose a provisional government to succeed the Provisional Council of Government appointed by the Commission. The constitutions of the States shall embody chapters 1 and 2 of the Declaration provided for in section C below and include inter alia provisions for:

(a) Establishing in each State a legislative body elected by universal suffrage and by secret ballot on the basis of proportional representation, and an executive body responsible to the legislature;

(b) Settling all international disputes in which the State may be involved by peaceful means in such a manner that international peace and security, and justice, are not endangered;

(c) Accepting the obligation of the State to refrain in its international relations from the threat or use of force against the territorial integrity of political independence of any State, or in any other manner inconsistent with the purposes of the

United Nations;

(d) Guaranteeing to all persons equal and non-discriminatory rights in civil, political, economic and religious matters and the enjoyment of human rights and fundamental freedoms, including freedom of religion, language, speech and publication, education, assembly and association; and

(e) Preserving freedom of transit and visit for all residents and citizens of the other State in Palestine and the City of Jerusalem, subject to considerations of national security, provided that each State shall control residence within its borders.

11. The Commission shall appoint a preparatory economic commission of three members to make whatever arrangements are possible for economic co-operation, with a view to establishing, as soon as practicable, the Economic Union and the Joint Economic Board, as provided in section D below.

12. During the period between the adoption of the recommendations on the question of Palestine by the General Assembly and the termination of the Mandate, the mandatory Power in Palestine shall maintain full responsibility for administration in areas from which it has not withdrawn its armed forces. The Commission shall assist the mandatory Power in the carrying out of these functions. Similarly the mandatory Power shall co-operate with the Commission in the execution of its functions.

13. With a view to ensuring that there shall be continuity in the functioning of administrative services and that, on the withdrawal of the armed forces of the mandatory Power, the whole administration shall be in the charge of the Provisional Councils and the Joint Economic Board, respectively, acting under the Commission, there shall be a progressive transfer, from the mandatory Power to the Commission, of responsibility for all the functions of government, including that of maintaining law and order in the areas from which the forces of the mandatory Power have been withdrawn.

14. The Commission shall be guided in its activities by the

recommendations of the General Assembly and by such instructions as the Security Council may consider necessary to issue. The measures taken by the Commission, within the recommendations of the General Assembly, shall become immediately effective unless the Commission has previously received contrary instructions from the Security Council. The Commission shall render periodic monthly progress reports, or more frequently if desirable, to the Security Council.

15. The Commission shall make its final report to the next regular session of the General Assembly and to the Security Council simultaneously.

C. Declaration

A declaration shall be made to the United Nations by the provisional government of each proposed State before independence. It shall contain inter alia the following clauses.

General Provision

The stipulations contained in the declaration are recognized as fundamental laws of the State and no law, regulation or official action shall conflict or interfere with these stipulations, nor shall any law, regulation or official action prevail over them.

Chapter 1: Holy Places, Religious Buildings and Sites

1. Existing rights in respect of Holy Places and religious buildings or sites shall not be denied or impaired.

2. In so far as Holy Places are concerned, the liberty of access, visit and transit shall be guaranteed, in conformity with existing rights, to all residents and citizens of the other State and of the City of Jerusalem, as well as to aliens, without distinction as to nationality, subject to requirements of national security, public order and decorum.

Similarly, freedom of worship shall be guaranteed in conformity with existing rights, subject to the maintenance of public order and decorum.

3. Holy Places and religious buildings or sites shall be preserved. No act shall be permitted which may in any way

impair their sacred character. If at any time it appears to the Government that any particular Holy Place, religious building or site is in need of urgent repair, the Government may call upon the community or communities concerned to carry out such repair. The Government may carry it out itself at the expense of the community or communities concerned if no action is taken within a reasonable time.

4. No taxation shall be levied in respect of any Holy Place, religious building or site which was exempt from taxation on the date of the creation of the State.

No change in the incidence of such taxation shall be made which would either discriminate between the owners or occupiers of Holy Places, religious buildings or sites, or would place such owners or occupiers in a position less favourable in relation to the general incidence of taxation than existed at the time of the adoption of the Assembly's recommendations.

5. The Governor of the City of Jerusalem shall have the right to determine whether the provisions of the Constitution of the State in relation to Holy Places, religious buildings and sites within the borders of the State and the religious rights appertaining thereto, are being properly applied and respected, and to make decisions on the basis of existing rights in cases of disputes which may arise between the different religious communities or the rites of a religious community with respect to such places, buildings and sites. He shall receive full co-operation and such privileges and immunities as are necessary for the exercise of his functions in the State.

Chapter 2: Religious and Minority Rights

1. Freedom of conscience and the free exercise of all forms of worship, subject only to the maintenance of public order and morals, shall be ensured to all.

2. No discrimination of any kind shall be made between the inhabitants on the ground of race, religion, language or sex.

3. All persons within the jurisdiction of the State shall be entitled to equal protection of the laws.

4. The family law and personal status of the various

minorities and their religious interests, including endowments, shall be respected.

5. Except as may be required for the maintenance of public order and good government, no measure shall be taken to obstruct or interfere with the enterprise of religious or charitable bodies of all faiths or to discriminate against any representative or member of these bodies on the ground of his religion or nationality.

6. The State shall ensure adequate primary and secondary education for the Arab and Jewish minority, respectively, in its own language and its cultural traditions.

The right of each community to maintain its own schools for the education of its own members in its own language, while conforming to such educational requirements of a general nature as the State may impose, shall not be denied or impaired. Foreign educational establishments shall continue their activity on the basis of their existing rights.

7. No restriction shall be imposed on the free use by any citizen of the State of any language in private intercourse, in commerce, in religion, in the Press or in publications of any kind, or at public meetings.

8. No expropriation of land owned by an Arab in the Jewish State (by a Jew in the Arab State) shall be allowed except for public purposes. In all cases of expropriation full compensation as fixed by the Supreme Court shall be paid previous to dispossession.

Chapter 3: Citizenship, International Conventions and Financial Obligations

1. Citizenship. Palestinian citizens residing in Palestine outside the City of Jerusalem, as well as Arabs and Jews who, not holding Palestinian citizenship, reside in Palestine outside the City of Jerusalem shall, upon the recognition of independence, become citizens of the State in which they are resident and enjoy full civil and political rights. Persons over the age of eighteen years may opt, within one year from the date of recognition of independence of the State in which they

reside, for citizenship of the other State, providing that no Arab residing in the area of the proposed Arab State shall have the right to opt for citizenship in the proposed Jewish State and no Jew residing in the proposed Jewish State shall have the right to opt for citizenship in the proposed Arab State. The exercise of this right of option will be taken to include the wives and children under eighteen years of age of persons so opting.

Arabs residing in the area of the proposed Jewish State and Jews residing in the area of the proposed Arab State who have signed a notice of intention to opt for citizenship of the other State shall be eligible to vote in the elections to the Constituent Assembly of that State, but not in the elections to the Constituent Assembly of the State in which they reside.

2. International conventions: (a) The State shall be bound by all the international agreements and conventions, both general and special, to which Palestine has become a party. Subject to any right of denunciation provided for therein, such agreements and conventions shall be respected by the State throughout the period for which they were concluded.

(b) Any dispute about the applicability and continued validity of international conventions or treaties signed or adhered to by the mandatory Power on behalf of Palestine shall be referred to the International Court of Justice in accordance with the provisions of the Statute of the Court.

3. Financial obligations: (a) The State shall respect and fulfil all financial obligations of whatever nature assumed on behalf of Palestine by the mandatory Power during the exercise of the Mandate and recognized by the State. This provision includes the right of public servants to pensions, compensation or gratuities.

(b) These obligations shall be fulfilled through participation in the Joint economic Board in respect of those obligations applicable to Palestine as a whole, and individually in respect of those applicable to, and fairly apportionable between, the States.

(c) A Court of Claims, affiliated with the Joint Economic Board, and composed of one member appointed by the United Nations, one representative of the United Kingdom and one representative of the State concerned, should be established. Any dispute between the United Kingdom and the State respecting claims not recognized by the latter should be referred to that Court.

(d) Commercial concessions granted in respect of any part of Palestine prior to the adoption of the resolution by the General Assembly shall continue to be valid according to their terms, unless modified by agreement between the concession-holder and the State.

Chapter 4: Miscellaneous Provisions

1. The provisions of chapters 1 and 2 of the declaration shall be under the guarantee of the United Nations, and no modifications shall be made in them without the assent of the General Assembly of the United Nations. Any Member of the United Nations shall have the right to bring to the attention of the General Assembly any infraction or danger of infraction of any of these stipulations, and the General Assembly may thereupon make such recommendations as it may deem proper in the circumstances.

2. Any dispute relating to the application or the interpretation of this declaration shall be referred, at the request of either party, to the International Court of Justice, unless the parties agree to another mode of settlement.

D. Economic Union and Transit

1. The Provisional Council of Government of each State shall enter into an undertaking with respect to economic union and transit. This undertaking shall be drafted by the commission provided for in section B, paragraph 1, utilizing to the greatest possible extent the advice and co-operation of representative organizations and bodies from each of the proposed States. It shall contain provisions to establish the Economic Union of Palestine and provide for other matters of

common interest. If by 1 April 1948 the Provisional Councils of Government have not entered into the undertaking, the undertaking shall be put into force by the Commission.

Economic Union of Palestine

2. Objectives of the Economic Union of Palestine shall be:

(a) A customs union;

(b) A joint currency system providing for a single foreign exchange rate;

(c) Operation in the common interest on a non-discriminatory basis of railways; inter-State highways; postal, telephone and telegraphic services, and port and airports involved in international trade and commerce;

(d) Joint economic development, especially in respect of irrigation, land reclamation and soil conservation; and

(e) Access for both States and for the City of Jerusalem on a non-discriminatory basis to water and power facilities.

3. There shall be established a Joint Economic Board, which shall consist of three representatives of each of the two States and three foreign members appointed by the Economic and Social Council of the United Nations. The foreign members shall be appointed in the first instance for a term of three years; they shall serve as individuals and not as representatives of States.

4. The functions of the Joint Economic Board shall be to implement either directly or by delegation the measures necessary to realize the objectives of the Economic Union. It shall have all powers of organization and administration necessary to fulfil its functions.

5. The States shall bind themselves to put into effect the decisions of the Joint Economic Board. The Board's decisions shall be taken by a majority vote.

6. In the event of failure of a State to take the necessary action the Board may, by a vote of six members, decide to withhold an appropriate portion of that part of the customs revenue to which the State in question is entitled under the Economic Union. Should the State persist in its failure to co-

operate, the Board may decide by a simple majority vote upon such further sanctions, including disposition of funds which it has withheld, as it may deem appropriate.

7. In relation to economic development, the functions of the Board shall be the planning, investigation and encouragement of joint development projects, but it shall not undertake such projects except with the assent of both States and the City of Jerusalem, in the event that Jerusalem is directly involved in the development project.

8. In regard to the joint currency system the currencies circulating in the two States and the City of Jerusalem shall be issued under the authority of the Joint Economic Board, which shall be the sole issuing authority and which shall determine the reserves to be held against such currencies.

9. So far as is consistent with paragraph 2 (b) above, each State may operate its own central bank, control its own fiscal and credit policy, its foreign exchange receipts and expenditures, the grant of import licenses, and may conduct international financial operations on its own faith and credit. During the first two years after the termination of the Mandate, the Joint Economic Board shall have the authority to take such measures as may be necessary to ensure that—to the extent that the total foreign exchange revenues of the two States from the export of goods and services permit, and provided that each State takes appropriate measures to conserve its own foreign exchange resources—each State shall have available, in any twelve months' period, foreign exchange sufficient to assure the supply of quantities of imported goods and services for consumption in its territory equivalent to the quantities of such goods and services consumed in that territory in the twelve months' period ending 31st December, 1947.

10. All economic authority not specifically vested in the Joint Economic Board is reserved to each State.

11. There shall be a common customs tariff with complete freedom of trade between the States, and between the States and the City of Jerusalem.

12. The tariff schedules shall be drawn up by a Tariff Commission, consisting of representatives of each of the States in equal numbers, and shall be submitted to the Joint Economic Board for approval by a majority vote. In case of disagreement in the Tariff Commission, the Joint Economic Board shall arbitrate the points of difference. In the event that the Tariff Commission fails to draw up any schedule by a date to be fixed, the Joint Economic Board shall determine the tariff schedule.

13. The following items shall be a first charge on the customs and other common revenue of the Joint Economic Board:

(a) The expenses of the customs service and of the operation of the joint services;

(b) The administrative expenses of the Joint Economic Board;

(c) The financial obligations of the Administration of Palestine consisting of:

(i) The service of the outstanding public debt; and

(ii) The cost of superannuation benefits, now being paid or falling due in the future, in accordance with the rules and to the extent established by paragraph 3 of chapter 3.

14. After these obligations have been met in full, the surplus revenue from the customs and other common services shall be divided in the following manner: not less than 5 percent and not more than 10 percent to the City of Jerusalem; the residue shall be allocated to each State by the Joint Economic Board equitably, with the objective of maintaining a sufficient and suitable level of government and social services in each State, except that the share of either State shall not exceed the amount of that State's contribution to the revenues of the Economic Union by more than approximately four million pounds in any year. The amount granted may be adjusted by the Board according to the price level in relation to the prices prevailing at the time of the establishment of the Union. After five years, the principles of the distribution of the

joint revenues may be revised by the Joint Economic Board on a basis of equity.

15. All international conventions and treaties affecting customs tariff rates, and those communications services under the jurisdiction of the Joint Economic Board, shall be entered into by both States. In these matters, the two States shall be bound to act in accordance with the majority vote of the Joint Economic Board.

16. The Joint Economic Board shall endeavour to secure for Palestine's export fair and equal access to world markets.

17. All enterprises operated by the Joint Economic Board shall pay fair wages on a uniform basis.

Freedom of transit and visit

18. The undertaking shall contain provisions preserving freedom of transit and visit for all residents or citizens of both States and of the City of Jerusalem, subject to security considerations; provided that each state and the City shall control residence within its borders.

Termination, modification and interpretation of the undertaking

19. The undertaking and any treaty issuing therefrom shall remain in force for a period of ten years. It shall continue in force until notice of termination, to take effect two years thereafter, is given by either of the parties.

20. During the initial ten-year period, the undertaking and any treaty issuing therefrom may not be modified except by consent of both parties and with the approval of the General Assembly.

21. Any dispute relating to the application or the interpretation of the undertaking and any treaty issuing therefrom shall be referred, at the request of either party, to the international Court of Justice, unless the parties agree to another mode of settlement.

E. Assets

1. The movable assets of the Administration of Palestine

shall be allocated to the Arab and Jewish States and the City of Jerusalem on an equitable basis. Allocations should be made by the United Nations Commission referred to in section B, paragraph 1, above. Immovable assets shall become the property of the government of the territory in which they are situated.

2. During the period between the appointment of the United Nations Commission and the termination of the Mandate, the mandatory Power shall, except in respect of ordinary operations, consult with the Commission on any measure which it may contemplate involving the liquidation, disposal or encumbering of the assets of the Palestine Government, such as the accumulated treasury surplus, the proceeds of Government bond issues, State lands or any other asset.

F. Admission to Membership in the United Nations

When the independence of either the Arab or the Jewish State as envisaged in this plan has become effective and the declaration and undertaking, as envisaged in this plan, have been signed by either of them, sympathetic consideration should be given to its application for admission to membership in the United Nations in accordance with Article 4 of the Charter of the United Nations.

Part II: Boundaries

The Arab State

The area of the Arab State in Western Galilee is bounded on the west by the Mediterranean and on the north by the frontier of the Lebanon from Ras en Naqura to a point north of Saliha. From there the boundary proceeds southwards, leaving the built-up area of Saliha in the Arab State, to join the southernmost point of this village. Thence it follows the western boundary line of the villages of Alma, Rihaniya and Teitaba, thence following the northern boundary line of Meirun village to join the Acre-Safad sub-district boundary line. It follows this line to a point west of Es Sammu'i village and joins it again at the northernmost point of Farradiya. Thence it follows the sub-district boundary line to the Acre-Safad main road. From here it follows the western boundary of Kafr I'nan village until it reaches the Tiberias-Acre sub-district boundary line, passing to the west of the junction of the Acre-Safad and Lubiya-Kafr I'nan roads. From south-west corner of Kafr I'nan village the boundary line follows the western boundary of the Tiberias sub-district to a point close to the boundary line between the villages of Maghar and Eilabun, thence bulging out to the west to include as much of the eastern part of the plain of Battuf as is necessary for the reservoir proposed by the Jewish Agency for the irrigation of lands to the south and east.

The boundary rejoins the Tiberias sub-district boundary at a point on the Nazareth-Tiberias road south-east of the built-up area of Tur'an; thence it runs southwards, at first following the sub-district boundary and then passing between the Kadoorie Agricultural School and Mount Tabor, to a point due south at the base of Mount Tabor. From here it runs due west, parallel to the horizontal grid line 230, to the north-east corner of the village lands of Tel Adashim. It then runs to the north-west corner of these lands, whence it turns south and west so as to include in the Arab State the sources of the Nazareth water supply in Yafa village. On reaching Ginneiger it follows the eastern, northern and western boundaries of the lands of this village to their south-west corner, whence it proceeds in a straight line to a point on the Haifa-Afula railway on the boundary between the villages of Sarid and El Mujeidil. This is the point of intersection.

The south-western boundary of the area of the Arab State in Galilee takes a line from this point, passing northwards along the eastern boundaries of Sarid and Gevat to the north-eastern corner of Nahalal, proceeding thence across the land of Kefar ha Horesh to a central point on the southern boundary of the village of Ilut, thence westwards along that village boundary to the eastern boundary of Beit Lahm, thence northwards and north-eastwards along its western boundary to the north-eastern corner of Waldheim and thence north-westwards across the village lands of Shafa 'Amr to the south-eastern corner of Ramat Yohanan'. From here it runs due north-north-east to a point on the Shafa 'Amr-Haifa road, west of its junction with the road to I'Billin. From there it proceeds north-east to a point on the southern boundary of I'Billin situated to the west of the I'Billin-Birwa road. Thence along that boundary to its westernmost point, whence it turns to the north, follows across the village land of Tamra to the north-westernmost corner and along the western boundary of Julis until it reaches the Acre-Safad road. It then runs westwards along the southern side of the Safad-Acre road to the Galilee-Haifa District boundary, from which point it follows that boundary to the sea.

The boundary of the hill country of Samaria and Judea starts on the Jordan River at the Wadi Malih south-east of Beisan and runs due west to meet the Beisan-Jericho road and then follows the western side of that road in a north-westerly direction to the junction of the boundaries of the sub-districts of Beisan, Nablus, and Jenin. From that point it follows the Nablus-Jenin sub-district boundary westwards for a distance of about three kilometres and then turns north-westwards, passing to the east of the built-up areas of the villages of Jalbun and Faqqu'a, to the boundary of the sub-districts of Jenin and Beisan at a point north-east of Nuris.

Thence it proceeds first north-westwards to a point due north of the built-up area of Zir'in and then westwards to the Afula-Jenin railway, thence north-westwards along the district boundary line to the point of intersection on the Hejaz railway. From here the boundary runs south-westwards, including the built-up area and some of the land of the village of Kh. Lid in the Arab State to cross the Haifa-Jenin road at a point on the district boundary between Haifa and Samaria west of El Mansi. It follows this boundary to the southernmost point of the village of El Buteimat. From here it follows the northern and eastern boundaries of the village of Ar'ara, rejoining the Haifa-Samaria district boundary at Wadi'Ara, and thence proceeding south-south-westwards in an approximately straight line joining up with the western boundary of Qaqun to a point east of the railway line on the eastern boundary of Qaqun village.

From here it runs along the railway line some distance to the east of it to a point just east of the Tulkarm railway station. Thence the boundary follows a line half-way between the railway and the Tulkarm-Qalqiliya-Jaljuliya and Ras el Ein road to a point just east of Ras el Ein station, whence it proceeds along the railway some distance to the east of it to the point on the railway line south of the junction of the Haifa-Lydda and Beit Nabala lines, whence it proceeds along the southern border of Lydda airport to its south-west corner, thence in a south-westerly direction to a point just west of the built-up area of Sarafand el'Amar, whence it turns south, passing just to the west of the built-up area of Abu el Fadil to the north-east corner of the lands of Beer Ya'Aqov. (The boundary line should be so demarcated as to allow direct access from the Arab State to the airport).

Thence the boundary line follows the western and southern boundaries of Ramle village, to the north-east corner of El Na'ana village, thence in a straight line to the southernmost point of El Barriya, along the eastern boundary of that village and the southern boundary of 'Innaba village. Thence it turns north to follow the southern side of the Jaffa-Jerusalem road until El Qubab, whence it follows the road to the boundary of Abu Shusha. It runs along the eastern boundaries of Abu Shusha, Seidun, Hulda to the southernmost point of Hulda, thence westwards in a straight line to the north-eastern corner of Umm Kalkha, thence following the northern boundaries of Umm Kalkha, Qazaza and the northern and western boundaries of Mukhezin to the Gaza District boundary and thence runs across the village lands of El Mismiya, El Kabira, and Yasur to the southern point of intersection, which is midway between the built-up areas of Yasur and Batani Sharqi.

From the southern point of intersection the boundary lines run north-westwards between the villages of Gan Yavne and Barqa to the sea at a point half way between Nabi Yunis and Minat el Qila, and south-eastwards to a point west of Qastina, whence it turns in a south-westerly direction, passing to the east of the built-up areas of Es Sawafir, Es Sharqiya and Ibdis. From the south-east corner of Ibdis village it runs to a point south-west of the built-up area of Beit 'Affa, crossing the Hebron-El Majdal road just to the west of the built-up area of Iraq Suweidan. Thence it proceeds southwards along the western village boundary of El Faluja to the Beersheba sub-district boundary.

It then runs across the tribal lands of Arab el Jubarat to a point on the boundary between the sub-districts of Beersheba and Hebron north of Kh. Khuweilifa, whence it proceeds in a south-westerly direction to a point on the Beersheba-Gaza main road two kilometres to the north-west of the town. It then turns south-eastwards to reach Wadi Sab at a point situated one kilometre to the west of it. From here it turns north-eastwards and proceeds along Wadi Sab and along the Beersheba-Hebron road for a distance of one kilometre, whence it turns eastwards and runs in a straight line to Kh. Kuseifa to join the Beersheba-Hebron sub-district boundary. It then follows the Beersheba-Hebron boundary eastwards to a point north of Ras Ez Zuweira, only departing from it so as to cut across the base of the indentation between vertical grid lines 150 and 160.

About five kilometres north-east of Ras ez Zuweira it turns north, excluding from the Arab State a strip along the coast of the Dead Sea not more than seven kilometres in depth, as far as Ein Geddi, whence it turns due east to join the Transjordan frontier in the Dead Sea.

The northern boundary of the Arab section of the coastal

plain runs from a point between Minat el Qila and Nabi Yunis, passing between the built-up areas of Gan Yavne and Barqa to the point of intersection. From here it turns south-westwards, running across the lands of Batani Sharqi, along the eastern boundary of the lands of Beit Daras and across the lands of Julis, leaving the built-up areas of Batani Sharqi and Julis to the westwards, as far as the north-west corner of the lands of Beit Tima. Thence it runs east of El Jiya across the village lands of El Barbara along the eastern boundaries of the villages of Beit Jirja, Deir Suneid and Dimra. From the south-east corner of Dimra the boundary passes across the lands of Beit Hanun, leaving the Jewish lands of Nir-Am to the eastwards. From the south-east corner of Dimra the boundary passes across the lands of Beit Hanun, leaving the Jewish lands of Nir-Am to the eastwards.

From the south-east corner of Beit Hanun the line runs south-west to a point south of the parallel grid line 100, then turns north-west for two kilometres, turning again in a south-westerly direction and continuing in an almost straight line to the north-west corner of the village lands of Kirbet Ikhza'a. From there it follows the boundary line of this village to its southernmost point. It then runs in a southerly direction along the vertical grid line 90 to its junction with the horizontal grid line 70. It then turns south-eastwards to Kh. el Ruheiba and then proceeds in a southerly direction to a point known as El Baha, beyond which it crosses the Beersheba-El 'Auja main road to the west of Kh. el Mushrifa. From there it joins Wadi El Zaiyatin just to the west of El Subeita. From there it turns to the north-east and then to the south-east following this Wadi and passes to the east of Abda to join Wadi Nafkh. It then bulges to the south-west along Wadi Nafkh. It then bulges to the south-west along Wadi Nafkh, Wadi Ajrim and Wadi Lassan to the point where Wadi Lassan crosses the Egyptian frontier.

The area of the Arab enclave of Jaffa consists of that part of the town-planning area of Jaffa which lies to the west of the

Jewish quarters lying south of Tel-Aviv, to the west of the continuation of Herzl street up to its junction with the Jaffa-Jerusalem road, to the south-west of the section of the Jaffa-Jerusalem road lying south-east of that junction, to the west of Miqve Israel lands, to the north-west of Holon local council area, to the north of the line linking up the north-west corner of Holon with the north-east corner of Bat Yam local council area and to the north of Bat Yam local council area. The question of Karton quarter will be decided by the Boundary Commission, bearing in mind among other considerations the desirability of including the smallest possible number of its Arab inhabitants and the largest possible number of its Jewish inhabitants in the Jewish State.

B. Jewish State

The north-eastern sector of the Jewish State (Eastern) Galilee) is bounded on the north and west by the Lebanese frontier and on the east by the frontiers of Syria and Transjordan. It includes the whole of the Hula Basin, Lake Tiberias, the whole of the Beisan sub-district, the boundary line being extended to the crest of the Gilboa mountains and the Wadi Malih. From there the Jewish State extends north-west, following the boundary described in respect of the Arab State.

The Jewish Section of the coastal plain extends from a point between Minat et Qila and Nabi Yunis in the Gaza sub-district and includes the towns of Haifa and Tel-Aviv, leaving Jaffa as an enclave of the Arab State. The eastern frontier of the Jewish State follows the boundary described in respect of the Arab State.

The Beersheba area comprises the whole of the Beersheba sub-district, including the Negeb and the eastern part of the Gaza sub-district, but excluding the town of Beersheba and those areas described in respect of the Arab State. It includes also a strip of land along the Dead Sea stretching from the Beersheba-Hebron sub-district boundary line to Ein Geddi, as described in respect of the Arab State.

C. City of Jerusalem

The boundaries of the City of Jerusalem are as defined in the recommendations on the City of Jerusalem. (See Part III, Section B, below).

Part III: City of Jerusalem

A. Special Regime

The City of Jerusalem shall be established as a *corpus separatum* under a special international regime and shall be administered by the United Nations. The Trusteeship Council shall be designated to discharge the responsibilities of the Administering Authority on behalf of the United Nations.

B. Boundaries of the City

The City of Jerusalem shall include the present municipality of Jerusalem plus the surrounding villages and towns, the most eastern of which shall be Abu Dis; the most southern, Bethlehem; the most western, Ein Karim (including also the built-up area of Motsa); and the most northern Shu'fat, as indicated on the sketch-map (annex B).

C. Statute of the City

The Trusteeship Council shall, within five months of the approval of the present plan, elaborate and approve a detailed Statute of the City which shall contain inter alia the substance of the following provisions:

1. *Government machinery; special objectives.* The Administering Authority in discharging its administrative obligations shall pursue the following special objectives:

(a) To protect and to preserve the unique spiritual and religious interests located in the city of the three great monotheistic faiths throughout the world, Christian, Jewish and Moslem; to this end to ensure that order and peace, and especially religious peace, reign in Jerusalem;

(b) To foster co-operation among all the inhabitants of the city in their own interests as well as in order to encourage and support the peaceful development of the mutual relations between the two Palestinian peoples throughout the Holy Land; to promote the security, well-being and any constructive measures of development of the residents, having regard to the special circumstances and customs of the various peoples and communities.

2. *Governor and administrative staff.* A Governor of the City of Jerusalem shall be appointed by the Trusteeship Council and shall be responsible to it. He shall be selected on the basis of special qualifications and without regard to nationality. He shall not, however, be a citizen of either State in Palestine.

The Governor shall represent the United Nations in the City and shall exercise on their behalf all powers of administration, including the conduct of external affairs. He shall be assisted by an administrative staff classed as international officers in the meaning of Article 100 of the Charter and chosen whenever practicable from the residents of the city and of the rest of Palestine on a non-discriminatory basis. A detailed plan for the organization of the administration of the city shall be submitted by the Governor to the Trusteeship Council and duly approved by it.

3. *Local autonomy.* (a) The existing local autonomous units in the territory of the city (villages, townships and municipalities) shall enjoy wide powers of local government and administration.

(b) The Governor shall study and submit for the consideration and decision of the Trusteeship Council a plan for the establishment of a special town units consisting respectively, of the Jewish and Arab sections of new Jerusalem. The new town units shall continue to form part of the present municipality of Jerusalem.

4. *Security measures:* (a) The City of Jerusalem shall be demilitarized; its neutrality shall be declared and preserved,

and no para-military formations, exercises or activities shall be permitted within its borders.

(b) Should the administration of the City of Jerusalem be seriously obstructed or prevented by the non-co-operation or interference of one or more sections of the population, the Governor shall have authority to take such measures as may be necessary to restore the effective functioning of the administration.

(c) To assist in the maintenance of internal law and order and especially for the protection of the Holy Places and religious buildings and sites in the city, the Governor shall organize a special police force of adequate strength, the members of which shall be recruited outside of Palestine. The Governor shall be empowered to direct such budgetary provision as may be necessary for the maintenance of this force.

5. *Legislative organization.* A Legislative Council, elected by adult residents of the city irrespective of nationality on the basis of universal and secret suffrage and proportional representation, shall have powers of legislation and taxation. No legislative measures shall, however, conflict or interfere with the provisions which will be set forth in the Statute of the City, nor shall any law, regulation, or official action prevail over them. The Statute shall grant to the Governor a right of vetoing bills inconsistent with the provisions referred to in the preceding sentence. It shall also empower him to promulgate temporary ordinances in case the council fails to adopt in time a bill deemed essential to the normal functioning of the administration.

6. *Administration of justice.* The Statute shall provide for the establishment of an independent judiciary system, including a court of appeal. All the inhabitants of the City shall be subject to it.

7. *Economic union and economic regime.* The City of Jerusalem shall be included in the Economic Union of Palestine and be bound by all stipulations of the undertaking

and of any treaties issued therefrom, as well as by the decision of the Joint Economic Board. The headquarters of the Economic Board shall be established in the territory of the City.

The Statute shall provide for the regulation of economic matters not falling within the regime of the Economic Union, on the basis of equal treatment and non-discrimination for all members of the United Nations and their nationals.

8. *Freedom of transit and visit; control of residents.* Subject to considerations of security, and of economic welfare as determined by the Governor under the directions of the Trusteeship Council, freedom of entry into, and residence within, the borders of the City shall be guaranteed for the residents or citizens of the Arab and Jewish States. Immigration into, and residence within, the borders of the city for nationals of other States shall be controlled by the Governor under the directions of the Trusteeship Council.

9. *Relations with the Arab and Jewish States.* Representatives of the Arab and Jewish States shall be accredited to the Governor of the City and charged with the protection of the interests of their States and nationals in connexion with the international administration of the City.

10. *Official languages.* Arabic and Hebrew shall be the official languages of the city. This will not preclude the adoption of one or more additional working languages, as may be required.

11. *Citizenship.* All the residents shall become ipso facto citizens of the City of Jerusalem unless they opt for citizenship of the State of which they have been citizens or, if Arabs or Jews, have filed notice of intention to become citizens of the Arab or Jewish State respectively, according to part I, section B, paragraph 9, of this plan.

The Trusteeship Council shall make arrangements for consular protection of the citizens of the City outside its territory.

12. *Freedoms of Citizens:* (a) Subject only to the

requirements of public order and morals, the inhabitants of the City shall be ensured the enjoyment of human rights and fundamental freedoms, including freedom of conscience, religion and worship, language, education, speech and press, assembly and association, and petition.

(b) No discrimination of any kind shall be made between the inhabitants on the grounds of race, religion, language or sex.

(c) All persons within the City shall be entitled to equal protection of the laws.

(d) The family law and personal status of the various persons and communities and their religious interests, including endowments, shall be respected.

(e) Except as may be required for the maintenance of public order and good government, no measure shall be taken to obstruct or interfere with the enterprise of religious or charitable bodies of all faiths or to discriminate against any representative or member of these bodies on the ground of his religion or nationality.

(f) The City shall ensure adequate primary and secondary education for the Arab and Jewish communities respectively, in their own languages and in accordance with their cultural traditions.

The right of each community to maintain its own schools for the education of its own members in its own language, while conforming to such educational requirements of a general nature as the City may impose, shall not be denied or impaired. Foreign educational establishments shall continue their activity on the basis of their existing rights.

(g) No restriction shall be imposed on the free use by any inhabitant of the City of any language in private intercourse, in commerce, in religion, in the Press or in publications of any kind, or at public meetings.

13. *Holy Places:* (a) Existing rights in respect of Holy Places and religious buildings or sites shall not be denied or impaired.

(b) Free access to the Holy Places and religious buildings or sites and the free exercise of worship shall be secured in conformity with existing rights and subject to the requirements of public order and decorum.

(c) Holy Places and religious buildings or sites shall be preserved. No act shall be permitted which may in any way impair their sacred character. If at any time it appears to the Governor that any particular Holy Place, religious building or site is in need of urgent repair, the Governor may call upon the community or communities concerned to carry out such repair. The Governor may carry it out himself at the expense of the community or communities concerned if no action is taken within a reasonable time.

(d) No taxation shall be levied in respect of any Holy Place, religious building or site which was exempt from taxation on the date of the creation of the City. No change in the incidence of such taxation shall be made which would either discriminate between the owners or occupiers of Holy Places, religious buildings or sites, or would place such owners or occupiers in a position less favourable in relation to the general incidence of taxation than existed at the time of the adoption of the Assembly's recommendations.

14. *Special powers of the Governor in respect of the Holy Places, religious buildings and sites in the City and in any part of Palestine:* (a) The protection of the Holy Places, religious buildings and sites located in the City of Jerusalem shall be a special concern of the Governor.

(b) With relation to such places, buildings and sites in Palestine outside the city, the Governor shall determine, on the ground of powers granted to him by the Constitutions of both States, whether the provisions of the Constitutions of the Arab and Jewish States in Palestine dealing therewith and the religious rights appertaining thereto are being properly applied and respected.

(c) The Governor shall also be empowered to make decisions on the basis of existing rights in cases of disputes which may arise between the different religious communities or the rites of a religious community in respect of the Holy Places, religious buildings and sites in any part of Palestine.

In this task he may be assisted by a consultative council of representatives of different denominations acting in an advisory capacity.

D. Duration of the Special Regime

The Statute elaborated by the Trusteeship Council on the aforementioned principles shall come into force not later than 1st October, 1948. It shall remain in force in the first instance for a period of ten years, unless the Trusteeship Council finds it necessary to undertake a re-examination of these provisions at an earlier date. After the expiration of this period the whole scheme shall be subject to re-examination by the Trusteeship Council in the light of the experience acquired with its functioning. The residents of the City shall be then free to express by means of a referendum their wishes as to possible modifications of the regime of the City.

Part IV: Capitulations

States whose nationals have in the past enjoyed in Palestine the privileges and immunities of foreigners, including the benefits of consular jurisdiction and protection, as formerly enjoyed by capitulation or usage in the Ottoman Empire, are invited to renounce any right pertaining to them to the re-establishment of such privileges and immunities in the proposed Arab and Jewish States and the City of Jerusalem.

Source: The United Nations Information Service on Palestine (UNISPAL) @http://unispal.un.org/unispal.nsf/udc.htm

Document II

Text of the United Nations General Assembly Resolution: 194 (III), December 11, 1948 Palestine: Progress Report of the United Nations Mediator

---

The General Assembly,

Having considered further the situation in Palestine,

1. *Expresses* its deep appreciation of the progress achieved through the good offices of the late United Nations Mediator in promoting a peaceful adjustment of the future situation of Palestine, for which cause he sacrificed his life; and

Extends its thanks to the Acting Mediator and his staff for their continued efforts and devotion to duty in Palestine;

2. *Establishes* a Conciliation Commission consisting of three States members of the United Nations which shall have the following functions:

(a) To assume, in so far as it considers necessary in existing circumstances, the functions given to the United Nations Mediator on Palestine by resolution 186 (S-2) of the General Assembly of 14th May 1948;

(b) To carry out the specific functions and directives given to it by the present resolution and such additional functions and directives as may be given to it by the General Assembly or by the Security Council;

(c) To undertake, upon the request of the Security Council, any of the functions now assigned to the United Nations Mediator on Palestine or to the United Nations Truce Commission by resolutions of the Security Council; upon such request to the Conciliation Commission by the Security Council with respect to all the remaining functions of the United Nations Mediator on Palestine under Security Council resolutions, the office of the Mediator shall be terminated;

3. *Decides* that a Committee of the Assembly, consisting of China, France, the Union of Soviet Socialist Republics, the United Kingdom and the United States of America, shall present, before the end of the first part of the present session of the General Assembly, for the approval of the Assembly, a proposal concerning the names of the three States which will constitute the Conciliation Commission;

4. *Requests* the Commission to begin its functions at once, with a view to the establishment of contact between the parties themselves and the Commission at the earliest possible date;

5. *Calls upon* the Governments and authorities concerned to extend the scope of the negotiations provided for in the Security Council's resolution of 16th November 1948 and to seek agreement by negotiations conducted either with the Conciliation Commission or directly, with a view to the final settlement of all questions outstanding between them;

6. *Instructs* the Conciliation Commission to take steps to assist the Governments and authorities concerned to achieve a final settlement of all questions outstanding between them;

7. *Resolves* that the Holy Places—including Nazareth—religious buildings and sites in Palestine should be protected and free access to them assured, in accordance with existing rights and historical practice; that arrangements to this end should be under effective United Nations supervision; that the United Nations Conciliation Commission, in presenting to the fourth regular session of the General Assembly its detailed proposals for a permanent international regime for the territory of Jerusalem, should include recommendations concerning the Holy Places in that territory; that with regard to the Holy Places in the rest of Palestine the Commission should call upon the political authorities of the areas concerned to give appropriate formal guarantees as to the protection of the Holy Places and access to them; and that these undertakings should be presented to the General Assembly for approval;

8. *Resolves* that, in view of its association with three world

religions, the Jerusalem area, including the present municipality of Jerusalem plus the surrounding villages and towns, the most eastern of which shall be Abu Dis; the most southern, Bethlehem; the most western, Ein Karim (including also the built-up area of Motsa); and the most northern, Shu'fat, should be accorded special and separate treatment from the rest of Palestine and should be placed under effective United Nations control;

Requests the Security Council to take further steps to ensure the demilitarization of Jerusalem at the earliest possible date;

Instructs the Conciliation Commission to present to the fourth regular session of the General Assembly detailed proposals for a permanent international regime for the Jerusalem area which will provide for the maximum local autonomy for distinctive groups consistent with the special international status of the Jerusalem area;

The Conciliation Commission is authorized to appoint a United Nations representative, who shall co-operate with the local authorities with respect to the interim administration of the Jerusalem area;

9. *Resolves* that, pending agreement on more detailed arrangements among the Governments and authorities concerned, the freest possible access to Jerusalem by road, rail or air should be accorded to all inhabitants of Palestine;

Instructs the Conciliation Commission to report immediately to the Security Council, for appropriate action by that organ, any attempt by any party to impede such access;

10. *Instructs* the Conciliation Commission to seek arrangements among the Governments and authorities concerned which will facilitate the economic development of the area, including arrangements for access to ports and airfields and the use of transportation and communication facilities;

11. *Resolves* that the refugees wishing to return to their homes and live at peace with their neighbours should be

permitted to do so at the earliest practicable date, and that compensation should be paid for the property of those choosing not to return and for loss of or damage to property which, under principles of international law or in equity, should be made good by the Governments or authorities responsible;

Instructs the Conciliation Commission to facilitate the repatriation, resettlement and economic and social rehabilitation of the refugees and the payment of compensation, and to maintain close relations with the Director of the United Nations Relief for Palestine Refugees and, through him, with the appropriate organs and agencies of the United Nations;

12. *Authorizes* the Conciliation Commission to appoint such subsidiary bodies and to employ such technical experts, acting under its authority, as it may find necessary for the effective discharge of its functions and responsibilities under the present resolution;

The Conciliation Commission will have its official headquarters at Jerusalem. The authorities responsible for maintaining order in Jerusalem will be responsible for taking all measures necessary to ensure the security of the Commission. The Secretary-General will provide a limited number of guards to the protection of the staff and premises of the Commission;

13. *Instructs* the Conciliation Commission to render progress reports periodically to the Secretary-General for transmission to the Security Council and to the Members of the United Nations;

14. *Calls upon* all Governments and authorities concerned to co-operate with the Conciliation Commission and to take all possible steps to assist in the implementation of the present resolution;

15. *Requests* the Secretary-General to provide the necessary staff and facilities and to make appropriate arrangements to provide the necessary funds required in

carrying out the terms of the present resolution.

At the 186th plenary meeting on 11th December, 1948, a committee of the Assembly consisting of the five States designated in paragraph 3 of the above resolution proposed that the following three States should constitute the Conciliation Commission:

France, Turkey, United States of America.

The proposal of the Committee having been adopted by the General Assembly at the same meeting, the Conciliation Commission is therefore composed of the above-mentioned three States.

Source: The United Nations Information Service on Palestine (UNISPAL) @ http://unispal.un.org/unispal.nsf/udc.htm.

Document III

Text of the United Nations Security Council Resolution 242 (1967), November 22, 1967

The Security Council,

Expressing its continuing concern with the grave situation in the Middle East,

Emphasizing the inadmissibility of the acquisition of territory by war and the need to work for a just and lasting peace in which every State in the area can live in security,

Emphasizing further that all Member States in their acceptance of the Charter of the United Nations have undertaken a commitment to act in accordance with Article 2 of the Charter,

1. *Affirms* that the fulfilment of Charter principles requires the establishment of a just and lasting peace in the Middle East which should include the application of both the following principles:

(i) Withdrawal of Israel armed forces from territories occupied in the recent conflict;

(ii) Termination of all claims or states of belligerency and respect for and acknowledgment of the sovereignty, territorial integrity and political independence of every State in the area and their right to live in peace within secure and recognized boundaries free from threats or acts of force;

2. *Affirms further* the necessity:

(a) For guaranteeing freedom of navigation through international waterways in the area;

(b) For achieving a just settlement of the refugee problem;

(c) For guaranteeing the territorial inviolability and political independence of every State in the area, through measures including the establishment of demilitarized zones;

3. *Requests* the Secretary-General to designate a Special

Representative to proceed to the Middle East to establish and maintain contacts with the States concerned in order to promote agreement and assist efforts to achieve a peaceful and accepted settlement in accordance with the provisions and principles in this resolution;

4. *Requests* the Secretary-General to report to the Security Council on the progress of the efforts of the Special Representative as soon as possible.

Adopted unanimously at the 1382nd meeting.

Source: The United Nations Information Service on Palestine (UNISPAL) @ http://unispal.un.org/unispal.nsf/udc.htm.

Document IV

Camp David Accords
Framework for Peace in the Middle East

Muhammad Anwar al-Sadat, President of the Arab Republic of Egypt, and Menachem Begin, Prime Minister of Israel, met with Jimmy Carter, President of the United States of America, at Camp David from September 5 to September 17, 1978, and have agreed on the following framework for peace in the Middle East. They invite other parties to the Arab-Israel conflict to adhere to it.

Preamble

The search for peace in the Middle East must be guided by the following:

- The agreed basis for a peaceful settlement of the conflict between Israel and its neighbours is United Nations Security Council Resolution 242, in all its parts.
- After four wars during 30 years, despite intensive human efforts, the Middle East, which is the cradle of civilization and the birthplace of three great religions, does not enjoy the blessings of peace. The people of the Middle East yearn for peace so that the vast human and natural resources of the region can be turned to the pursuits of peace and so that this area can become a model for coexistence and cooperation among nations.
- The historic initiative of President Sadat in visiting Jerusalem and the reception accorded to him by the parliament, government and people of Israel, and the reciprocal visit of Prime Minister Begin to Ismailia, the peace proposals made by both leaders, as well as the warm reception of these missions by the peoples of both countries, have created an unprecedented opportunity for

peace which must not be lost if this generation and future generations are to be spared the tragedies of war.

- The provisions of the Charter of the United Nations and the other accepted norms of international law and legitimacy now provide accepted standards for the conduct of relations among all states.
- To achieve a relationship of peace, in the spirit of Article 2 of the United Nations Charter, future negotiations between Israel and any neighbour prepared to negotiate peace and security with it are necessary for the purpose of carrying out all the provisions and principles of Resolutions 242 and 338.
- Peace requires respect for the sovereignty, territorial integrity and political independence of every state in the area and their right to live in peace within secure and recognized boundaries free from threats or acts of force. Progress toward that goal can accelerate movement toward a new era of reconciliation in the Middle East marked by cooperation in promoting economic development, in maintaining stability and in assuring security.
- Security is enhanced by a relationship of peace and by cooperation between nations which enjoy normal relations. In addition, under the terms of peace treaties, the parties can, on the basis of reciprocity, agree to special security arrangements such as demilitarized zones, limited armaments areas, early warning stations, the presence of international forces, liaison, agreed measures for monitoring and other arrangements that they agree are useful.

Framework

Taking these factors into account, the parties are determined to reach a just, comprehensive, and durable settlement of the Middle East conflict through the conclusion of peace treaties based on Security Council Resolutions 242 and 338 in all their parts. Their purpose is to achieve peace and good neighbourly relations. They recognize that for peace to endure, it must involve all those who have been most deeply affected by the conflict. They therefore agree that this framework, as appropriate, is intended by them to constitute a basis for peace not only between Egypt and Israel, but also between Israel and each of its other neighbours which is prepared to negotiate peace with Israel on this basis. With that objective in mind, they have agreed to proceed as follows:

West Bank and Gaza

Egypt, Israel, Jordan and the representatives of the Palestinian people should participate in negotiations on the resolution of the Palestinian problem in all its aspects. To achieve that objective, negotiations relating to the West Bank and Gaza should proceed in three stages:

1. Egypt and Israel agree that, in order to ensure a peaceful and orderly transfer of authority, and taking into account the security concerns of all the parties, there should be transitional arrangements for the West Bank and Gaza for a period not exceeding five years. In order to provide full autonomy to the inhabitants, under these arrangements the Israeli military government and its civilian administration will be withdrawn as soon as a self-governing authority has been freely elected by the inhabitants of these areas to replace the existing military government. To negotiate the details of a transitional arrangement, Jordan will be invited to join the negotiations on the basis of this framework. These new arrangements should give due consideration both to the principle of self-government by the inhabitants of these territories and to the legitimate security concerns of the parties involved.

2. Egypt, Israel, and Jordan will agree on the modalities for establishing elected self-governing authority in the West Bank and Gaza. The delegations of Egypt and Jordan may include Palestinians from the West Bank and Gaza or other Palestinians as mutually agreed. The parties will negotiate an agreement which will define the powers and responsibilities of

the self-governing authority to be exercised in the West Bank and Gaza. A withdrawal of Israeli armed forces will take place and there will be a redeployment of the remaining Israeli forces into specified security locations. The agreement will also include arrangements for assuring internal and external security and public order. A strong local police force will be established, which may include Jordanian citizens. In addition, Israeli and Jordanian forces will participate in joint patrols and in the manning of control posts to assure the security of the borders.

3. When the self-governing authority (administrative council) in the West Bank and Gaza is established and inaugurated, the transitional period of five years will begin. As soon as possible, but not later than the third year after the beginning of the transitional period, negotiations will take place to determine the final status of the West Bank and Gaza and its relationship with its neighbours and to conclude a peace treaty between Israel and Jordan by the end of thc transitional period. These negotiations will be conducted among Egypt, Israel, Jordan and the elected representatives of the inhabitants of the West Bank and Gaza. Two separate but related committees will be convened, one committee, consisting of representatives of the four parties which will negotiate and agree on the final status of the West Bank and Gaza, and its relationship with its neighbours, and the second committee, consisting of representatives of Israel and representatives of Jordan to be joined by the elected representatives of the inhabitants of the West Bank and Gaza, to negotiate the peace treaty between Israel and Jordan, taking into account the agreement reached in the final status of the West Bank and Gaza. The negotiations shall be based on all the provisions and principles of UN Security Council Resolution 242. The negotiations will resolve, among other matters, the location of the boundaries and the nature of the security arrangements. The solution from the negotiations must also recognize the legitimate right of the Palestinian

peoples and their just requirements. In this way, the Palestinians will participate in the determination of their own future through:

1. The negotiations among Egypt, Israel, Jordan and the representatives of the inhabitants of the West Bank and Gaza to agree on the final status of the West Bank and Gaza and other outstanding issues by the end of the transitional period.
2. Submitting their agreements to a vote by the elected representatives of the inhabitants of the West Bank and Gaza.
3. Providing for the elected representatives of the inhabitants of the West Bank and Gaza to decide how they shall govern themselves consistent with the provisions of their agreement.
4. Participating as stated above in the work of the committee negotiating the peace treaty between Israel and Jordan.
5. All necessary measures will be taken and provisions made to assure the security of Israel and its neighbours during the transitional period and beyond. To assist in providing such security, a strong local police force will be constituted by the self-governing authority. It will be composed of inhabitants of the West Bank and Gaza. The police will maintain liaison on internal security matters with the designated Israeli, Jordanian, and Egyptian officers.
6. During the transitional period, representatives of Egypt, Israel, Jordan, and the self-governing authority will constitute a continuing committee to decide by agreement on the modalities of admission of persons displaced from the West Bank and Gaza in 1967, together with necessary measures to prevent disruption and disorder. Other matters of common concern may also be dealt with by this committee.
7. Egypt and Israel will work with each other and with other interested parties to establish agreed procedures for a

prompt, just and permanent implementation of the resolution of the refugee problem.

Egypt-Israel

Egypt-Israel undertake not to resort to the threat or the use of force to settle disputes. Any disputes shall be settled by peaceful means in accordance with the provisions of Article 33 of the U.N. Charter.

In order to achieve peace between them, the parties agree to negotiate in good faith with a goal of concluding within three months from the signing of the Framework a peace treaty between them while inviting the other parties to the conflict to proceed simultaneously to negotiate and conclude similar peace treaties with a view the achieving a comprehensive peace in the area. The Framework for the Conclusion of a Peace Treaty between Egypt and Israel will govern the peace negotiations between them. The parties will agree on the modalities and the timetable for the implementation of their obligations under the treaty.

Associated Principles

Egypt and Israel state that the principles and provisions described below should apply to peace treaties between Israel and each of its neighbours—Egypt, Jordan, Syria and Lebanon.

Signatories shall establish among themselves relationships normal to states at peace with one another. To this end, they should undertake to abide by all the provisions of the U.N. Charter. Steps to be taken in this respect include:

- full recognition;
- abolishing economic boycotts;
- guaranteeing that under their jurisdiction the citizens of the other parties shall enjoy the protection of the due process of law.

Signatories should explore possibilities for economic development in the context of final peace treaties, with the objective of contributing to the atmosphere of peace, cooperation and friendship which is their common goal.

Claims commissions may be established for the mutual settlement of all financial claims.

The United States shall be invited to participate in the talks on matters related to the modalities of the implementation of the agreements and working out the timetable for the carrying out of the obligations of the parties.

The United Nations Security Council shall be requested to endorse the peace treaties and ensure that their provisions shall not be violated. The permanent members of the Security Council shall be requested to underwrite the peace treaties and ensure respect or the provisions. They shall be requested to conform their policies and actions with an undertaking contained in this Framework.

Camp David Accords

Framework for the Conclusion of a Peace Treaty between Egypt and Israel

In order to achieve peace between them, Israel and Egypt agree to negotiate in good faith with a goal of concluding within three months of the signing of this framework a peace treaty between them:

It is agreed that:

- The site of the negotiations will be under a United Nations flag at a location or locations to be mutually agreed.
- All of the principles of U.N. Resolution 242 will apply in this resolution of the dispute between Israel and Egypt.
- Unless otherwise mutually agreed, terms of the peace treaty will be implemented between two and three years after the peace treaty is signed.
- The following matters are agreed between the parties:

1. The full exercise of Egyptian sovereignty up to the internationally recognized border between Egypt and mandated Palestine;

2. The withdrawal of Israeli armed forces from the Sinai;

3. The use of airfields left by the Israelis near al-Arish,

Rafah, Ras en-Naqb, and Sharm el-Sheikh for civilian purposes only, including possible commercial use only by all nations;

4. The right of free passage by ships of Israel through the Gulf of Suez and the Suez Canal on the basis of the Constantinople Convention of 1888 applying to all nations; the Strait of Tiran and Gulf of Aqaba are international waterways to be open to all nations for unimpeded and non-suspendable freedom of navigation and overflight;

5. The construction of a highway between the Sinai and Jordan near Eilat with guaranteed free and peaceful passage by Egypt and Jordan; and

6. The stationing of military forces listed below.

Stationing of Forces

- No more than one division (mechanized or infantry) of Egyptian armed forces will be stationed within an area lying approximately 50 km. (30 miles) east of the Gulf of Suez and the Suez Canal.
- Only United Nations forces and civil police equipped with light weapons to perform normal police functions will be stationed within an area lying west of the international border and the Gulf of Aqaba, varying in width from 20 km. (12 miles) to 40 km. (24 miles).
- In the area within 3 km. (1.8 miles) east of the international border there will be Israeli limited military forces not to exceed four infantry battalions and United Nations observers.
- Border patrol units not to exceed three battalions will supplement the civil police in maintaining order in the area not included above.
- The exact demarcation of the above areas will be as decided during the peace negotiations.
- Early warning stations may exist to insure compliance with the terms of the agreement.
- United Nations forces will be stationed:

1. In part of the area in the Sinai lying within about 20 km. of the Mediterranean Sea and adjacent to the international border, and

2. In the Sharm el-Sheikh area to insure freedom of passage through the Strait of Tiran; and these forces will not be removed unless such removal is approved by the Security Council of the United Nations with a unanimous vote of the five permanent members.

- After a peace treaty is signed, and after the interim withdrawal is complete, normal relations will be established between Egypt and Israel, including full recognition, including diplomatic, economic and cultural relations; termination of economic boycotts and barriers to the free movement of goods and people; and mutual protection of citizens by the due process of law.

Interim Withdrawal

Between three months and nine months after the signing of the peace treaty, all Israeli forces will withdraw east of a line extending from a point east of El-Arish to Ras Muhammad, the exact location of this line to be determined by mutual agreement.

Document V

Hamas Covenant 1988: The Covenant of the Islamic Resistance Movement, August 18, 1988

In the Name of the Most Merciful Allah

"Ye are the best nation that hath been raised up unto mankind: ye command that which is just, and ye forbid that which is unjust, and ye believe in Allah. And if they who have received the scriptures had believed, it had surely been the better for them: there are believers among them, but the greater part of them are transgressors. They shall not hurt you, unless with a slight hurt; and if they fight against you, they shall turn their backs to you, and they shall not be helped. They are smitten with vileness wheresoever they are found; unless they obtain security by entering into a treaty with Allah, and a treaty with men; and they draw on themselves indignation from Allah, and they are afflicted with poverty. This they suffer, because they disbelieved the signs of Allah, and slew the prophets unjustly; this, because they were rebellious, and transgressed" (Al-Imran; verses 109-111).

Israel will exist and will continue to exist until Islam will obliterate it, just as it obliterated others before it" (The Martyr, Imam Hassan al-Banna, of blessed memory).

"The Islamic world is on fire. Each of us should pour some water, no matter how little, to extinguish whatever one can without waiting for the others" (Sheikh Amjad al-Zahawi, of blessed memory).

In the Name of the Most Merciful Allah

Introduction

Praise be unto Allah, to whom we resort for help, and whose forgiveness, guidance and support we seek; Allah bless the Prophet and grant him salvation, his companions and supporters, and to those who carried out his message and adopted his laws—everlasting prayers and salvation as long as the earth and heaven will last. Hereafter:

O People:

Out of the midst of troubles and the sea of suffering, out of the palpitations of faithful hearts and cleansed arms; out of the sense of duty, and in response to Allah's command, the call has gone out rallying people together and making them follow the ways of Allah, leading them to have determined will in order to fulfil their role in life, to overcome all obstacles, and surmount the difficulties on the way. Constant preparation has continued and so has the readiness to sacrifice life and all that is precious for the sake of Allah.

Thus it was that the nucleus (of the movement) was formed and started to pave its way through the tempestuous sea of hopes and expectations, of wishes and yearnings, of troubles and obstacles, of pain and challenges, both inside and outside.

When the idea was ripe, the seed grew and the plant struck root in the soil of reality, away from passing emotions, and hateful haste. The Islamic Resistance Movement emerged to carry out its role through striving for the sake of its Creator, its arms intertwined with those of all the fighters for the liberation of Palestine. The spirits of its fighters meet with the spirits of all the fighters who have sacrificed their lives on the soil of Palestine, ever since it was conquered by the companions of the Prophet, Allah bless him and grant him salvation, and until this day.

This Covenant of the Islamic Resistance Movement (HAMAS), clarifies its picture, reveals its identity, outlines its stand, explains its aims, speaks about its hopes, and calls for its support, adoption and joining its ranks. Our struggle against the Jews is very great and very serious. It needs all sincere efforts. It is a step that inevitably should be followed by other steps. The Movement is but one squadron that should be supported by more and more squadrons from this vast Arab and Islamic world, until the enemy is vanquished and Allah's victory is realised.

Thus we see them coming on the horizon "and you shall learn about it hereafter" "Allah hath written, Verily I will prevail, and my apostles: for Allah is strong and mighty" (The Dispute; verse 21).

"Say to them, This is my way: I invite you to Allah, by an evident demonstration; both I and he who followeth me; and, praise be unto Allah! I am not an idolator" (Joseph; verse 107).

Hamas (means) ***strength and bravery*****—(according to) Al-Mua'jam al-Wasit: c1.** Definition of the Movement

Ideological Starting Points

Article One:

The Islamic Resistance Movement: The Movement's programme is Islam. From it, it draws its ideas, ways of thinking and understanding of the universe, life and man. It resorts to it for judgement in all its conduct, and it is inspired by it for guidance of its steps.

Islamic Resistance Movement's Relation with the Moslem Brotherhood Group:

Article Two:

The Islamic Resistance Movement is one of the wings of Moslem Brotherhood in Palestine. Moslem Brotherhood Movement is a universal organization which constitutes the largest Islamic movement in modern times. It is characterised by its deep understanding, accurate comprehension and its complete embrace of all Islamic concepts of all aspects of life, culture, creed, politics, economics, education, society, justice and judgement, the spreading of Islam, education, art, information, science of the occult and conversion to Islam.

Structure and Formation

Article Three:

The basic structure of the Islamic Resistance Movement

consists of Moslems who have given their allegiance to Allah whom they truly worship—"I have created the jinn and humans only for the purpose of worshipping"—who know their duty towards themselves, their families and country. In all that, they fear Allah and raise the banner of Jihad in the face of the oppressors, so that they would rid the land and the people of their uncleanliness, vileness and evils.

"But we will oppose truth to vanity, and it shall confound the same; and behold, it shall vanish away". (Prophets; verse 18).

Article Four:

The Islamic Resistance Movement welcomes every Moslem who embraces its faith, ideology, follows its programme, keeps its secrets, and wants to belong to its ranks and carry out the duty. Allah will certainly reward such one.

Time and Place Extent of the Islamic Resistance Movement

Article Five:

Time extent of the Islamic Resistance Movement: By adopting Islam as its way of life, the Movement goes back to the time of the birth of the Islamic message, of the righteous ancestor, for Allah is its target, the Prophet is its example and the Koran is its constitution. Its extent in place is anywhere that there are Moslems who embrace Islam as their way of life everywhere in the globe. This being so, it extends to the depth of the earth and reaches out to the heaven.

"Dost thou not see how Allah putteth forth a parable; representing a good word, as a good tree, whose root is firmly fixed in the earth, and whose branches reach unto heaven; which bringeth forth its fruit in all seasons, by the will of its Lord? Allah propoundeth parables unto men, that they may be instructed" (Abraham; verses 24-25).

Characteristics and Independence

Article Six:

The Islamic Resistance Movement is a distinguished

Palestinian movement, whose allegiance is to Allah, and whose way of life is Islam. It strives to raise the banner of Allah over every inch of Palestine, for under the wing of Islam followers of all religions can coexist in security and safety where their lives, possessions and rights are concerned. In the absence of Islam, strife will be rife, oppression spreads, evil prevails and schisms and wars will break out.

How excellent was the Moslem poet, Mohamed Ikbal, when he wrote:

"If faith is lost, there is no security and there is no life for him who does not adhere to religion. He who accepts life without religion, has taken annihilation as his companion for life".

The Universality of the Islamic Resistance Movement
Article Seven:

As a result of the fact that those Moslems who adhere to the ways of the Islamic Resistance Movement spread all over the world, rally support for it and its stands, strive towards enhancing its struggle, the Movement is a universal one. It is well-equipped for that because of the clarity of its ideology, the nobility of its aim and the loftiness of its objectives.

On this basis, the Movement should be viewed and evaluated, and its role be recognised. He who denies its right, evades supporting it and turns a blind eye to facts, whether intentionally or unintentionally, would awaken to see that events have overtaken him and with no logic to justify his attitude. One should certainly learn from past examples.

The injustice of next-of-kin is harder to bear than the smite of the Indian sword.

"We have also sent down unto thee the book of the Koran with truth, confirming that scripture which was revealed before it; and preserving the same safe from corruption. Judge therefore between them according to that which Allah hath revealed; and follow not their desires, by swerving from the truth which hath come unto thee. Unto every of you have we given a law, and an open path; and if Allah had pleased, he had surely made you one people; but he hath thought it fit to give you different laws, that he might try you in that which he hath given you respectively. Therefore strive to excel each other in good works; unto Allah shall ye all return, and then will he declare unto you that concerning which ye have disagreed" (The Table; verse 48).

The Islamic Resistance Movement is one of the links in the chain of the struggle against the Zionist invaders. It goes back to 1939, to the emergence of the martyr Izz al-Din al Kissam and his brethren the fighters, members of Moslem Brotherhood. It goes on to reach out and become one with another chain that includes the struggle of the Palestinians and Moslem Brotherhood in the 1948 war and the Jihad operations of the Moslem Brotherhood in 1968 and after.

Moreover, if the links have been distant from each other and if obstacles, placed by those who are the lackeys of Zionism in the way of the fighters obstructed the continuation of the struggle, the Islamic Resistance Movement aspires to the realisation of Allah's promise, no matter how long that should take. The Prophet, Allah bless him and grant him salvation, has said:

"The Day of Judgement will not come about until Moslems fight the Jews (killing the Jews), when the Jew will hide behind stones and trees. The stones and trees will say O Moslems, O Abdulla, there is a Jew behind me, come and kill him. Only the Gharkad tree, (evidently a certain kind of tree) would not do that because it is one of the trees of the Jews" (related by al-Bukhari and Moslem).

The Slogan of the Islamic Resistance Movement
Article Eight:

Allah is its target, the Prophet is its model, the Koran its constitution: Jihad is its path and death for the sake of Allah is the loftiest of its wishes.

Objectives

Incentives and Objectives:

Article Nine:

The Islamic Resistance Movement found itself at a time when Islam has disappeared from life. Thus rules shook, concepts were upset, values changed and evil people took control, oppression and darkness prevailed, cowards became like tigers: homelands were usurped, people were scattered and were caused to wander all over the world, the state of justice disappeared and the state of falsehood replaced it. Nothing remained in its right place. Thus, when Islam is absent from the arena, everything changes. From this state of affairs the incentives are drawn.

As for the objectives: They are the fighting against the false, defeating it and vanquishing it so that justice could prevail, homelands be retrieved and from its mosques would the voice of the mu'azen emerge declaring the establishment of the state of Islam, so that people and things would return each to their right places and Allah is our helper.

"...and if Allah had not prevented men, the one by the other, verily the earth had been corrupted: but Allah is beneficent towards his creatures" (The Cow; verse 251).

Article Ten:

As the Islamic Resistance Movement paves its way, it will back the oppressed and support the wronged with all its might. It will spare no effort to bring about justice and defeat injustice, in word and deed, in this place and everywhere it can reach and have influence therein.

Strategies and Methods

Strategies of the Islamic Resistance Movement: Palestine Is Islamic aqf

Article Eleven:

The Islamic Resistance Movement believes that the land of Palestine is an Islamic Waqf consecrated for future Moslem generations until Judgement Day. It, or any part of it, should not be squandered: it, or any part of it, should not be given up.

Neither a single Arab country nor all Arab countries, neither any king or president, nor all the kings and presidents, neither any organization nor all of them, be they Palestinian or Arab, possess the right to do that. Palestine is an Islamic Waqf land consecrated for Moslem generations until Judgement Day. This being so, who could claim to have the right to represent Moslem generations till Judgement Day?

This is the law governing the land of Palestine in the Islamic Sharia (law) and the same goes for any land the Moslems have conquered by force, because during the times of (Islamic) conquests, the Moslems consecrated these lands to Moslem generations till the Day of Judgement.

It happened like this: When the leaders of the Islamic armies conquered Syria and Iraq, they sent to the Caliph of the Moslems, Umar bin-el-Khatab, asking for his advice concerning the conquered land - whether they should divide it among the soldiers, or leave it for its owners, or what? After consultations and discussions between the Caliph of the Moslems, Omar bin-el-Khatab and companions of the Prophet, Allah bless him and grant him salvation, it was decided that the land should be left with its owners who could benefit by its fruit. As for the real ownership of the land and the land itself, it should be consecrated for Moslem generations till Judgement Day. Those who are on the land, are there only to benefit from its fruit. This Waqf remains as long as earth and heaven remain. Any procedure in contradiction to Islamic Sharia, where Palestine is concerned, is null and void.

"Verily, this is a certain truth. Wherefore praise the name of thy Lord, the great Allah" (The Inevitable; verse 95).

Homeland and Nationalism from the Point of View of the Islamic Resistance Movement in Palestine
Article Twelve:

Nationalism, from the point of view of the Islamic Resistance Movement, is part of the religious creed. Nothing in nationalism is more significant or deeper than in the case when an enemy should tread Moslem land. Resisting and quelling the enemy become the individual duty of every Moslem, male or female. A woman can go out to fight the enemy without her husband's permission, and so does the slave: without his master's permission.

Nothing of the sort is to be found in any other regime. This is an undisputed fact. If other nationalist movements are connected with materialistic, human or regional causes, nationalism of the Islamic Resistance Movement has all these elements as well as the more important elements that give it soul and life. It is connected to the source of spirit and the granter of life, hoisting in the sky of the homeland the heavenly banner that joins earth and heaven with a strong bond.

If Moses comes and throws his staff, both witch and magic are annulled.

"Now is the right direction manifestly distinguished from deceit: whoever therefore shall deny Tagut, and believe in Allah, he shall surely take hold with a strong handle, which shall not be broken; Allah is he who heareth and seeth" (The Cow; verse 256).

Peaceful Solutions, Initiatives and International Conferences

Article Thirteen:

Initiatives, and so-called peaceful solutions and international conferences, are in contradiction to the principles of the Islamic Resistance Movement. Abusing any part of Palestine is abuse directed against part of religion. Nationalism of the Islamic Resistance Movement is part of its religion. Its members have been fed on that. For the sake of hoisting the banner of Allah over their homeland they fight. "Allah will be prominent, but most people do not know".

Now and then the call goes out for the convening of an international conference to look for ways of solving the (Palestinian) question. Some accept, others reject the idea, for this or other reason, with one stipulation or more for consent to convening the conference and participating in it. Knowing the parties constituting the conference, their past and present attitudes towards Moslem problems, the Islamic Resistance Movement does not consider these conferences capable of realising the demands, restoring the rights or doing justice to the oppressed. These conferences are only ways of setting the infidels in the land of the Moslems as arbitrators. When did the infidels do justice to the believers?

"But the Jews will not be pleased with thee, neither the Christians, until thou follow their religion; say, The direction of Allah is the true direction. And verily if thou follow their desires, after the knowledge which hath been given thee, thou shalt find no patron or protector against Allah" (The Cow; verse 120).

There is no solution for the Palestinian question except through Jihad. Initiatives, proposals and international conferences are all a waste of time and vain endeavours. The Palestinian people know better than to consent to having their future, rights and fate toyed with. As in said in the honourable Hadith:

"The people of Syria are Allah's lash in His land. He wreaks His vengeance through them against whomsoever He wishes among His slaves It is unthinkable that those who are double-faced among them should prosper over the faithful. They will certainly die out of grief and desperation".

The Three Circles

Article Fourteen:

The question of the liberation of Palestine is bound to three circles: the Palestinian circle, the Arab circle and the Islamic circle. Each of these circles has its role in the struggle against Zionism. Each has its duties, and it is a horrible mistake and a sign of deep ignorance to overlook any of these circles. Palestine is an Islamic land which has the first of the two kiblahs (direction to which Moslems turn in praying), the third of the holy (Islamic) sanctuaries, and the point of departure for Mohamed's midnight journey to the seven heavens (i.e. Jerusalem).

"Praise be unto him who transported his servant by night, from the sacred temple of Mecca to the farther temple of Jerusalem, the circuit of which we have blessed, that we might show him some of our signs; for Allah is he who heareth, and seeth" (The Night-Journey; verse 1).

Since this is the case, liberation of Palestine is then an individual duty for very Moslem wherever he may be. On this basis, the problem should be viewed. This should be realised by every Moslem.

The day the problem is dealt with on this basis, when the three circles mobilize their capabilities, the present state of affairs will change and the day of liberation will come nearer. "Verily ye are stronger than they, by reason of the terror cast into their breasts from Allah. This, because they are not people of prudence" (The Emigration; verse 13).

The Jihad for the Liberation of Palestine is an Individual Duty

Article Fifteen:

The day that enemies usurp part of Moslem land, Jihad becomes the individual duty of every Moslem. In face of the Jews' usurpation of Palestine, it is compulsory that the banner of Jihad be raised. To do this requires the diffusion of Islamic consciousness among the masses, both on the regional, Arab and Islamic levels. It is necessary to instil the spirit of Jihad in the heart of the nation so that they would confront the enemies and join the ranks of the fighters.

It is necessary that scientists, educators and teachers, information and media people, as well as the educated masses, especially the youth and sheikhs of the Islamic movements, should take part in the operation of awakening (the masses). It is important that basic changes be made in the school curriculum, to cleanse it of the traces of ideological invasion that affected it as a result of the orientalists and missionaries who infiltrated the region following the defeat of the Crusaders at the hands of Salah el-Din (Saladin). The Crusaders realised that it was impossible to defeat the Moslems without first having ideological invasion pave the way by upsetting their thoughts, disfiguring their heritage and violating their ideals. Only then could they invade with soldiers. This, in its turn, paved the way for the imperialistic invasion that made Allenby declare on entering Jerusalem: "Only now have the Crusades ended" General Guru stood at Salah el-Din's grave and said: "We have returned, O Salah el-Din". Imperialism has helped towards the strengthening of ideological invasion, deepening, and still does, its roots. All this has paved the way towards the loss of Palestine.

It is necessary to instil in the minds of the Moslem generations that the Palestinian problem is a religious problem, and should be dealt with on this basis. Palestine contains Islamic holy sites. In it there is al-Aqsa Mosque which is bound to the great Mosque in Mecca in an inseparable bond as long as heaven and earth speak of Isra (Mohammed's midnight journey to the seven heavens) and Mi'raj (Mohammed's ascension to the seven heavens from Jerusalem).

"The bond of one day for the sake of Allah is better than the world and whatever there is on it. The place of one's whip in Paradise is far better than the world and whatever there is on it. A worshipper's going and coming in the service of Allah is better than the world and whatever there is on it" (As related by al-Bukhari, Moslem, al-Tarmdhi and Ibn Maja).

"I swear by the holder of Mohammed's soul that I would like to invade and be killed for the sake of Allah, then invade and be killed, and then invade again and be killed" (As related by al-Bukhari and Moslem).

The Education of the Generations
Article Sixteen:

It is necessary to follow Islamic orientation in educating

the Islamic generations in our region by teaching the religious duties, comprehensive study of the Koran, the study of the Prophet's Sunna (his sayings and doings), and learning about Islamic history and heritage from their authentic sources. This should be done by specialised and learned people, using a curriculum that would healthily form the thoughts and faith of the Moslem student. Side by side with this, a comprehensive study of the enemy, his human and financial capabilities, learning about his points of weakness and strength, and getting to know the forces supporting and helping him, should also be included. Also, it is important to be acquainted with the current events, to follow what is new and to study the analysis and commentaries made of these events. Planning for the present and future, studying every trend appearing, is a must so that the fighting Moslem would live knowing his aim, objective and his way in the midst of what is going on around him.

"O my son, verily every matter, whether good or bad, though it be the weight of a grain of mustard-seed, and be hidden in a rock, or in the heavens, or in the earth, Allah will bring the same to light; for Allah is clear-sighted and knowing. O my son, be constant at prayer, and command that which is just, and forbid that which is evil: and be patient under the afflictions which shall befall thee; for this is a duty absolutely incumbent on all men. Distort not thy face out of contempt to men, neither walk in the earth with insolence; for Allah loveth no arrogant, vain-glorious person" (Lokman; verses 16-18).

The Role of the Moslem Woman
Article Seventeen:

The Moslem woman has a role no less important than that of the moslem man in the battle of liberation. She is the maker of men. Her role in guiding and educating the new generations is great. The enemies have realised the importance of her role. They consider that if they are able to direct and bring her up they way they wish, far from Islam, they would have won the battle. That is why you find them giving these attempts constant attention through information campaigns, films, and the school curriculum, using for that purpose their lackeys who are infiltrated through Zionist organizations under various names and shapes, such as Freemasons, Rotary Clubs, espionage groups and others, which are all nothing more than cells of subversion and saboteurs. These organizations have ample resources that enable them to play their role in societies for the purpose of achieving the Zionist targets and to deepen the concepts that would serve the enemy. These organizations operate in the absence of Islam and its estrangement among its people. The Islamic peoples should perform their role in confronting the conspiracies of these saboteurs. The day Islam is in control of guiding the affairs of life, these organizations, hostile to humanity and Islam, will be obliterated.

Article Eighteen:

Woman in the home of the fighting family, whether she is a mother or a sister, plays the most important role in looking after the family, rearing the children and embuing them with moral values and thoughts derived from Islam. She has to teach them to perform the religious duties in preparation for the role of fighting awaiting them. That is why it is necessary to pay great attention to schools and the curriculum followed in educating Moslem girls, so that they would grow up to be good mothers, aware of their role in the battle of liberation.

She has to be of sufficient knowledge and understanding where the performance of housekeeping matters are concerned, because economy and avoidance of waste of the family budget, is one of the requirements for the ability to continue moving forward in the difficult conditions surrounding us. She should put before her eyes the fact that the money available to her is just like blood which should never flow except through the veins so that both children and grown-ups could continue to live.

"Verily, the Moslems of either sex, and the true believers of either sex, and the devout men, and the devout women, and the men of veracity, and the women of veracity, and the patient men, and the patient women, and the humble men, and the humble women, and the alms-givers of either sex who remember Allah frequently; for them hath Allah prepared forgiveness and a great reward" (The Confederates; verse 25).

The Role of Islamic Art in the Battle of Liberation
Article Nineteen:

Art has regulations and measures by which it can be determined whether it is Islamic or pre-Islamic (Jahili) art. The issues of Islamic liberation are in need of Islamic art that would take the spirit high, without raising one side of human nature above the other, but rather raise all of them harmoniously an in equilibrium.

Man is a unique and wonderful creature, made out of a handful of clay and a breath from Allah. Islamic art addresses man on this basis, while pre-Islamic art addresses the body giving preference to the clay component in it.

The book, the article, the bulletin, the sermon, the thesis, the popular poem, the poetic ode, the song, the play and others, contain the characteristics of Islamic art, then these are among the requirements of ideological mobilization, renewed food for the journey and recreation for the soul. The road is long and suffering is plenty. The soul will be bored, but Islamic art renews the energies, resurrects the movement, arousing in them lofty meanings and proper conduct. "Nothing can improve the self if it is in retreat except shifting from one mood to another".

All this is utterly serious and no jest, for those who are fighters do not jest.

Social Mutual Responsibility
Article Twenty:

Moslem society is a mutually responsible society. The Prophet, prayers and greetings be unto him, said: "Blessed are the generous, whether they were in town or on a journey, who have collected all that they had and shared it equally among themselves".

The Islamic spirit is what should prevail in every Moslem society. The society that confronts a vicious enemy which acts in a way similar to Nazism, making no differentiation between man and woman, between children and old people—such a society is entitled to this Islamic spirit. Our enemy relies on the methods of collective punishment. He has deprived people of their homeland and properties, pursued them in their places of exile and gathering, breaking bones, shooting at women, children and old people, with or without a reason. The enemy has opened detention camps where thousands and thousands of people are thrown and kept under sub-human conditions. Added to this, are the demolition of houses, rendering children orphans, meting cruel sentences against thousands of young people, and causing them to spend the best years of their lives in the dungeons of prisons.

In their Nazi treatment, the Jews made no exception for women or children. Their policy of striking fear in the heart is meant for all. They attack people where their breadwinning is concerned, extorting their money and threatening their honour. They deal with people as if they were the worst war criminals. Deportation from the homeland is a kind of murder.

To counter these deeds, it is necessary that social mutual responsibility should prevail among the people. The enemy should be faced by the people as a single body which if one member of it should complain, the rest of the body would respond by feeling the same pains.

Article Twenty-One:

Mutual social responsibility means extending assistance, financial or moral, to all those who are in need and joining in the execution of some of the work. Members of the Islamic Resistance Movement should consider the interests of the masses as their own personal interests. They must spare no effort in achieving and preserving them. They must prevent any foul play with the future of the upcoming generations and anything that could cause loss to society. The masses are part of them and they are part of the masses. Their strength is theirs, and their future is theirs. Members of the Islamic Resistance Movement should share the people's joy and grief, adopt the demands of the public and whatever means by which they could be realised. The day that such a spirit prevails, brotherliness would deepen, cooperation, sympathy and unity will be enhanced and the ranks will be solidified to confront the enemies.

Supportive Forces Behind the Enemy
Article Twenty-Two:

For a long time, the enemies have been planning, skilfully and with precision, for the achievement of what they have attained. They took into consideration the causes affecting the current of events. They strived to amass great and substantive material wealth which they devoted to the realisation of their dream. With their money, they took control of the world media, news agencies, the press, publishing houses, broadcasting stations, and others. With their money they stirred revolutions in various parts of the world with the purpose of achieving their interests and reaping the fruit therein. They were behind the French Revolution, the Communist revolution and most of the revolutions we heard and hear about, here and there. With their money they formed secret societies, such as Freemasons, Rotary Clubs, the Lions and others in different parts of the world for the purpose of sabotaging societies and achieving Zionist interests. With their money they were able to control imperialistic countries and instigate them to colonize many countries in order to enable them to exploit their resources and spread corruption there.

You may speak as much as you want about regional and world wars. They were behind World War I, when they were able to destroy the Islamic Caliphate, making financial gains and controlling resources. They obtained the Balfour Declaration, formed the League of Nations through which they could rule the world. They were behind World War II, through which they made huge financial gains by trading in armaments, and paved the way for the establishment of their state. It was they who instigated the replacement of the League of Nations with the United Nations and the Security Council to enable them to rule the world through them. There is no war going on anywhere, without having their finger in it.

"So often as they shall kindle a fire for war, Allah shall extinguish it; and they shall set their minds to act corruptly in the earth, but Allah loveth not the corrupt doers" (The Table; verse 64).

The imperialistic forces in the Capitalist West and Communist East, support the enemy with all their might, in money and in men. These forces take turns in doing that. The day Islam appears, the forces of infidelity would unite to challenge it, for the infidels are of one nation.

"O true believers, contract not an intimate friendship with any besides yourselves: they will not fail to corrupt you. They wish for that which may cause you to perish: their hatred hath already appeared from out of their mouths; but what their breasts conceal is yet more inveterate. We have already shown you signs of their ill will towards you, if ye understand" (The Family of Imran; verse 118).

It is not in vain that the verse is ended with Allah's words "if ye understand".

Our Attitudes Towards

A. Islamic Movements

Article Twenty-Three:

The Islamic Resistance Movement views other Islamic movements with respect and appreciation. If it were at variance with them on one point or opinion, it is in agreement with them on other points and understandings. It considers these movements, if they reveal good intentions and dedication to Allah, that they fall into the category of those who are trying hard since they act within the Islamic circle. Each active person has his share.

The Islamic Resistance Movement considers all these movements as a fund for itself. It prays to Allah for guidance and directions for all and it spares no effort to keep the banner of unity raised, ever striving for its realisation in accordance with the Koran and the Prophet's directives.

"And cleave all of you unto the covenant of Allah, and depart not from it, and remember the favour of Allah towards you: since ye were enemies, and he reconciled your hearts, and ye became companions and brethren by his favour: and ye were on the brink of a pit of fire, and he delivered you thence. Allah declareth unto you his signs, that ye may be directed" (The Family of Imran; verse 102).

Article Twenty-Four:

The Islamic Resistance Movement does not allow slandering or speaking ill of individuals or groups, for the believer does not indulge in such malpractices. It is necessary to differentiate between this behaviour and the stands taken by certain individuals and groups. Whenever those stands are erroneous, the Islamic Resistance Movement preserves the right to expound the error and to warn against it. It will strive to show the right path and to judge the case in question with objectivity. Wise conduct is indeed the target of the believer who follows it wherever he discerns it.

"Allah loveth not the speaking ill of anyone in public, unless he who is injured call for assistance; and Allah heareth and knoweth: whether ye publish a good action, or conceal it, or forgive evil, verily Allah is gracious and powerful" (Women; verses 147-148).

B. Nationalist Movements in the Palestinian Arena

Article Twenty-Five:

The Islamic Resistance Movement respects these

movements and appreciates their circumstances and the conditions surrounding and affecting them. It encourages them as long as they do not give their allegiance to the Communist East or the Crusading West. It confirms to all those who are integrated in it, or sympathetic towards it, that the Islamic Resistance Movement is a fighting movement that has a moral and enlightened look of life and the way it should cooperate with the other (movements). It detests opportunism and desires only the good of people, individuals and groups alike. It does not seek material gains, personal fame, nor does it look for a reward from others. It works with its own resources and whatever is at its disposal "and prepare for them whatever force you can", for the fulfilment of the duty, and the earning of Allah's favour. It has no other desire than that.

The Movement assures all the nationalist trends operating in the Palestinian arena for the liberation of Palestine, that it is there for their support and assistance. It will never be more than that, both in words and deeds, now and in the future. It is there to bring together and not to divide, to preserve and not to squander, to unify and not to throw asunder. It evaluates every good word, sincere effort and good offices. It closes the door in the face of side disagreements and does not lend an ear to rumours and slanders, while at the same time fully realising the right for self-defence.

Anything contrary or contradictory to these trends, is a lie disseminated by enemies or their lackeys for the purpose of sowing confusion, disrupting the ranks and occupy them with side issues.

"O true believers, if a wicked man come unto you with a tale, inquire strictly into the truth thereof; lest ye hurt people through ignorance, and afterwards repent of what ye have done" (The Inner Apartments; verse 6).

Article Twenty-Six:

In viewing the Palestinian nationalist movements that give allegiance neither to the East nor the West, in this positive way, the Islamic Resistance Movement does not refrain from discussing new situations on the regional or international levels where the Palestinian question is concerned. It does that in such an objective manner revealing the extent of how much it is in harmony or contradiction with the national interests in the light of the Islamic point of view.

C. The Palestinian Liberation Organization
Article Twenty-Seven:

The Palestinian Liberation Organization is the closest to the heart of the Islamic Resistance Movement. It contains the father and the brother, the next of kin and the friend. The Moslem does not estrange himself from his father, brother, next of kin or friend. Our homeland is one, our situation is one, our fate is one and the enemy is a joint enemy to all of us.

Because of the situations surrounding the formation of the Organization, of the ideological confusion prevailing in the Arab world as a result of the idcological invasion under whose influence the Arab world has fallen since the defeat of the Crusaders and which was, and still is, intensified through orientalists, missionaries and imperialists, the Organization adopted the idea of the secular state. And that it how we view it.

Secularism completely contradicts religious ideology. Attitudes, conduct and decisions stem from ideologies.

That is why, with all our appreciation for The Palestinian Liberation Organization—and what it can develop into—and without belittling its role in the Arab-Israeli conflict, we are unable to exchange the present or future Islamic Palestine with the secular idea. The Islamic nature of Palestine is part of our religion and whoever takes his religion lightly is a loser.

"Who will be adverse to the religion of Abraham, but he whose mind is infatuated? (The Cow; verse 130).

The day The Palestinian Liberation Organization adopts Islam as its way of life, we will become its soldiers, and fuel for its fire that will burn the enemies.

Until such a day, and we pray to Allah that it will be soon, the Islamic Resistance Movement's stand towards the PLO is that of the son towards his father, the brother towards his brother, and the relative to relative, suffers his pain and supports him in confronting the enemies, wishing him to be wise and well-guided.

"Stand by your brother, for he who is brotherless is like the fighter who goes to battle without arms. One's cousin is the wing one flies with—could the bird fly without wings"?

D. Arab and Islamic Countries
Article Twenty-Eight:

The Zionist invasion is a vicious invasion. It does not refrain from resorting to all methods, using all evil and contemptible ways to achieve its end. It relies greatly in its infiltration and espionage operations on the secret organizations it gave rise to, such as the Freemasons, The Rotary and Lions clubs, and other sabotage groups. All these organizations, whether secret or open, work in the interest of Zionism and according to its instructions. They aim at undermining societies, destroying values, corrupting consciences, deteriorating character and annihilating Islam. It is behind the drug trade and alcoholism in all its kinds so as to facilitate its control and expansion.

Arab countries surrounding Israel are asked to open their borders before the fighters from among the Arab and Islamic nations so that they could consolidate their efforts with those of their Moslem brethren in Palestine.

As for the other Arab and Islamic countries, they are asked to facilitate the movement of the fighters from and to it, and this is the least thing they could do.

We should not forget to remind every Moslem that when the Jews conquered the Holy City in 1967, they stood on the threshold of the Aqsa Mosque and proclaimed that "Mohammed is dead, and his descendants are all women".

Israel, Judaism and Jews challenge Islam and the Moslem people. "May the cowards never sleep".

E. Nationalist and Religious Groupings, Institutions, Intellectuals, The Arab and Islamic World

The Islamic Resistance Movement hopes that all these groupings will side with it in all spheres, would support it, adopt its stand and solidify its activities and moves, work towards rallying support for it so that the Islamic people will be a base and a stay for it, supplying it with strategic depth an all human material and informative spheres, in time and in place. This should be done through the convening of solidarity conferences, the issuing of explanatory bulletins, favourable articles and booklets, enlightening the masses regarding the Palestinian issue, clarifying what confronts it and the conspiracies woven around it. They should mobilize the Islamic nations, ideologically, educationally and culturally, so that these peoples would be equipped to perform their role in the decisive battle of liberation, just as they did when they vanquished the Crusaders and the Tatars and saved human civilization. Indeed, that is not difficult for Allah.

"Allah hath written, Verily I will prevail, and my apostles: for Allah is strong and mighty" (The Dispute; verse 21).

Article Thirty:

Writers, intellectuals, media people, orators, educaters and teachers, and all the various sectors in the Arab and Islamic world—all of them are called upon to perform their role, and to fulfil their duty, because of the ferocity of the Zionist offensive and the Zionist influence in many countries exercised through financial and media control, as well as the consequences that all this lead to in the greater part of the world.

Jihad is not confined to the carrying of arms and the confrontation of the enemy. The effective word, the good article, the useful book, support and solidarity—together with the presence of sincere purpose for the hoisting of Allah's banner higher and higher—all these are elements of the Jihad for Allah's sake.

"Whosoever mobilises a fighter for the sake of Allah is

himself a fighter. Whosoever supports the relatives of a fighter, he himself is a fighter" (related by al-Bukhari, Moslem, Abu-Dawood and al-Tarmadhi).

F. Followers of Other Religions: The Islamic Resistance Movement Is A Humanistic Movement

Article Thirty-One:

The Islamic Resistance Movement is a humanistic movement. It takes care of human rights and is guided by Islamic tolerance when dealing with the followers of other religions. It does not antagonize anyone of them except if it is antagonized by it or stands in its way to hamper its moves and waste its efforts.

Under the wing of Islam, it is possible for the followers of the three religions—Islam, Christianity and Judaism—to co-exist in peace and quiet with each other. Peace and quiet would not be possible except under the wing of Islam. Past and present history is the best witness to that.

It is the duty of the followers of other religions to stop disputing the sovereignty of Islam in this region, because the day these followers should take over there will be nothing but carnage, displacement and terror. Everyone of them is at variance with his fellow-religionists, not to speak about followers of other religionists. Past and present history is full of examples to prove this fact.

"They will not fight against you in a body, except in fenced towns, or from behind walls. Their strength in war among themselves is great: thou thinkest them to be united; but their hearts are divided. This, because they are people who do not understand" (The Emigration; verse 14).

Islam confers upon everyone his legitimate rights. Islam prevents the incursion on other people's rights. The Zionist Nazi activities against our people will not last for long. "For the state of injustice lasts but one day, while the state of justice lasts till Doomsday".

"As to those who have not borne arms against you on

account of religion, nor turned you out of your dwellings, Allah forbiddeth you not to deal kindly with them, and to behave justly towards them; for Allah loveth those who act justly" (The Tried; verse 8).

The Attempt to Isolate the Palestinian People
Article Thirty-Two:

World Zionism, together with imperialistic powers, try through a studied plan and an intelligent strategy to remove one Arab state after another from the circle of struggle against Zionism, in order to have it finally face the Palestinian people only. Egypt was, to a great extent, removed from the circle of the struggle, through the treacherous Camp David Agreement. They are trying to draw other Arab countries into similar agreements and to bring them outside the circle of struggle.

The Islamic Resistance Movement calls on Arab and Islamic nations to take up the line of serious and persevering action to prevent the success of this horrendous plan, to warn the people of the danger eminating from leaving the circle of struggle against Zionism. Today it is Palestine, tomorrow it will be one country or another. The Zionist plan is limitless. After Palestine, the Zionists aspire to expand from the Nile to the Euphrates. When they will have digested the region they overtook, they will aspire to further expansion, and so on. Their plan is embodied in the "Protocols of the Elders of Zion", and their present conduct is the best proof of what we are saying.

Leaving the circle of struggle with Zionism is high treason, and cursed be he who does that..."for whoso shall turn his back unto them on that day, unless he turneth aside to fight, or retreateth to another party of the faithful, shall draw on himself the indignation of Allah, and his abode shall be hell; an ill journey shall it be thither" (The Spoils; verse 16). There is no way out except by concentrating all powers and energies to face this Nazi, vicious Tatar invasion. The alternative is loss of one's country, the dispersion of citizens, the spread of vice on earth and the destruction of religious values. Let every person know that he is responsible before Allah, for "the doer of the slightest good deed is rewarded in like, and the does of the slightest evil deed is also rewarded in like".

The Islamic Resistance Movement considers itself to be the spearhead of the circle of struggle with world Zionism and a step on the road. The Movement adds its efforts to the efforts of all those who are active in the Palestinian arena. Arab and Islamic Peoples should augment by further steps on their part; Islamic groupings all over the Arab world should also do the same, since all of these are the best-equipped for the future role in the fight with the warmongering Jews.

"..and we have put enmity and hatred between them, until the day of resurrection. So often as they shall kindle a fire of war, Allah shall extinguish it; and they shall set their minds to act corruptly in the earth, but Allah loveth not the corrupt doers" (The Table; verse 64).

Article Thirty-Three:

The Islamic Resistance Movement, being based on the common coordinated and interdependent conceptions of the laws of the universe, and flowing in the stream of destiny in confronting and fighting the enemies in defence of the Moslems and Islamic civilization and sacred sites, the first among which is the Aqsa Mosque, urges the Arab and Islamic peoples, their governments, popular and official groupings, to fear Allah where their view of the Islamic Resistance Movement and their dealings with it are concerned. They should back and support it, as Allah wants them to, extending to it more and more funds till Allah's purpose is achieved when ranks will close up, fighters join other fighters and masses everywhere in the Islamic world will come forward in response to the call of duty while loudly proclaiming: Hail to Jihad. Their cry will reach the heavens and will go on being resounded until liberation is achieved, the invaders vanquished and Allah's victory comes about.

"And Allah will certainly assist him who shall be on his side: for Allah is strong and mighty" (The Pilgrimage; verse 40).

The Testimony of History

Across History in Confronting the Invaders

Article Thirty-Four:

Palestine is the navel of the globe and the crossroad of the continents. Since the dawn of history, it has been the target of expansionists. The Prophet, Allah bless him and grant him salvation, had himself pointed to this fact in the noble Hadith in which he called on his honourable companion, Ma'adh ben-Jabal, saying: O Ma'ath, Allah throw open before you, when I am gone, Syria, from Al-Arish to the Euphrates. Its men, women and slaves will stay firmly there till the Day of Judgement. Whoever of you should choose one of the Syrian shores, or the Holy Land, he will be in constant struggle till the Day of Judgement".

Expansionists have more than once put their eye on Palestine which they attacked with their armies to fulfil their designs on it. Thus, it was that the Crusaders came with their armies, bringing with them their creed and carrying their Cross. They were able to defeat the Moslems for a while, but the Moslems were able to retrieve the land only when they stood under the wing of their religious banner, united their word, hallowed the name of Allah and surged out fighting under the leadership of Salah ed-Din al-Ayyubi. They fought for almost twenty years and at the end the Crusaders were defeated and Palestine was liberated.

"Say unto those who believe not, Ye shall be overcome, and thrown together into hell; an unhappy couch it shall be" (The Family of Imran; verse 12).

This is the only way to liberate Palestine. There is no doubt about the testimony of history. It is one of the laws of the universe and one of the rules of existence. Nothing can overcome iron except iron. Their false futile creed can only be defeated by the righteous Islamic creed. A creed could not be fought except by a creed, and in the last analysis, victory is for the just, for justice is certainly victorious.

"Our word hath formerly been given unto our servants the apostles; that they should certainly be assisted against the infidels, and that our armies should surely be the conquerors" (Those Who Rank Themselves; verses 171-172).

Article Thirty-Five:

The Islamic Resistance Movement views seriously the defeat of the Crusaders at the hands of Salah ed-Din al-Ayyubi and the rescuing of Palestine from their hands, as well as the defeat of the Tatars at Ein Galot, breaking their power at the hands of Qataz and Al-Dhaher Bivers and saving the Arab world from the Tatar onslaught which aimed at the destruction of every meaning of human civilization. The Movement draws lessons and examples from all this.

The present Zionist onslaught has also been preceded by Crusading raids from the West and other Tatar raids from the East. Just as the Moslems faced those raids and planned fighting and defeating them, they should be able to confront the Zionist invasion and defeat it. This is indeed no problem for the Almighty Allah, provided that the intentions are pure, the determination is true and that Moslems have benefited from past experiences, rid themselves of the effects of ideological invasion and followed the customs of their ancestors.

The Islamic Resistance Movement is Composed of Soldiers
Article Thirty-Six:

While paving its way, the Islamic Resistance Movement, emphasizes time and again to all the sons of our people, to the Arab and Islamic nations, that it does not seek personal fame, material gain, or social prominence. It does not aim to compete against any one from among our people, or take his place. Nothing of the sort at all. It will not act against any of the sons of Moslems or those who are peaceful towards it from among non-Moslems, be they here or anywhere else. It will only serve as a support for all groupings and organizations operating against the Zionist enemy and its lackeys.

The Islamic Resistance Movement adopts Islam as its way of life. Islam is its creed and religion. Whoever takes Islam as his way of life, be it an organization, a grouping, a country or any other body, the Islamic Resistance Movement considers itself as their soldiers and nothing more.

We ask Allah to show us the right course, to make us an example to others and to judge between us and our people with truth. "O Lord, do thou judge between us and our nation with truth; for thou art the best judge" (Al Araf; verse 89).

The last of our prayers will be praise to Allah, the Master of the Universe.

Source: The Avalon Project at Yale Law School @ http://avalon.law.yale.edu.

Document VI

Declaration of Principles on Interim Self-Government Arrangements (Also Known as the Oslo Accords) September 13, 1993

The Government of the State of Israel and the P.L.O. team (in the Jordanian-Palestinian delegation to the Middle East Peace Conference) (the "Palestinian Delegation"), representing the Palestinian people, agree that it is time to put an end to decades of confrontation and conflict, recognize their mutual legitimate and political rights, and strive to live in peaceful coexistence and mutual dignity and security and achieve a just, lasting and comprehensive peace settlement and historic reconciliation through the agreed political process.

Accordingly, the two sides agree to the following principles:

Article I: Aim of the Negotiations

The aim of the Israeli-Palestinian negotiations within the current Middle East peace process is, among other things, to establish a Palestinian Interim Self-Government Authority, the elected Council (the "Council"), for the Palestinian people in the West Bank and the Gaza Strip, for a transitional period not exceeding five years, leading to a permanent settlement based on Security Council Resolution 242 and 338.

It is understood that the interim arrangements are an integral part of the whole peace process and that the negotiations on the permanent status will lead to the implementation of Security Council Resolutions 242 and 338.

Article II: Framework for the Interim Period

The agreed framework for the interim period is set forth in

this Declaration of Principles.

Article III: Elections

1. In order that the Palestinian people in the West Bank and Gaza Strip may govern themselves according to democratic principles, direct, free and general political elections will be held for the Council under agreed supervision and international observation, while the Palestinian police will ensure public order.

2. An agreement will be concluded on the exact mode and conditions of the elections in accordance with the protocol attached as Annex I, with the goal of holding the elections not later than nine months after the entry into force of this Declarations of Principles.

3. These elections will constitute a significant interim preparatory step toward the realization of the legitimate rights of the Palestinian people and their just requirements.

Article IV: Jurisdiction

Jurisdiction of the Council will cover West Bank and Gaza Strip territory, except for issues that will be negotiated in the permanent status negotiations. The two sides view the West Bank and the Gaza Strip as a single territorial unit, whose integrity will be preserved during the interim period.

Article V: Transitional period and permanent status negotiations

The five-year transitional period will begin upon the withdrawal from the Gaza Strip and Jericho area.

1. Permanent status negotiations will commence as soon as possible, but not later than the beginning of the third year of the interim period, between the Government of Israel and the Palestinian people representatives.

2. It is understood that these negotiations shall cover remaining issues, including: Jerusalem, refugees, settlements, security arrangements, borders, relations and cooperation with

other neighbours, and other issues of common interest.

3. The two parties agree that the outcome of the permanent status negotiations should not be prejudiced or pre-empted by agreements reached for the interim period.

Article VI: Preparatory transfer of powers and responsibilities

Upon the entry into force of this Declaration of Principles and the withdrawal from the Gaza Strip and the Jericho area, a transfer of authority from the Israeli military government and its Civil Administration to the authorized Palestinians for this task, as detailed herein, will commence. This transfer of authority will be of a preparatory nature until the inauguration of the Council.

1. Immediately after the entry into force of this Declaration of Principles and the withdrawal from the Gaza Strip and Jericho area, with the view to promoting economic development in the West Bank and Gaza Strip, authority will be transferred to the Palestinians on the following spheres: education and culture, health, Social welfare, direct taxation, and tourism. The Palestinian side will commence in building the Palestinian police force, as agreed upon. Pending the inauguration of the Council, the two parties may negotiate the transfer of additional powers and responsibilities, as agreed upon.

Article VII: Interim Agreement

The Israeli and Palestinian delegations will negotiate an agreement on the interim period (the "Interim Agreement").

1. The Interim Agreement shall specify, among other things, the structure of the Council, the number of its members, and the transfer of powers and responsibilities from the Israeli military government and its Civil Administration to the Council. The Interim Agreement shall also specify the Council's executive authority, legislative authority in accordance with Article IX below, and the independent Palestinian judicial organs.

2. The Interim Agreement shall include arrangements, to be implemented upon the inauguration of the Council, for the assumption by the Council of all of the powers and responsibilities transferred previously in accordance with Article VI above.

3. In order to enable the Council to promote economic growth, upon its inauguration, the Council will establish, among other things, a Palestinian Electricity Authority, a Gaza Sea Port Authority, a Palestinian Development Bank, a Palestinian Export Promotion Board, a Palestinian Environmental Authority, a Palestinian Land Authority and a Palestinian Water Administration Authority, and any other Authorities agreed upon, in accordance with the Interim Agreement that will specify their powers and responsibilities.

4. After the inauguration of the Council, the Civil Administration will be dissolved, and the Israeli military government will be withdrawn.

Article VIII: Public order and security

In order to guarantee public order and internal security for the Palestinians of the West Bank and the Gaza Strip, the Council will establish a strong police force, while Israel will continue to carry the responsibility for overall security of Israelis for the purpose of safeguarding their internal security and public order.

Article IX: Laws and military orders

The Council will be empowered to legislate, in accordance with the Interim Agreement, within all authorities transferred to it.

1. Both parties will review jointly laws and military orders presently in force in remaining spheres.

Article X: Joint Israeli-Palestinian liaison committee

In order to provide for a smooth implementation of this Declaration of Principles and any subsequent agreements pertaining to the interim period, upon the entry into force of this Declaration of Principles, a Joint Israeli-Palestinian Liaison Committee will be established in order to deal with issues requiring coordination, other issues of common interest, and disputes.

Article XI: Israeli-Palestinian Co-operation in Economic Fields

Recognizing the mutual benefit of cooperation in promoting the development of the West Bank, the Gaza Strip and Israel, upon the entry into force of this Declaration of Principles, an Israeli-Palestinian Economic Cooperation Committee will be established in order to develop and implement in a cooperative manner the programs identified in the protocols attached as Annex III and Annex IV.

Article XII: Liaison and cooperation with Jordan and Egypt

The two parties will invite the Governments of Jordan and Egypt to participate in establishing further liaison and cooperation arrangements between the Government of Israel and the Palestinian representatives, on the one hand, and the Government of Jordan and Egypt, on the other hand, to promote cooperation between them. These arrangements will include the constitution of a Continuing Committee that will decide by agreement on the modalities of admission of persons displaced from the West Bank and Gaza Strip in 1967, together with necessary measures to prevent disruption and disorder. Other matters of common concern will be dealt with by this Committee.

Article XIII: Redeployment of Israeli forces

1. After the entry into force of this Declaration of Principles, and not later than the eve of elections for the Council, a redeployment of Israeli military forces in the West Bank and the Gaza Strip will take place, in addition to withdrawal of Israeli forces carried out in accordance with

Article XIV.

2. In redeploying its military forces, Israel will be guided by the principle that its military forces should be redeployed outside populated areas.

3. Further redeployments to specified locations will be gradually implemented commensurate with the assumption of responsibility for public order and internal security by the Palestinian police force pursuant to Article VIII above.

Article XIV: Israeli withdrawal from the Gaza Strip and Jericho Area

Israel will withdraw from the Gaza Strip and Jericho area, as detailed in the protocol attached as Annex II.

Article XV: Resolution of disputes

1. Disputes arising out of the application or interpretation of this Declaration of Principles, or any subsequent agreement pertaining to the interim period, shall be resolved by negotiations through the Joint Liaison Committee to be established pursuant to Article X above.

2. Disputes which cannot be settled by negotiations may be resolved by a mechanism of conciliation to be agreed upon by the parties.

3. The parties may agree to submit to arbitration disputes relating to the interim period, which cannot be settled through conciliation. To this end, upon the agreement of both parties, the parties will establish an Arbitration Committee.

Article XVI: Israeli-Palestinian Co-operation Concerning Regional Programmes

Both parties view the multilateral working groups as an appropriate instrument for promoting a "Marshal Plan," the regional programs and other programs, including special programs for the West Bank and Gaza Strip, as indicated in the protocol attached as Annex IV.

Article XVII: Miscellaneous provisions

1. This Declaration of Principles will enter into force one month after its signing.

2. All protocols annexed to this Declaration of Principles and Agreed Minutes pertaining thereto shall be regarded as an integral part hereof.

Done at Washington, D.C., this thirteenth day of September, 1993.

For the Government of Israel: [Shimon Perez]

For the P.L.O.: [Mahmoud Abbas]

Witnessed by:

The United States of America: [Warren Christopher]

The Russian Federation: [Andrei Kozyrev]

Document VII

Trilateral Statement on the Middle East Peace Summit at Camp David, July 25, 2000

Between July 11 and 24, under the auspices of President Clinton, Prime Minister Barak and Chairman Arafat met at Camp David in an effort to reach an agreement on permanent status. While they were not able to bridge the gaps and reach an agreement, their negotiations were unprecedented in both scope and detail. Building on the progress achieved at Camp David, the two leaders agreed on the following principles to guide their negotiations:

1. The two sides agreed that the aim of their negotiations is to put an end to decades of conflict and achieve a just and lasting peace.
2. The two sides commit themselves to continue their efforts to conclude an agreement on all permanent status issues as soon as possible.
3. Both sides agree that negotiations based on UN Security Council Resolutions 242 and 338 are the only way to achieve such an agreement and they undertake to create an environment for negotiations free from pressure, intimidation and threats of violence.
4. The two sides understand the importance of avoiding unilateral actions that prejudge the outcome of negotiations and that their differences will be resolved only by good faith negotiations.
5. Both sides agree that the United States remains a vital partner in the search for peace and will continue to consult closely with President Clinton and Secretary Albright in the period ahead.

Source: The United Nations Information Service on Palestine (UNISPAL) @ http://unispal.un.org/unispal.nsf/udc.htm.

Document VIII

Clinton's Speech on Mideast Peace Parameters, January 8, 2001

THE PRESIDENT: Thank you very much. Thank you (applause). I want to thank all of you for making me feel so welcome tonight, and also for making Hillary and Chelsea feel welcome. I thank Michael Sonnenfeldt who, like me, is going out after eight years (laughter) and will doubtless find some other useful activity. But he has done a superb job, and I'm very grateful to him (applause).

I thank my friend, Jack Bendheim, for his many kindnesses to me and to Hillary. Yesterday, he had a birthday and now, like me, he's 54. Unlike me, he has enough children to be elected President of the United States (laughter). And he's had a wonderful family and a wonderful life, and I'm delighted that he's so active in the Israel Policy Forum (applause). I'd like to thank Judith Stern Peck for making me feel so welcome and for her leadership.

I thank Lesley Stahl; it's good to see you, and thank you for your kind remarks. I thank the many members of Congress who are here; and also the members of my Middle East peace team, Secretary Albright and Sandy Berger and others have been introduced. But Secretary Dan Glickman is here and Kerry Kennedy Cuomo is here, and I thank them for being here (applause).

I want to thank the New York officials who are here—Carl McCall, Mark Green and any others who may be in the crowd for your many kindnesses to me over the last eight years. New York has been great to me and Al Gore and even greater to my wife on Election Day, so I thank you for that (applause).

We just re-enacted her swearing-in at Madison Square

Garden. And I was reminded of one of the many advantages of living in New York—Jessye Norman sang, Toni Morrison read and Billy Joel sang. Meanwhile, at least at half time, the Giants were ahead (laughter and applause). And so I said, I felt sort of like Garrison Keillor did about Lake Wobegone. I was glad to be in New York where all the writers, artists and sports teams were above average (laughter) and all the votes were always counted (applause).

Let me also say a word of warm welcome and profound respect to the Speaker of the Knesset, Speaker Burg, for his wonderful and kind comments to me (applause); And to Cabinet Secretary Herzog, for his message from the government of Israel. I want to say a little more about that in a moment.

I want to congratulate Dwayne Andreas, my good friend—I wish he were here tonight—and thank him for his many kindnesses to me. Congratulations, Louis Perlmutter; Susan Stern who has been such a great friend to Hillary, and you gave a good talk tonight, I think you've got a real future in this business. And your mother sat by me and she gave you a good grade, too (laughter).

And Alan Solomont, who has done as much for me as I suppose any American, and he and Susan and their children have been great friends, and I thank you for what you've done, sir. I thank all of you (applause).

I'd also like to say how much I appreciated and was moved by the words of Prime Minister Barak. He was dealt the hard hand by history. And he came to office with absolute conviction that in the end, Israel could not be secure unless a just and lasting peace could be reached with its neighbours, beginning with the Palestinians. That if that turned out not to be possible, then the next best thing was to be as strong as possible and as effective in the use of that strength.

But his knowledge of war has fed a passion for peace. And his understanding of the changing technology of war has made him more passionate, not because he thinks the existence of

Israel is less secure—if anything, it's more secure—but because the sophisticated weapons available to terrorists today mean even though they still lose, they can exact a higher price along the way.

I've been in enough political fights in my life to know that sometimes you just have to do the right thing—and it may work out and it may not. Most people thought I had lost my mind when we passed the economic plan to get rid of the deficit in 1993.

And no one in the other party voted for it, and they just talked about how it would bring the world to an end and America's economy would be a disaster. I think the only Republican who thought it would work was Alan Greenspan (laughter). He was relieved of the burden of having to say anything about it.

But no dilemma I have ever faced approximates in difficulty or comes close to the choice that Prime Minister Barak had to make when he took office. He realized that he couldn't know for sure what the final intentions of the Palestinian leadership were without testing them.

He further realized that even if the intentions were there, there was a lot of competition among the Palestinians and from outside forces, from people who are enemies of peace because they don't give a rip how the ordinary Palestinians have to live and they're pursuing a whole different agenda.

He knew nine things could go wrong and only one thing could go right. But he promised himself that he would have to try. And as long as he knew Israel in the end could defend itself and maintain its security, he would keep taking risks. And that's what he's done, down to these days. There may be those who disagree with him, but he has demonstrated as much bravery in the office of Prime Minister as he ever did on the field of battle and no one should ever question that (applause).

Now, I imagine this has been a tough time for those of you who have been supporting the IPF, out of conviction for a long time. All the dreams we had in '93 that were revived when we had the peace with Jordan, revived again when we had the Wye River accords—that was, I think, the most interesting peace talks I was ever involved in. My strategy was the same used to break prisoners of war, I just didn't let anybody sleep for nine days and, finally, out of exhaustion, we made a deal—just so people could go home and go to bed (laughter). I've been looking for an opportunity to employ it again, ever since.

There have been a lot of positive things, and I think it's worth remembering that there have been positive developments along the way. But this is heartbreaking, what we've been through these last few months, for all of you who have believed for eight years in the Oslo process; all of you whose hearts soared on September 19, 1993, when Yasser Arafat and Yitzhak Rabin signed that agreement.

For over three months we have lived through a tragic cycle of violence that has cost hundreds of lives. It has shattered the confidence in the peace process. It has raised questions in some people's minds about whether Palestinians and Israelis could ever really live and work together, support each other's peace and prosperity and security. It's been a heartbreaking time for me, too. But we have done our best to work with the parties to restore calm, to end the bloodshed and to get back to working on an agreement to address the underlying causes that continuously erupt in conflicts.

Whatever happens in the next two weeks I've got to serve, I think it's appropriate for me tonight, before a group of Americans and friends from the Middle East who believe profoundly in the peace process and have put their time and heart and money where their words are, to reflect on the lessons I believe we've all learned over the last eight years, and how we can achieve the long sought peace.

From my first day as President, we have worked to advance interests in the Middle East that are long standing and historically bipartisan. I was glad to hear of Senator Hagel's recitation of President-elect Bush's commitment to peace in the Middle East. Those historic commitments include an ironclad commitment to Israel's security and a just, comprehensive and lasting agreement between the Palestinians and Israelis.

Along the way since '93, through the positive agreements that have been reached between those two sides, through the peace between Israel and Jordan, through last summer's withdrawal from Lebanon in which Israel fulfilled its part of implementing U.N. Security Council resolution 425—along this way we have learned some important lessons, not only because of the benchmarks of progress, because of the occasional eruption of terrorism, bombing, death and then these months of conflict. I think these lessons have to guide any effort, now or in the future, to reach a comprehensive peace. Here's what I think they are. Most of you probably believed in them, up to the last three months. I still do. First, the Arab-Israeli conflict is not just a morality play between good and evil. It is a conflict with a complex history, whose resolution requires balancing the needs of both sides, including respect for their national identities and religious beliefs.

Second, there is no place for violence, and no military solution to this conflict. The only path to a just and durable resolution is through negotiation. Third, there will be no lasting peace or regional stability without a strong and secure Israel, secure enough to make peace, strong enough to deter the adversaries which will still be there, even if a peace is made in complete good faith. And clearly that is why the United States must maintain its commitment to preserving Israel's qualitative edge in military superiority.

Fourth, talks must be accompanied by acts—acts which show trust and partnership. For goodwill at the negotiating table cannot survive forever ill intent on the ground. And it is important that each side understands how the other reads actions.

For example, on the one hand, the tolerance of violence and incitement of hatred in classrooms and the media in the Palestinian communities, or on the other hand, humiliating treatment on the streets or at checkpoints by Israelis are real obstacles to even getting people to talk about building a genuine peace.

Fifth, in the resolution of remaining differences, whether they come today or after several years of heartbreak and bloodshed, the fundamental, painful, but necessary choices will almost certainly remain the same whenever the decision is made. The parties will face the same history, the same geography, the same neighbours, the same passions, the same hatreds. This is not a problem time will take care of.

And I would just like to go off the script here, because a lot of you have more personal contacts than I do with people that will be dealing with this for a long time to come, whatever happens in the next two weeks.

Among the really profound and difficult problems of the world that I have dealt with, I find that they tend to fall into two categories. And if I could use sort of a medical analogy, some are like old wounds with scabs on them, and some are like abscessed teeth.

What do I mean by that? Old wounds with scabs eventually will heal if you just leave them alone. And if you fool with them too much, you might open the scab and make them worse. Abscessed teeth, however, will only get worse if you leave them alone, and if you wait and wait and wait, they'll just infect the whole rest of your mouth.

Northern Ireland, I believe, is becoming more like the scab. There are very difficult things. If you followed my trip over there, you know I was trying to help them resolve some of their outstanding problems, and we didn't get it all done. But what I really wanted to do was to remind people of the benefits of peace and to keep everybody in a good frame of mind and going on so that all the politicians know that if they really let the wheel run off over there, the people will throw them out on their ears.

Now, why is that? Because the Irish Republic is now the fastest-growing economy in Europe, and Northern Ireland is the fastest-growing economy within the United Kingdom. So the people are benefiting from peace, and they can live with the fact that they can't quite figure out what to do about the police force and the reconciliation of the various interests and passions of the Protestants and Catholics. And the other three or four things. Because the underlying reality has changed their lives.

So even though I wish I could solve it all, eventually it will heal, if it just keeps going in the same direction. The Middle East is not like that. Why? Because there are all these independent actors—that is, independent of the Palestinian Authority and not under the direct control of any international legal body—who don't want this peace to work. So that even if we can get an agreement, and the Palestinian Authority works as hard as they can, and the Israelis works as hard as they can, we're all going to have to pitch in, send in an international force like we did in the Sinai, and hang tough, because there are enemies of peace out there, number one.

Number two, because the enemies of peace know they can drive the Israelis to close the borders if they can blow up enough bombs. They do it periodically to make sure that the Palestinians in the street cannot enjoy the benefits of peace that have come to the people in Northern Ireland. So as long as they can keep the people miserable, and they can keep the fundamental decisions from being made, they still have a hope, the enemies of peace, of derailing the whole thing. That's why it's more like an abscessed tooth.

The fundamental realities are not going to be changed by delays. And that's why I said what I did about Ehud Barak. I know that— I don't think it's appropriate for the United States to deal with anybody else's politics, but I know why—you can't expect poll ratings to be very good when the voters in the moment wonder if they're going to get peace or security, and think they can no longer have both and may have to choose one. I understand that.

But I'm telling you, the reason he has continued to push ahead on this is that he has figured out, this is one of those political problems that is like the abscessed tooth. The realities are not going to change. We can wait until all these handsome young people at this table are the same age as the honorees tonight, and me, we can wait until they've got kids their age, and we've got a whole lot more bodies and a lot more funerals, a lot more crying and a lot more hatred, and I'll swear the decisions will still be the same ones that will have to be made that have to be made today.

That's the fundamental deal here. And this is a speech I have given, I might add, to all my Israeli friends who question what we have done, and to the Palestinians. And in private, God forgive me, my language is sometimes somewhat more graphic than it has been tonight. But anybody that ever kneeled at the grave of a person who died in the Middle East knows that what we've been through these last three months is not what Yitzhak Rabin died for and not what I went to Gaza two years ago to speak to the Palestinian National Council for either, for that matter.

So those are the lessons I think are still operative, and I'm a little concerned that we could draw the wrong lessons from this tragic, still relatively brief, chapter in the history of the Middle East. The violence does not demonstrate that the quest for peace has gone too far or too fast. It demonstrates what happens when you've got a problem that is profoundly difficult and you never quite get to the end, so there is no settlement, no resolution, anxiety prevailed, and at least some people never get any concrete benefits out of it.

And I believe that the last few months demonstrate the futility of force or terrorism as an ultimate solution; that's what I believe (applause). I think the last few months show that unilateralism will exacerbate, not abate, mutual hostility. I believe that the violence confirms the need to do more to prepare both publics for the requirements of peace, not to condition people for the so-called glory of further conflict.

Now, what are we going to do now? The first priority, obviously, has got to be to drastically reduce the current cycle of violence. But beyond that, on the Palestinian side, there must be an end to the culture of violence and the culture of incitement that, since Oslo, has not gone unchecked (applause). Young children still are being educated to believe in confrontation with Israel, and multiple militia-like groups carry and use weapons with impunity. Voices of reason in that kind of environment will be drowned out too often by voices of revenge.

Such conduct is inconsistent with the Palestinian leadership's commitment to Oslo's non-violent path to peace and its persistence sends the wrong message to the Israeli people, and makes it much more difficult for them to support their leaders in making the compromises necessary to get a lasting agreement.

For their part, the Israeli people also must understand that they're creating a few problems, too; that the settlement enterprise and building bypass roads in the heart of what they already know will one day be part of a Palestinian state is inconsistent with the Oslo commitment that both sides negotiate a compromise (applause).

And restoring confidence requires the Palestinians being able to lead a normal existence, and not be subject to daily, often humiliating reminders that they lack basic freedom and control over their lives.

These, too, make it harder for the Palestinians to believe the commitments made to them will be kept. Can two peoples with this kind of present trouble and troubling history still conclude a genuine and lasting peace? I mean, if I gave you this as a soap opera, you would say they're going to divorce court. But they can't, because they share such a small piece of land with such a profound history of importance to more than a billion people around the world. So I believe with all my heart not only that they can, but that they must.

At Camp David, I saw Israeli and Palestinian negotiators who knew how many children each other had, who knew how many grandchildren each other had, who knew how they met their spouses, who knew what their family tragedies were, who trusted each other in their word. It was almost shocking to see what could happen and how people still felt on the ground when I saw how their leaders felt about each other and the respect and the confidence they had in each other when they were talking.

The alternative to getting this peace done is being played out before our very eyes. But amidst the agony, I will say again, there are signs of hope. And let me try to put this into what I think is a realistic context.

Camp David was a transformative event, because the two sides faced the core issue of their dispute in a forum that was official for the first time. And they had to debate the tradeoffs required to resolve the issues. Just as Oslo forced Israelis and Palestinians to come to terms with each other's existence, the discussions of the past six months have forced them to come to terms with each other's needs and the contours of a peace that ultimately they will have to reach.

That's why Prime Minister Barak, I think, has demonstrated real courage and vision in moving toward peace in difficult circumstances while trying to find a way to continue to protect Israel's security and vital interests.

So that's a fancy way of saying we know what we have to do and we've got a mess on our hands. So where do we go from here? Given the impasse and the tragic deterioration on the ground, a couple of weeks ago both sides asked me to present my ideas. So I put forward parameters that I wanted to be guide toward a comprehensive agreement; parameters based on eight years of listening carefully to both sides and hearing them describe with increasing clarity their respective grievances and needs.

Both Prime Minister Barak and Chairman Arafat have now accepted these parameters as the basis for further efforts. Both have expressed some reservations. At their request, I am using my remaining time in office to narrow the differences between the parties to the greatest degree possible (applause). For which I deserve no applause. Believe me, it beats packing up all my old books (laughter).

The parameters I put forward contemplate a settlement in response to each side's essential needs, if not to their utmost desires. A settlement based on sovereign homelands, security, peace and dignity for both Israelis and Palestinians. These parameters don't begin to answer every question, they just narrow the questions that have to be answered.

Here they are. First, I think there can be no genuine resolution to the conflict without a sovereign, viable, Palestinian state that accommodates Israeli's security requirements and the demographic realities. That suggests Palestinian sovereignty over Gaza, the vast majority of the West Bank, the incorporation into Israel of settlement blocks, with the goal of maximizing the number of settlers in Israel while minimizing the land annex for Palestine to be viable must be a geographically contiguous state (applause).

Now, the land annexed into Israel into settlement blocks should include as few Palestinians as possible, consistent with the logic of two separate homelands. And to make the agreement durable, I think there will have to be some territorial swaps and other arrangements.

Second, a solution will have to be found for the Palestinian refugees who have suffered a great deal—particularly some of them. A solution that allows them to return to a Palestinian state that will provide all Palestinians with a place they can safely and proudly call home. All Palestinian refugees who wish to live in this homeland should have the right to do so. All others who want to find new homes, whether in their current locations or in third countries, should be able to do so, consistent with those countries' sovereign decisions. And that includes Israel.

All refugees should receive compensation from the international community for their losses, and assistance in building new lives.

Now, you all know what the rub is. That was a lot of artful

language for saying that you cannot expect Israel to acknowledge an unlimited right of return to present day Israel, and at the same time, to give up Gaza and the West Bank and have the settlement blocks as compact as possible, because of where a lot of these refugees came from. We cannot expect Israel to make a decision that would threaten the very foundations of the state of Israel, and would undermine the whole logic of peace. And it shouldn't be done (applause).

But I have made it very clear that the refugees will be a high priority, and that the United States will take a lead in raising the money necessary to relocate them in the most appropriate manner (applause). If the government of Israel or a subsequent government of Israel ever—will be in charge of their immigration policy, just as we and the Canadians and the Europeans and others who would offer Palestinians a home would be, they would be obviously free to do that, and I think they've indicated that they would do that, to some extent. But there cannot be an unlimited language in an agreement that would undermine the very foundations of the Israeli state or the whole reason for creating the Palestinian state (applause). So that's what we're working on.

Third, there will be no peace, and no peace agreement, unless the Israeli people have lasting security guarantees (applause). These need not and should not come at the expense of Palestinian sovereignty, or interfere with Palestinian territorial integrity. So my parameters rely on an international presence in Palestine to provide border security along the Jordan Valley and to monitor implementation of the final agreement. They rely on a non-militarized Palestine, a phased Israeli withdrawal, to address Israeli security needs in the Jordan Valley, and other essential arrangements to ensure Israel's ability to defend itself.

Fourth, I come to the issue of Jerusalem, perhaps the most emotional and sensitive of all. It is a historic, cultural and political centre for both Israelis and Palestinians, a unique city sacred to all three monotheistic religions. And I believe the parameters I have established flow from four fair and logical propositions.

First, Jerusalem should be an open and undivided city, with assured freedom of access and worship for all. It should encompass the internationally recognized capitals of two states, Israel and Palestine. Second, what is Arab should be Palestinian, for why would Israel want to govern in perpetuity the lives of hundreds of thousands of Palestinians? Third, what is Jewish should be Israeli. That would give rise to a Jewish Jerusalem, larger and more vibrant than any in history. Fourth, what is holy to both requires a special care to meet the needs of all. I was glad to hear what the Speaker said about that. No peace agreement will last if not premised on mutual respect for the religious beliefs and holy shrines of Jews, Muslims and Christians.

I have offered formulations on the Haram Ash-Shareef, and the area holy to the Jewish people, an area which for 2,000 years, as I said at Camp David, has been the focus of Jewish yearning, that I believed fairly addressed the concerns of both sides.

Fifth and, finally, any agreement will have to mark the decision to end the conflict, for neither side can afford to make these painful compromises, only to be subjected to further demands. They are both entitled to know that if they take the last drop of blood out of each other's turnip, that's it. It really will have to be the end of the struggle that has pitted Palestinians and Israelis against one another for too long. And the end of the conflict must manifest itself with concrete acts that demonstrate a new attitude and a new approach by Palestinians and Israelis toward each other, and by other states in the region toward Israel, and by the entire region toward Palestine, to help it get off to a good start.

The parties' experience with interim accords has not always been happy—too many deadlines missed, too many commitments unfulfilled on both sides. So for this to signify a real end of the conflict, there must be effective mechanisms to provide guarantees of implementation. That's a lot of stuff, isn't it? It's what I think is the outline of a fair agreement. (Applause)

Let me say this, I am well aware that it will entail real pain and sacrifices for both sides. I am well aware that I don't even have to run for re-election in the United States on the basis of these ideas. I have worked for eight years without laying such ideas down. I did it only when both sides asked me to, and when it was obvious that we had come to the end of the road, and somebody had to do something to break out of the impasse.

Now, I still think the benefits of the agreement, based on these parameters, far outweigh the burdens. For the people of Israel, they are an end to conflict, secure and defensible borders, the incorporation of most of the settlers into Israel, and the Jewish capital of Jerusalem, recognized by all, not just the United States, by everybody in the world. It's a big deal, and it needs to be done (applause).

For the Palestinian people, it means the freedom to determine their own future on their own land, a new life for the refugees, an independent and sovereign state with al Quds as its capital, recognized by all (applause). And for America, it means that we could have new flags flying over new embassies in both these capitals (applause).

Now that the sides have accepted the parameters with reservations, what's going to happen? Well, each side will try to do a little better than I did (laughter). You know, that's just natural. But a peace viewed as imposed by one party upon the other, that puts one side up and the other down, rather than both ahead, contains the seeds of its own destruction.

Let me say those who believe that my ideas can be altered to one party's exclusive benefit are mistaken. I think to press for more will producc less. There can be no peace without compromise. Now, I don't ask Israelis or Palestinians to agree with everything I said. If they can come up with a completely different agreement, it would suit me just fine. But I doubt it.

I have said what I have out of a profound lifetime commitment to and love for the state of Israel, out of a conviction that the Palestinian people have been ignored or used as political footballs by others for long enough, and they ought to have a chance to make their own life with dignity (applause). And out of a belief that in the homeland of the world's three great religions that believe we are all the creatures of one God, we ought to be able to prove that one person's win is not, by definition, another's loss; that one person's dignity is not, by definition, another's humiliation; that one person's work of God is not, by definition, another's heresy. There has to be a way for us to find a truth we can share. (Applause)

There has to be a way for us to reach those young Palestinian kids who, unlike the young people in this audience, don't imagine a future in which they would ever put on clothes like this and sit at a dinner like this.

There has to be a way for us to say to them, struggle and pain and destruction and self-destruction are way overrated, and not the only option. There has to be a way for us to reach those people in Israel who have paid such a high price and believe, frankly, that people who embrace the ideas I just outlined are nuts, because Israel is a little country and this agreement would make it smaller; to understand that the world in which we live and the technology of modern weaponry no longer make defence primarily a matter of geography and of politics and the human feeling and the interdependence and the cooperation and the shared values and the shared interests are more important and worth the considered risk, especially if the United States remains committed to the military capacity of the state of Israel (applause).

So I say to the Palestinians: there will always be those who are sitting outside in the peanut gallery of the Middle East, urging you to hold out for more, or to plant one more bomb. But all the people who do that, they're not the refugees languishing in those camps—you are. They're not the ones with children growing up in poverty whose income is lower today than it was the day we had the signing on the White House Lawn in 1993—you are.

All the people that are saying to the Palestinian people: Stay on the path of no, are people that have a vested interest in the failure of the peace process that has nothing to do with how those kids in Gaza and the West Bank are going to grow up and live and raise their own children (applause).

To the citizens of Israel who have returned to an ancient homeland after 2,000 years, whose hopes and dreams almost vanished in the Holocaust, who have hardly had one day of peace and quiet since the state of Israel was created, I understand, I believe, something of the disillusionment, the anger, the frustration that so many feel when, just at the moment peace seemed within reach, all this violence broke out and raised the question of whether it is ever possible.

The fact is that the people of Israel dreamed of a homeland. The dream came through; but when they came home, the land was not all vacant. Your land is also their land, it is the homeland of two people. And, therefore, there is no choice but to create two states and make the best of it.

If it happens today, it will be better than if it happens tomorrow, because fewer people will die. And after it happens, the motives of those who continue the violence will be clearer to all than they are today.

Today, Israel is closer than ever to ending a 100-year-long era of struggle. It could be Israel's finest hour. And I hope and pray that the people of Israel will not give up the hope of peace.

Now, I've got 13 days and I'll do what I can. We're working with Egypt and the parties to try to end the violence. I'm sending Dennis Ross to the region this week. I met with both sides this week. I hope we can really do something. And I appreciate more than I can say the kind, personal things that you said about me.

But here's what I want you to think about. New York has

its own high-tech corridor called "Silicon Alley". The number one foreign recipient of venture capital from Silicon Alley is Israel. Palestinians who have come to the United States, to Chile, to Canada, to Europe, have done fabulously well—in business, in the sciences, in academia.

If we could ever let a lot of this stuff go and realize that a lot of—that the enemies of peace in the Middle East are overlooking not only what the Jewish people have done beyond Israel, but what has happened to the state of Israel since its birth, and how fabulously well the people of Palestinian descent have done everywhere else in the world except in their homeland, where they are in the grip of forces that have not permitted them to reconcile with one another and with the people of Israel—listen, if you guys ever got together, 10 years from now we would all wonder what the heck happened for 30 years before.

And the centre of energy and creativity and economic power and political influence in the entire region would be with the Israelis and the Palestinians because of their gifts. It could happen. But somebody has got to take the long leap, and they have to be somebodies on both sides.

All I can tell you is, whether you do it now or whether you do it later, whether I'm the President or just somebody in the peanut gallery, I'll be there, cheering and praying and working along the way (applause). And I think America will be there. I think America will always be there for Israel's security. But Israel's lasting security rests in a just and lasting peace. I pray that the day will come sooner, rather than later, where all the people of the region will see that they can share the wisdom of God in their common humanity and give up their conflict.

Thank you and God bless you (applause).

Source: US Embassy in Israel Press Section @
http://israel.usembassy.gov/news-events.html.

Document IX

Obama's Speech in Cairo
The New York Times, June 4, 2009

The following is a text of President Obama's prepared remarks to the Muslim world, delivered on June 4, 2009, as released by the White House.

I am honoured to be in the timeless city of Cairo, and to be hosted by two remarkable institutions. For over a thousand years, Al-Azhar has stood as a beacon of Islamic learning, and for over a century, Cairo University has been a source of Egypt's advancement. Together, you represent the harmony between tradition and progress. I am grateful for your hospitality, and the hospitality of the people of Egypt. I am also proud to carry with me the goodwill of the American people, and a greeting of peace from Muslim communities in my country: assalaamu alaykum.

We meet at a time of tension between the United States and Muslims around the world—tension rooted in historical forces that go beyond any current policy debate. The relationship between Islam and the West includes centuries of co-existence and cooperation, but also conflict and religious wars. More recently, tension has been fed by colonialism that denied rights and opportunities to many Muslims, and a Cold War in which Muslim-majority countries were too often treated as proxies without regard to their own aspirations. Moreover, the sweeping change brought by modernity and globalization led many Muslims to view the West as hostile to the traditions of Islam.

Violent extremists have exploited these tensions in a small but potent minority of Muslims. The attacks of September 11th, 2001 and the continued efforts of these extremists to engage in violence against civilians has led some in my country to view Islam as inevitably hostile not only to America and Western countries, but also to human rights. This has bred more fear and mistrust.

So long as our relationship is defined by our differences, we will empower those who sow hatred rather than peace, and who promote conflict rather than the cooperation that can help all of our people achieve justice and prosperity. This cycle of suspicion and discord must end.

I have come here to seek a new beginning between the United States and Muslims around the world; one based upon mutual interest and mutual respect; and one based upon the truth that America and Islam are not exclusive, and need not be in competition. Instead, they overlap, and share common principles—principles of justice and progress; tolerance and the dignity of all human beings.

I do so recognizing that change cannot happen overnight. No single speech can eradicate years of mistrust, nor can I answer in the time that I have all the complex questions that brought us to this point. But I am convinced that in order to move forward, we must say openly the things we hold in our hearts, and that too often are said only behind closed doors. There must be a sustained effort to listen to each other; to learn from each other; to respect one another; and to seek common ground. As the Holy Koran tells us, "Be conscious of God and speak always the truth". That is what I will try to do—to speak the truth as best I can, humbled by the task before us, and firm in my belief that the interests we share as human beings are far more powerful than the forces that drive us apart.

Part of this conviction is rooted in my own experience. I am a Christian, but my father came from a Kenyan family that includes generations of Muslims. As a boy, I spent several years in Indonesia and heard the call of the azaan at the break of dawn and the fall of dusk. As a young man, I worked in Chicago communities where many found dignity and peace in their Muslim faith.

As a student of history, I also know civilization's debt to

Islam. It was Islam—at places like Al-Azhar University—that carried the light of learning through so many centuries, paving the way for Europe's Renaissance and Enlightenment. It was innovation in Muslim communities that developed the order of algebra; our magnetic compass and tools of navigation; our mastery of pens and printing; our understanding of how disease spreads and how it can be healed. Islamic culture has given us majestic arches and soaring spires; timeless poetry and cherished music; elegant calligraphy and places of peaceful contemplation. And throughout history, Islam has demonstrated through words and deeds the possibilities of religious tolerance and racial equality.

I know, too, that Islam has always been a part of America's story. The first nation to recognize my country was Morocco. In signing the Treaty of Tripoli in 1796, our second President John Adams wrote, "The United States has in itself no character of enmity against the laws, religion or tranquillity of Muslims". And since our founding, American Muslims have enriched the United States. They have fought in our wars, served in government, stood for civil rights, started businesses, taught at our Universities, excelled in our sports arenas, won Nobel Prizes, built our tallest building, and lit the Olympic Torch. And when the first Muslim-American was recently elected to Congress, he took the oath to defend our Constitution using the same Holy Koran that one of our Founding Fathers—Thomas Jefferson—kept in his personal library.

So I have known Islam on three continents before coming to the region where it was first revealed. That experience guides my conviction that partnership between America and Islam must be based on what Islam is, not what it isn't. And I consider it part of my responsibility as President of the United States to fight against negative stereotypes of Islam wherever they appear.

But that same principle must apply to Muslim perceptions of America. Just as Muslims do not fit a crude stereotype,

America is not the crude stereotype of a self-interested empire. The United States has been one of the greatest sources of progress that the world has ever known. We were born out of revolution against an empire. We were founded upon the ideal that all are created equal, and we have shed blood and struggled for centuries to give meaning to those words—within our borders, and around the world. We are shaped by every culture, drawn from every end of the Earth, and dedicated to a simple concept: E pluribus unum: "Out of many, one".

Much has been made of the fact that an African-American with the name Barack Hussein Obama could be elected President. But my personal story is not so unique. The dream of opportunity for all people has not come true for everyone in America, but its promise exists for all who come to our shores—that includes nearly seven million American Muslims in our country today who enjoy incomes and education that are higher than average.

Moreover, freedom in America is indivisible from the freedom to practice one's religion. That is why there is a mosque in every state of our union, and over 1,200 mosques within our borders. That is why the U.S. government has gone to court to protect the right of women and girls to wear the hijab, and to punish those who would deny it.

So let there be no doubt: Islam is a part of America. And I believe that America holds within her the truth that regardless of race, religion, or station in life, all of us share common aspirations—to live in peace and security; to get an education and to work with dignity; to love our families, our communities, and our God. These things we share. This is the hope of all humanity.

Of course, recognizing our common humanity is only the beginning of our task. Words alone cannot meet the needs of our people. These needs will be met only if we act boldly in the years ahead; and if we understand that the challenges we face are shared, and our failure to meet them will hurt us all.

For we have learned from recent experience that when a financial system weakens in one country, prosperity is hurt everywhere. When a new flu infects one human being, all are at risk. When one nation pursues a nuclear weapon, the risk of nuclear attack rises for all nations. When violent extremists operate in one stretch of mountains, people are endangered across an ocean. And when innocents in Bosnia and Darfur are slaughtered, that is a stain on our collective conscience. That is what it means to share this world in the 21st century. That is the responsibility we have to one another as human beings.

This is a difficult responsibility to embrace. For human history has often been a record of nations and tribes subjugating one another to serve their own interests. Yet in this new age, such attitudes are self-defeating. Given our interdependence, any world order that elevates one nation or group of people over another will inevitably fail. So whatever we think of the past, we must not be prisoners of it. Our problems must be dealt with through partnership; progress must be shared.

That does not mean we should ignore sources of tension. Indeed, it suggests the opposite: we must face these tensions squarely. And so in that spirit, let me speak as clearly and plainly as I can about some specific issues that I believe we must finally confront together.

The first issue that we have to confront is violent extremism in all of its forms.

In Ankara, I made clear that America is not—and never will be—at war with Islam. We will, however, relentlessly confront violent extremists who pose a grave threat to our security. Because we reject the same thing that people of all faiths reject: the killing of innocent men, women, and children. And it is my first duty as President to protect the American people.

The situation in Afghanistan demonstrates America's goals, and our need to work together. Over seven years ago, the United States pursued Al-Qaeda and the Taliban with broad international support. We did not go by choice, we went because of necessity. I am aware that some question or justify the events of 9/11. But let us be clear: Al-Qaeda killed nearly 3,000 people on that day. The victims were innocent men, women and children from America and many other nations who had done nothing to harm anybody. And yet Al-Qaeda chose to ruthlessly murder these people, claimed credit for the attack, and even now states their determination to kill on a massive scale. They have affiliates in many countries and are trying to expand their reach. These are not opinions to be debated; these are facts to be dealt with.

Make no mistake: we do not want to keep our troops in Afghanistan. We seek no military bases there. It is agonizing for America to lose our young men and women. It is costly and politically difficult to continue this conflict. We would gladly bring every single one of our troops home if we could be confident that there were not violent extremists in Afghanistan and Pakistan determined to kill as many Americans as they possibly can. But that is not yet the case.

That's why we're partnering with a coalition of forty-six countries. And despite the costs involved, America's commitment will not weaken. Indeed, none of us should tolerate these extremists. They have killed in many countries. They have killed people of different faiths—more than any other, they have killed Muslims. Their actions are irreconcilable with the rights of human beings, the progress of nations, and with Islam. The Holy Koran teaches that whoever kills an innocent, it is as if he has killed all mankind; and whoever saves a person, it is as if he has saved all mankind. The enduring faith of over a billion people is so much bigger than the narrow hatred of a few. Islam is not part of the problem in combating violent extremism—it is an important part of promoting peace.

We also know that military power alone is not going to solve the problems in Afghanistan and Pakistan. That is why we plan to invest US$ 1.5 billion each year over the next five years to partner with Pakistanis to build schools and hospitals, roads and businesses, and hundreds of millions to help those who have been displaced. And that is why we are providing more than US$ 2.8 billion to help Afghans develop their economy and deliver services that people depend upon.

Let me also address the issue of Iraq. Unlike Afghanistan, Iraq was a war of choice that provoked strong differences in my country and around the world. Although I believe that the Iraqi people are ultimately better off without the tyranny of Saddam Hussein, I also believe that events in Iraq have reminded America of the need to use diplomacy and build international consensus to resolve our problems whenever possible. Indeed, we can recall the words of Thomas Jefferson, who said: "I hope that our wisdom will grow with our power, and teach us that the less we use our power the greater it will be".

Today, America has a dual responsibility: to help Iraq forge a better future—and to leave Iraq to Iraqis. I have made it clear to the Iraqi people that we pursue no bases, and no claim on their territory or resources. Iraq's sovereignty is its own. That is why I ordered the removal of our combat brigades by next August. That is why we will honour our agreement with Iraq's democratically-elected government to remove combat troops from Iraqi cities by July, and to remove all our troops from Iraq by 2012. We will help Iraq train its Security Forces and develop its economy. But we will support a secure and united Iraq as a partner, and never as a patron.

And finally, just as America can never tolerate violence by extremists, we must never alter our principles. 9/11 was an enormous trauma to our country. The fear and anger that it provoked was understandable, but in some cases, it led us to act contrary to our ideals. We are taking concrete actions to change course. I have unequivocally prohibited the use of torture by the United States, and I have ordered the prison at Guantanamo Bay closed by early next year.

So America will defend itself respectful of the sovereignty

of nations and the rule of law. And we will do sc in partnership with Muslim communities which are also threatened. The sooner the extremists are isolated and unwelcome in Muslim communities, the sooner we will all be safer. The second major source of tension that we need to discuss is the situation between Israelis, Palestinians and the Arab world.

America's strong bonds with Israel are well known. This bond is unbreakable. It is based upon cultural and historical ties, and the recognition that the aspiration for a Jewish homeland is rooted in a tragic history that cannot be denied.

Around the world, the Jewish people were persecuted for centuries, and anti-Semitism in Europe culminated in an unprecedented Holocaust. Tomorrow, I will visit Buchenwald, which was part of a network of camps where Jews were enslaved, tortured, shot and gassed to death by the Third Reich. Six million Jews were killed—more than the entire Jewish population of Israel today. Denying that fact is baseless, ignorant, and hateful. Threatening Israel with destruction—or repeating vile stereotypes about Jews—is deeply wrong, and only serves to evoke in the minds of Israelis this most painful of memories while preventing the peace that the people of this region deserve.

On the other hand, it is also undeniable that the Palestinian people—Muslims and Christians—have suffered in pursuit of a homeland. For more than sixty years they have endured the pain of dislocation. Many wait in refugee camps in the West Bank, Gaza, and neighbouring lands for a life of peace and security that they have never been able to lead. They endure the daily humiliations—large and small—that come with occupation. So let there be no doubt: the situation for the Palestinian people is intolerable. America will not turn our backs on the legitimate Palestinian aspiration for dignity, opportunity, and a state of their own.

For decades, there has been a stalemate: two peoples with legitimate aspirations, each with a painful history that makes compromise elusive. It is easy to point fingers—for Palestinians to point to the displacement brought by Israel's founding, and for Israelis to point to the constant hostility and attacks throughout its history from within its borders as well as beyond. But if we see this conflict only from one side or the other, then we will be blind to the truth: the only resolution is for the aspirations of both sides to be met through two states, where Israelis and Palestinians each live in peace and security. That is in Israel's interest, Palestine's interest, America's interest, and the world's interest. That is why I intend to personally pursue this outcome with all the patience that the task requires. The obligations that the parties have agreed to under the Road Map are clear. For peace to come, it is time for them—and all of us—to live up to our responsibilities.

Palestinians must abandon violence. Resistance through violence and killing is wrong and does not succeed. For centuries, black people in America suffered the lash of the whip as slaves and the humiliation of segregation. But it was not violence that won full and equal rights. It was a peaceful and determined insistence upon the ideals at the centre of America's founding. This same story can be told by people from South Africa to South Asia; from Eastern Europe to Indonesia. It's a story with a simple truth: that violence is a dead end. It is a sign of neither courage nor power to shoot rockets at sleeping children, or to blow up old women on a bus. That is not how moral authority is claimed; that is how it is surrendered.

Now is the time for Palestinians to focus on what they can build. The Palestinian Authority must develop its capacity to govern, with institutions that serve the needs of its people. Hamas does have support among some Palestinians, but they also have responsibilities. To play a role in fulfilling Palestinian' aspirations, and to unify the Palestinian people, Hamas must put an end to violence, recognize past agreements, and recognize Israel's right to exist.

At the same time, Israelis must acknowledge that just as

Israel's right to exist cannot be denied, neither can Palestine's. The United States does not accept the legitimacy of continued Israeli settlements. This construction violates previous agreements and undermines efforts to achieve peace. It is time for these settlements to stop.

Israel must also live up to its obligations to ensure that Palestinians can live, and work, and develop their society. And just as it devastates Palestinian families, the continuing humanitarian crisis in Gaza does not serve Israel's security; neither does the continuing lack of opportunity in the West Bank. Progress in the daily lives of the Palestinian people must be part of a road to peace, and Israel must take concrete steps to enable such progress.

Finally, the Arab States must recognize that the Arab Peace Initiative was an important beginning, but not the end of their responsibilities. The Arab-Israeli conflict should no longer be used to distract the people of Arab nations from other problems. Instead, it must be a cause for action to help the Palestinian people develop the institutions that will sustain their state; to recognize Israel's legitimacy; and to choose progress over a self-defeating focus on the past.

America will align our policies with those who pursue peace, and say in public what we say in private to Israelis and Palestinians and Arabs. We cannot impose peace. But privately, many Muslims recognize that Israel will not go away. Likewise, many Israelis recognize the need for a Palestinian state. It is time for us to act on what everyone knows to be true.

Too many tears have flowed. Too much blood has been shed. All of us have a responsibility to work for the day when the mothers of Israelis and Palestinians can see their children grow up without fear; when the Holy Land of three great faiths is the place of peace that God intended it to be; when Jerusalem is a secure and lasting home for Jews and Christians and Muslims, and a place for all of the children of Abraham to mingle peacefully together as in the story of Isra, when Moses,

Jesus, and Mohammed (peace be upon them) joined in prayer. The third source of tension is our shared interest in the rights and responsibilities of nations on nuclear weapons.

This issue has been a source of tension between the United States and the Islamic Republic of Iran. For many years, Iran has defined itself in part by its opposition to my country, and there is indeed a tumultuous history between us. In the middle of the Cold War, the United States played a role in the overthrow of a democratically-elected Iranian government. Since the Islamic Revolution, Iran has played a role in acts of hostage-taking and violence against U.S. troops and civilians. This history is well known. Rather than remain trapped in the past, I have made it clear to Iran's leaders and people that my country is prepared to move forward. The question, now, is not what Iran is against, but rather what future it wants to build.

It will be hard to overcome decades of mistrust, but we will proceed with courage, rectitude and resolve. There will be many issues to discuss between our two countries, and we are willing to move forward without preconditions on the basis of mutual respect. But it is clear to all concerned that when it comes to nuclear weapons, we have reached a decisive point. This is not simply about America's interests. It is about preventing a nuclear arms race in the Middle East that could lead this region and the world down a hugely dangerous path.

I understand those who protest that some countries have weapons that others do not. No single nation should pick and choose which nations hold nuclear weapons. That is why I strongly reaffirmed America's commitment to seek a world in which no nations hold nuclear weapons. And any nation—including Iran—should have the right to access peaceful nuclear power if it complies with its responsibilities under the nuclear Non-Proliferation Treaty. That commitment is at the core of the Treaty, and it must be kept for all who fully abide by it. And I am hopeful that all countries in the region can share in this goal.

The fourth issue that I will address is democracy.

I know there has been controversy about the promotion of democracy in recent years, and much of this controversy is connected to the war in Iraq. So let me be clear: no system of government can or should be imposed upon one nation by any other.

That does not lessen my commitment, however, to governments that reflect the will of the people. Each nation gives life to this principle in its own way, grounded in the traditions of its own people. America does not presume to know what is best for everyone, just as we would not presume to pick the outcome of a peaceful election. But I do have an unyielding belief that all people yearn for certain things: the ability to speak your mind and have a say in how you are governed; confidence in the rule of law and the equal administration of justice; government that is transparent and doesn't steal from the people; the freedom to live as you choose. Those are not just American ideas, they are human rights, and that is why we will support them everywhere.

There is no straight line to realize this promise. But this much is clear: governments that protect these rights are ultimately more stable, successful and secure. Suppressing ideas never succeeds in making them go away. America respects the right of all peaceful and law-abiding voices to be heard around the world, even if we disagree with them. And we will welcome all elected, peaceful governments—provided they govern with respect for all their people.

This last point is important because there are some who advocate for democracy only when they are out of power; once in power, they are ruthless in suppressing the rights of others. No matter where it takes hold, government of the people and by the people sets a single standard for all who hold power: you must maintain your power through consent, not coercion; you must respect the rights of minorities, and participate with a spirit of tolerance and compromise; you must place the interests of your people and the legitimate workings of the political process above your party. Without these ingredients, elections alone do not make true democracy.

The fifth issue that we must address together is religious freedom.

Islam has a proud tradition of tolerance. We see it in the history of Andalusia and Cordoba during the Inquisition. I saw it firsthand as a child in Indonesia, where devout Christians worshiped freely in an overwhelmingly Muslim country. That is the spirit we need today. People in every country should be free to choose and live their faith based upon the persuasion of the mind, heart, and soul. This tolerance is essential for religion to thrive, but it is being challenged in many different ways.

Among some Muslims, there is a disturbing tendency to measure one's own faith by the rejection of another's. The richness of religious diversity must be upheld—whether it is for Maronites in Lebanon or the Copts in Egypt. And fault lines must be closed among Muslims as well, as the divisions between Sunni and Shia have led to tragic violence, particularly in Iraq.

Freedom of religion is central to the ability of peoples to live together. We must always examine the ways in which we protect it. For instance, in the United States, rules on charitable giving have made it harder for Muslims to fulfil their religious obligation. That is why I am committed to working with American Muslims to ensure that they can fulfil zakat.

Likewise, it is important for Western countries to avoid impeding Muslim citizens from practicing religion as they see fit—for instance, by dictating what clothes a Muslim woman should wear. We cannot disguise hostility towards any religion behind the pretence of liberalism.

Indeed, faith should bring us together. That is why we are forging service projects in America that bring together Christians, Muslims, and Jews. That is why we welcome efforts like Saudi Arabian King Abdullah's Interfaith dialogue and Turkey's leadership in the Alliance of Civilizations. Around the world, we can turn dialogue into Interfaith service, so bridges between peoples lead to action—whether it is combating malaria in Africa, or providing relief after a natural disaster.

The sixth issue that I want to address is women's rights.

I know there is debate about this issue. I reject the view of some in the West that a woman who chooses to cover her hair is somehow less equal, but I do believe that a woman who is denied an education is denied equality. And it is no coincidence that countries where women are well-educated are far more likely to be prosperous.

Now let me be clear: issues of women's equality are by no means simply an issue for Islam. In Turkey, Pakistan, Bangladesh and Indonesia, we have seen Muslim-majority countries elect a woman to lead. Meanwhile, the struggle for women's equality continues in many aspects of American life, and in countries around the world.

Our daughters can contribute just as much to society as our sons, and our common prosperity will be advanced by allowing all humanity—men and women—to reach their full potential. I do not believe that women must make the same choices as men in order to be equal, and I respect those women who choose to live their lives in traditional roles. But it should be their choice. That is why the United States will partner with any Muslim-majority country to support expanded literacy for girls, and to help young women pursue employment through micro-financing that helps people live their dreams.

Finally, I want to discuss economic development and opportunity.

I know that for many, the face of globalization is contradictory. The Internet and television can bring knowledge and information, but also offensive sexuality and mindless violence. Trade can bring new wealth and opportunities, but also huge disruptions and changing communities. In all nations —including my own—this change can bring fear. Fear that because of modernity we will lose of control over our economic choices, our politics, and most importantly our identities—those things we most cherish about our communities, our families, our traditions, and our faith.

But I also know that human progress cannot be denied.

There need not be contradiction between development and tradition. Countries like Japan and South Korea grew their economies while maintaining distinct cultures. The same is true for the astonishing progress within Muslim-majority countries from Kuala Lumpur to Dubai. In ancient times and in our times, Muslim communities have been at the forefront of innovation and education.

This is important because no development strategy can be based only upon what comes out of the ground, nor can it be sustained while young people are out of work. Many Gulf States have enjoyed great wealth as a consequence of oil, and some are beginning to focus it on broader development. But all of us must recognize that education and innovation will be the currency of the 21st century, and in too many Muslim communities there remains underinvestment in these areas. I am emphasizing such investments within my country. And while America in the past has focused on oil and gas in this part of the world, we now seek a broader engagement.

On education, we will expand exchange programs, and increase scholarships, like the one that brought my father to America, while encouraging more Americans to study in Muslim communities. And we will match promising Muslim students with internships in America; invest in on-line learning for teachers and children around the world; and create a new online network, so a teenager in Kansas can communicate instantly with a teenager in Cairo.

On economic development, we will create a new corps of business volunteers to partner with counterparts in Muslim-majority countries. And I will host a Summit on Entrepreneurship this year to identify how we can deepen ties between business leaders, foundations and social entrepreneurs in the United States and Muslim communities around the world.

On science and technology, we will launch a new fund to support technological development in Muslim-majority countries, and to help transfer ideas to the marketplace so they can create jobs. We will open centres of scientific excellence in Africa, the Middle East and Southeast Asia, and appoint new Science Envoys to collaborate on programs that develop new sources of energy, create green jobs, digitize records, clean water, and grow new crops. And today I am announcing a new global effort with the Organization of the Islamic Conference to eradicate polio. And we will also expand partnerships with Muslim communities to promote child and maternal health.

All these things must be done in partnership. Americans are ready to join with citizens and governments; community organizations, religious leaders, and businesses in Muslim communities around the world to help our people pursue a better life.

The issues that I have described will not be easy to address. But we have a responsibility to join together on behalf of the world we seek—a world where extremists no longer threaten our people, and American troops have come home; a world where Israelis and Palestinians are each secure in a state of their own, and nuclear energy is used for peaceful purposes; a world where governments serve their citizens, and the rights of all God's children are respected. Those are mutual interests. That is the world we seek. But we can only achieve it together. I know there are many—Muslim and non-Muslim—who question whether we can forge this new beginning. Some are eager to stoke the flames of division, and to stand in the way of progress. Some suggest that it isn't worth the effort—that we are fated to disagree, and civilizations are doomed to clash. Many more are simply sceptical that real change can occur. There is so much fear, so much mistrust. But if we choose to be bound by the past, we will never move forward. And I want to particularly say this to young people of every faith, in every country—you, more than anyone, have the ability to remake this world.

All of us share this world for but a brief moment in time. The question is whether we spend that time focused on what pushes us apart, or whether we commit ourselves to an effort—a sustained effort—to find common ground, to focus on the future we seek for our children, and to respect the dignity of all human beings.

It is easier to start wars than to end them. It is easier to blame others than to look inward; to see what is different about someone than to find the things we share. But we should choose the right path, not just the easy path. There is also one rule that lies at the heart of every religion—that we do unto others as we would have them do unto us. This truth transcends nations and peoples—a belief that isn't new; that isn't black or white or brown; that isn't Christian, or Muslim or Jew. It's a belief that pulsed in the cradle of civilization, and that still beats in the heart of billions. It's a faith in other people, and it's what brought me here today.

We have the power to make the world we seek, but only if we have the courage to make a new beginning, keeping in mind what has been written.

The Holy Koran tells us, "O mankind! We have created you male and a female; and we have made you into nations and tribes so that you may know one another".

The Talmud tells us: "The whole of the Torah is for the purpose of promoting peace".

The Holy Bible tells us, "Blessed are the peacemakers, for they shall be called sons of God".

The people of the world can live together in peace. We know that is God's vision. Now, that must be our work here on Earth. Thank you. And may God's peace be upon you.

Source: The New York Times @ www.nytimes.com.

Document X

Netanyahu's Foreign Policy Speech at BarIlan, June 14, 2009

Honoured guests, citizens of Israel.

Peace was always the desire of our people. Our prophets had a vision of peace, we greet each other with peace, our prayers end with the word peace. This evening we are in the centre named for two leaders who were groundbreakers for peace—Menachem Begin and Anwar Sadat—and we share their vision.

Two and a half months ago, I was sworn in at the Knesset as the Prime Minister of Israel. I promised that I would establish a unity government, and did so. I believed, and still believe, that we need unity now more than ever before.

We are currently facing three tremendous challenges: The Iranian threat, the financial crisis, and the promotion of peace.

The Iranian threat still is before us in full force, as it became quite clear yesterday. The greatest danger to Israel, to the Middle East, and to all of humanity, is the encounter between extremist Islam and nuclear weapons. I discussed this with President Obama on my visit to Washington, and will be discussing it next week on my visit with European leaders. I have been working tirelessly for many years to form an international front against Iran arming itself with nuclear armaments.

With the world financial crisis, we acted immediately to bring about stability to the Israeli economy. We passed a two-year budget in the government and will pass it through the Knesset very soon. The second challenge, rather, the third, so very important challenge, facing us today, is promoting peace. I discussed this also with President Obama. I strongly support the idea of regional peace that he is advancing. I share the

President of the U.S.A's desire to bring about a new era of reconciliation in our region.

I discussed this in my meetings with President Mubarak in Egypt and with King Abdullah in Jordan to obtain the assistance of these leaders in the effort to expand the circle of peace in our region.

I appeal tonight to the leaders of the Arab countries and say: Let us meet. Let us talk about peace. Let us make peace. I am willing to meet at any time, at any place, in Damascus, in Riyadh, in Beirut, and in Jerusalem as well (applause).

I call upon the leaders of the Arab countries to join together with the Palestinians and with us to promote economic peace. Economic peace is not a substitute for peace, but it is a very important component in achieving it. Together we can advance projects that can overcome the problems facing our region. For example, water desalinization. And we can utilize the advantages of our region, such as maximizing the use of solar energy, or utilizing its geographical advantages to lay pipelines, pipelines to Africa and Europe.

Together we can realize the initiatives that I see in the Persian Gulf, which amaze the entire world, and also amaze me. I call upon the talented entrepreneurs of the Arab world, to come and invest here, to assist the Palestinians and us, to give the economy a jump-start. Together we can develop industrial zones, we can create thousands of jobs, and foster tourism that will draw millions, people who want to walk in the footsteps of history, in Nazareth and Bethlehem, in the heights of Jericho and on the walls of Jerusalem, on the shore of the Sea of Galilee, and at the baptismal site of the Jordan. There is a huge potential for the development of tourism potential here. If you only agree to work together.

I appeal to you, our Palestinian neighbours, and to the leadership of the Palestinian Authority. Let us begin peace negotiations immediately without prior conditions. Israel is committed to international agreements, and expects all sides to fulfil their obligations. I say to the Palestinians: We want to live with you in peace, quiet, and good neighbourly relations. We want our children and your children to 'know war no more'.

We do not want parents and wives, sons and daughters, brothers and sisters, to know the sorrow of bereavement. We want our children to dream of a better future for humankind. We want us and our neighbours to devote our efforts to 'ploughshares and pruning hooks' and not to "swords and spears"? I know the terror of war, I participated in battles, I lost good friends who fell [in battle], I lost a brother. I saw the pain of bereaved families from up close—very many times. I do not want war. No one in Israel wants war (applause).

Let us join hands and work together in peace, together with our neighbours. There is no limit to the flourishing growth that we can achieve for both peoples—in the economy, in agriculture, in commerce, tourism, education—but, above all, in the ability to give our younger generation hope to live in a place that's good to live in, a life of creative work, a peaceful life with much of interest, with opportunity and hope.

Friends, with the advantages of peace so clear, so obvious, we must ask ourselves why is peace still so far from us, even though our hands are extended for peace? Why has the conflict going on for over 60 years? To bring an end to it, there must be a sincere, genuine answer to the question: what is the root of the conflict? In his speech at the Zionist Congress in Basel, in speaking of his grand vision of a Jewish homeland for the Jewish People, Theodor Herzl, the visionary of the State of Israel, said: This is so big, we must talk about it only in the simplest words possible.

I now am asking that when we speak of the huge challenge of peace, we must use the simplest words possible, using person to person terms. Even with our eyes on the horizon, we must have our feet on the ground, firmly rooted in truth. The simple truth is that the root of the conflict has been—and remains—the refusal to recognize the right of the Jewish People to its own state in its historical homeland.

In 1947 when the United Nations proposed the Partition Plan for a Jewish state and an Arab state, the entire Arab world rejected the proposal, while the Jewish community accepted it with great rejoicing and dancing. The Arabs refused any Jewish state whatsoever, with any borders whatsoever.

Whoever thinks that the continued hostility to Israel is a result of our forces in Judea, Samaria and Gaza is confusing cause and effect. The attacks on us began in the 1920s, became an overall attack in 1948 when the state was declared, continued in the 1950s with the fedaayyin attacks, and reached their climax in 1967 on the eve of the Six-Day War, with the attempt to strangle Israel. All this happened nearly 50 years before a single Israeli soldier went into Judea and Samaria.

To our joy, Egypt and Jordan left this circle of hostility. They signed peace agreements with us which ended their hostility to Israel. It brought about peace.

To our deep regret, this is not happening with the Palestinians. The closer we get to a peace agreement with them, the more they are distancing themselves from peace. They raise new demands. They are not showing us that they want to end the conflict.

A great many people are telling us that withdrawal is the key to peace with the Palestinians. But the fact is that all our withdrawals were met by huge waves of suicide bombers.

We tried withdrawal by agreement, withdrawal without an agreement; we tried partial withdrawal and full withdrawal. In 2000, and once again last year, the government of Israel, based on good will, tried a nearly complete withdrawal, in exchange for the end of the conflict, and were twice refused.

We withdrew from the Gaza Strip to the last centimetre; we uprooted dozens of settlements and turned thousands of Israelis out of their homes. In exchange, what we received were missiles raining down on our cities, our towns and our children. The argument that withdrawal would bring peace closer did not stand up to the test of reality.

With Hamas in the south and Hezbollah in the north, they

keep on saying that they want to 'liberate' Ashkelon in the south and Haifa and Tiberias. Even the moderates among the Palestinians are not ready to say the most simplest things: The State of Israel is the national homeland of the Jewish People and will remain so (applause).

Friends, in order to achieve peace, we need courage and integrity on the part of the leaders of both sides. I am speaking today with courage and honesty. We need courage and sincerity not only on the Israeli side: we need the Palestinian leadership to rise and say, simply "We have had enough of this conflict. We recognize the right of the Jewish People to a state its own in this Land. We will live side by side in true peace". I am looking forward to this moment.

We want them to say the simplest things, to our people and to their people. This will then open the door to solving other problems, no matter how difficult. The fundamental condition for ending the conflict is the public, binding and sincere Palestinian recognition of Israel as the national homeland of the Jewish People (applause).

For this to have practical meaning, we need a clear agreement to solve the Palestinian refugee problem outside of the borders of the State of Israel. For it is clear to all that the demand to settle the Palestinian refugees inside of Israel, contradicts the continued existence of the State of Israel as the state of the Jewish People. We must solve the problem of the Arab refugees. And I believe that it is possible to solve it. Because we have proven that we ourselves solved a similar problem. Tiny Israel took in the hundreds of thousands of Jewish refugees from Arab countries who were uprooted from their homes.

Therefore, justice and logic dictates that the problem of the Palestinian refugees must be solved outside the borders of the State of Israel. There is broad national agreement on this (applause).

I believe that with good will and international investment of we can solve this humanitarian problem once and for all.

Friends, up to now, I have been talking about the need for the Palestinians to recognize our rights. Now I will talk about the need for us to recognize their rights.

The connection of the Jewish People to the Land has been in existence for more than 3,500 years. Judea and Samaria, the places where our forefathers Abraham, Isaac and Jacob walked, our forefathers David, Solomon, Isaiah and Jeremiah—this is not a foreign land, this is the Land of our Forefathers (applause).

The right of the Jewish People to a state in the Land of Israel does not arise from the series of disasters that befell the Jewish People over 2,000 years—persecutions, expulsions, pogroms, blood libels, murders, which reached its climax in the Holocaust, an unprecedented tragedy in the history of nations. There are those who say that without the Holocaust the State would not have been established, but I say that if the State of Israel had been established in time, the Holocaust would not have taken place (applause). The tragedies that arose from the Jewish People's helplessness show very sharply that we need a protective state. The right to establish our sovereign state here, in the Land of Israel, arises from one simple fact: Eretz Israel is the birthplace of the Jewish People (applause).

As the first PM David Ben Gurion in the declaration of the State, the State of Israel was established here in Eretz Israel, where the People of Israel created the Book of Books, and gave it to the world.

But, friends, we must state the whole truth here. The truth is that in the area of our homeland, in the heart of our Jewish Homeland, now lives a large population of Palestinians. We do not want to rule over them. We do not want to run their lives. We do not want to force our flag and our culture on them. In my vision of peace, there are two free peoples living side by side in this small land, with good neighbourly relations and mutual respect, each with its flag, anthem and government, with neither one threatening its neighbour's security and existence.

These two facts—our link to the Land of Israel, and the Palestinian population who live here, have created deep disagreements within Israeli society. But the truth is that we have much more unity than disagreement.

I came here tonight to talk about the agreement and security that are broad consensus within Israeli society. This is what guides our policy. This policy must take into account the international situation. We have to recognize international agreements but also principles important to the State of Israel. I spoke tonight about the first principle—recognition. Palestinians must truly recognize Israel as the state of the Jewish people. The second principle is demilitarization. Any area in Palestinian hands has to be demilitarization, with solid security measures.

Without this condition, there is a real fear that there will be an armed Palestinian state which will become a terrorist base against Israel, as happened in Gaza. We do not want missiles on Petah Tikva, or Grads on the Ben-Gurion international airport. We want peace. (Applause) And, to ensure peace we don't want them to bring in missiles or rockets or have an army, or control of airspace, or make treaties with countries like Iran, or Hezbollah. There is broad agreement on this in Israel. We cannot be expected to agree to a Palestinian state without ensuring that it is demilitarized. This is crucial to the existence of Israel—we must provide for our security needs.

This is why we are now asking our friends in the international community, headed by the USA, for what is necessary for our security, that in any peace agreement, the Palestinian area must be demilitarized. No army, no control of air space. Real effective measures to prevent arms coming in, not what's going on now in Gaza. The Palestinians cannot make military treaties.

Without this, sooner or later, we will have another Hamastan. We can't agree to this. Israel must govern its own fate and security. I told President Obama in Washington, if we get a guarantee of demilitarization, and if the Palestinians recognize Israel as the Jewish state, we are ready to agree to a real peace agreement, a demilitarized Palestinian state side by side with the Jewish state (applause).

Whenever we discuss a permanent arrangement, Israel needs defensible borders with Jerusalem remaining the united capital of Israel (applause).

The territorial issues will be discussed in a permanent agreement. Till then we have no intention to build new settlements or set aside land for new settlements. But there is a need to have people live normal lives and let mothers and fathers raise their children like everyone in the world. The settlers are not enemies of peace. They are our brothers and sisters (applause).

Friends, unity among us is, to my view, vital, and unity will help with reconciliation with our neighbours. Reconciliation must begin now. A strong Palestinian government will strengthen peace. If they truly want peace, and educate their children for peace and stop incitement, we for our part will make every effort, allow them freedom of movement and accessibility, making their lives easier and this will help bring peace. But above all, they must decide: the Palestinians must decide between path of peace and path of Hamas. They must overcome Hamas. Israel will not sit down at conference table with terrorist who seek to destroy it (applause).

Hamas are not willing to even let the Red Cross visit our abducted soldier Gilad Shalit who has been in captivity three years, cut off from his family and his country. We want to bring him back whole and well. With help of the international community, there is no reason why we can't have peace. With help of USA, we can do we can do the unbelievable. In 61 years, with constant threats to our existence we have achieved so much. Our microchips power the world's computers unbelievable, we have found cures for incurable diseases. Israeli drip irrigation waters barren lands throughout the world. Israeli researchers are making worldwide breakthroughs. If our neighbours only work for peace, we can achieve peace (applause).

I call upon Arab leaders and Palestinian leaders: Let's go in the path of Menachem Begin and Anwar Sadat, Yitzhak Rabin and King Hussein. Let's go in the path of Prophet Isaiah, who spoke thousands of years ago, they shall beat their swords into ploughshares and know war no more. Let us know war no more. Let us know peace.

Source: Ha'aretz (Israel) @ www.haaretz.com.

Document XI

Obama's Speech in Israel, March 21, 2013

The welcome that I've received from the people of Israel (cheers, applause)...thank you. I bring with me the support of the American people (cheers, applause) and the friendship that binds us together (cheers, applause).

You know, over the last two days I've reaffirmed the bonds between our countries with Prime Minister Netanyahu and President Peres. I've borne witness to the ancient history of the Jewish people at the Shrine of the Book, and I've seen Israel's shining future in your scientists and your entrepreneurs. This is a nation of museums and patents, timeless holy sites, groundbreaking innovation. Only in Israel could you see the Dead Sea Scrolls and the place where the technology onboard the Mars rover originated at the same time (cheers, applause).

But what I've most looked forward to is the ability to speak directly to you, the Israeli people, especially so many young people who are here today (cheers, applause) to talk to you about the history that brought us here today and the future that you will make in the years to come.

Now, I know that in Israel's vibrant democracy, every word, every gesture is carefully scrutinized (laughter). But I—I want to clear something up, just so you know: Any drama between me and my friend Bibi over the years was just a plot to create material for Eretz Nehederet (cheers, applause). That's the only—only thing that was going on. We just—we just wanted to make sure the writers had good material (laughter).

I also know that I come to Israel on the eve of a sacred holiday—the celebration of Passover. And that is where I would like to begin today. Just a few days from now Jews here in Israel and around the world will sit with family and friends at the Seder table and celebrate with songs, wine and symbolic foods. After enjoying Seders with family and friends in Chicago and on the campaign trail, I'm proud that I've now brought this tradition into the White House.

And I did so (applause) I did so because I wanted my daughters to experience the Haggadah and the story at the centre of Passover that makes this time of year so powerful. It's a story of centuries of slavery and years of wandering in the desert; a story of perseverance amidst persecution and faith in God and the Torah.

It's a story about finding freedom in your own land. And for the Jewish people, this story is central to who you've become.

But it's also a story that holds within it the universal human experience, with all of its suffering but also all of its salvation. It's a part of the three great religions—Judaism, Christianity and Islam—that trace their origins to Abraham and see Jerusalem as sacred. And it's a story that's inspired communities across the globe, including me and my fellow Americans.

In the United States, a nation made of up people who crossed oceans to start anew, we're naturally drawn to the idea of finding freedom in our land. To African-Americans, the story of the exodus was perhaps the central story, the most powerful image, about emerging from the grip of bondage to reach for liberty and human dignity—a tale that was carried from slavery through the civil rights movement into today.

For generations, this promise helped people weather poverty and persecution while holding on to the hope that a better day was on the horizon. For me personally, growing up in far-flung parts of the world and without firm roots, the story spoke to a yearning within every human being for a home (applause).

Of course, even as we draw strength from the story of God's will and his gift of freedom expressed on Passover, we also know that here on Earth we must bear our responsibilities in an imperfect world.

That means accepting our measure of sacrifice and struggle, just like previous generations. It means us working through generation after generation on behalf of that ideal of freedom. As Dr. Martin Luther King said on the day before he was killed, "I may not get there with you. But I want you to know that we, as a people, will get to the promised land". So just (applause) so just as Joshua carried on after Moses, the work goes on for all of you, the Joshua generation—for justice and dignity, for opportunity and freedom.

For the Jewish people, the journey to the promise of the state of Israel wound through countless generations. It involved centuries of suffering and exile, prejudice and pogroms and even genocide. Through it all, the Jewish people sustained their unique identity and traditions, as well as a longing to return home. And while Jews achieved extraordinary success in many parts of the world, the dream of true freedom finally found its full expression in the Zionist idea—to be a free people in your homeland.

And that's why I believe that Israel is rooted not just in history and tradition but also in a simple and profound idea: the—the idea that people deserve to be free in a land of their own (cheers, applause).

Over the last 65 years, when Israel has been at its best, Israelis have demonstrated that responsibility does not end when you reach the promised land, it only begins.

And so Israel has been a refuge for the diaspora, welcoming Jews from Europe, from the former Soviet Union, from Ethiopia, from North Africa (applause).

Israel has built a prosperous nation, through kibbutzeem that made the desert bloom, business that broadened the middle class, innovators who reached new frontiers, from the smallest microchip to the orbits of space.

Israel has established a thriving democracy with a spirited civil society and proud political parties and a tireless free press and a lively public debate—lively may be an understatement (applause).

And Israel has achieved all this even as it's overcome relentless threats to its security, through the courage of the Israel Defence Forces and a citizenry that is so resilient in the face of terror.

This is the story of Israel. This is the work that has brought the dreams of so many generations to life. And every step of the way, Israel has built unbreakable bonds of friendship with my country, the United States of America (applause).

Those ties began only eleven minutes after Israeli independence, when the United States was the first nation to recognize the State of Israel (applause).

As President Truman said in explaining his decision to recognize Israel, he said, "I believe it has a glorious future before it, not just as another sovereign nation, but as an embodiment of the great ideals of our civilization".

And since then, we've built a friendship that advances our shared interests. Together, we share a commitment to security for our citizens and the stability of the Middle East and North Africa. Together, we share a focus on advancing economic growth around the globe and strengthening the middle class within our own countries. Together, we share a stake in the success of democracy.

But the source of our friendship extends beyond mere interests, just as it has transcended political parties and individual leaders. America's a nation of immigrants. America's strengthened by diversity. America's enriched by faith. We are governed not simply by men and women but by laws. We're fuelled by entrepreneurship and innovation, and we are defined by a democratic discourse that allows each generation to re-imagine and renew our union once more. So in Israel, we see values that we share, even as we recognize what makes us different. That is an essential part of our bond.

Now, I stand here today mindful that for both our nations, these are some complicated times. We have difficult issues to work through within our own countries, and we face dangers and upheaval around the world. And when I look at young people within the United States, I think about the choices that they must make in their lives to define who we'll be as a nation in this 21st century, particularly as we emerge from two wars and the worst recession since the Great Depression.

But part of the reason I like talking to young people is because no matter how great the challenges are, their idealism, their energy, their ambition always gives me hope (cheers, applause).

And I see the same spirit in the young people here today. (Cheers, applause.) I believe that you will shape our future. And given the ties between our countries, I believe your future is bound to ours.

This is part of the lively debate that we talked about (cheers, applause). This is good (cheers, applause); (chuckles). The you know (cheers, applause) (chuckles) (continued cheers and applause) you know, I'd (chuckles) I have to say we actually arranged for that because it made me feel at home (laughter, cheers, applause). You know, I wouldn't feel comfortable if I didn't have at least one heckler (laughter) (chuckles).

I'd like to focus on how we—and when I say we, in particular young people—can work together to make progress in three areas that will define our times: security, peace, and prosperity (applause).

Let me begin with security. I'm proud that the security relationship between the United States and Israel has never been stronger (cheers, applause). Never. More exercises between our militaries. More exchanges among our political and military and intelligence officials than ever before. The largest program to date to help you retain your qualitative military edge. These are the facts; these aren't my opinions. These are facts.

But to me, this is not simply measured on a balance sheet. I know that here, in Israel, security is something personal.

Here's what I think about when I consider these issues.

When I consider Israel's security, I think about children like Osher Twito, who I met in Sderot (applause).

Children, the same age as my own daughters, who went to bed at night fearful that a rocket would land in their bedroom simply because of who they are and where they live (applause).

That reality is why we've invested in the Iron Dome system, to save countless lives, because those children deserve to sleep better at night (cheers, applause).

That's why we've made it clear time and again that Israel cannot accept rocket attacks from Gaza, and we have stood up for Israel's right to defend itself (cheers, applause). And that's why Israel has a right to expect Hamas to renounce violence and recognize Israel's right to exist (cheers, applause).

When I think about Israel's security, I think about five Israelis who boarded a bus in Bulgaria, who were blown up because of where they came from, robbed of the ability to live and love and raise families.

That's why every country that values justice should call Hezbollah what it truly is, a terrorist organization (cheers, applause) because the world cannot tolerate an organization that murders innocent civilians, stockpiles rockets to shoot at cities and supports the massacre of men and women and children in Syria right now (applause).

The fact that Hezbollah's ally, the Assad regime, has stockpiles of chemical weapons only heightens the urgency. We will continue to cooperate closely to guard against that danger. I've made it clear to Bashar al-Assad and all who follow his orders: We will not tolerate the use of chemical weapons against the Syrian people or the transfer of those weapons to terrorists. The world is watching. We will hold you accountable (cheers, applause).

The Syrian people have the right to be freed from the grip of a dictator who would rather kill his own people than relinquish power.

(Cheers, applause) Assad must go so that Syria's future can begin, because true stability in Syria depends upon establishing a government that is responsible to its people, one that protects all communities within its borders, while making peace with countries beyond them. These are the things I think about when I think about Israel's security.

When I consider Israel's security, I also think about a people who have a living memory of the Holocaust, faced with the prospect of a nuclear-armed Iranian government that has called for Israel's destruction. It's no wonder Israelis view this as an existential threat.

But this is not simply a challenge for Israel; it is a danger for the entire world, including the United States (cheers, applause). A nuclear-armed Iran would raise the risk of nuclear terrorism. It would undermine the non-proliferation regime. It would spark an arms race in a volatile region. And it would embolden a government that has shown no respect for the rights of its own people or the responsibilities of nations.

And that's why America has built a coalition to increase the cost to Iran of failing to meet their obligations. The Iranian government is now under more pressure than ever before, and that pressure is increasing. It is isolated. Its economy is in dire straits. It (sic) leadership is divided. And its position in the region and the world has only grown weaker (applause).

I do believe that all of us have an interest in resolving this issue peacefully.

Strong and principled diplomacy (applause) strong and principled diplomacy is the best way to ensure that the Iranian government forsakes nuclear weapons (applause). Peace is far more preferable to war, and the inevitable costs, the unintended consequences that would come with war means that we have to do everything we can to try to resolve this diplomatically. Because of the cooperation between our governments, we know that there remains time to pursue a diplomatic resolution. That's what America will do, with clear eyes, working with a world that's united and with the sense of urgency that's required.

But Iran must know this time is not unlimited, and I've made the position of the United States of America clear. Iran must not get a nuclear weapon. This is not a danger that can be contained (applause) and as president, I've said all options are on the table for achieving our objectives. America will do what we must to prevent a nuclear-armed Iran (cheers, applause).

For young Israelis, I know that these issues of security are rooted in an experience that's even more fundamental than the pressing threat of the day. You live in a neighbourhood where many of your neighbours have rejected the right of your nation to exist, and your grandparents had to risk their lives and all that they had to make a place for themselves in this world.

Your parents lived through war after war to ensure the survival of the Jewish state. Your children grow up knowing that people they've never met may hate them because of who they are, in a region that is full of turmoil and changing underneath your feet.

So that's what I think about when Israel's faced with these challenges—that sense of an Israel that is surrounded by many in this region who reject it and many in the world who refuse to accept it.

That's why the security of the Jewish people in Israel is so important; it cannot be taken for granted. But make no mistake: Those who adhere to the ideology of rejecting Israel's right to exist—they might as well reject the earth beneath them and the sky above, because Israel's not going anywhere (cheers, applause).

And today I want to tell you, particularly the young people, so that—so that there's no mistake here, so long as there is a United States of America, "Ah-tem lo lah-vahd" (cheers, applause). You are not alone (applause).

The question is what kind of future Israel will look forward to.

Israel's not going anywhere, but especially for the young people in this audience, the question is, what does its future hold? And that brings me to the subject of peace (applause).

I know Israel has taken risks for peace. Brave leaders—Menachem Begin, Yitzhak Rabin—reached treaties with two of your neighbours. You made credible proposals to the Palestinians at Annapolis. You withdrew from Gaza and Lebanon and then faced terror and rockets. Across the region, you've extended a hand of friendship, and all too often you've been confronted with rejection and, in some cases, the ugly reality of anti-Semitism. So I believe that the Israeli people do want peace, and I also understand why too many Israelis, maybe an increasing number, maybe a lot of young people here today, are sceptical that it can be achieved.

But today, Israel is at a crossroads. It can be tempting to put aside the frustrations and sacrifices that come with the pursuit of peace, particularly when Iron Dome repels rockets, barriers keep out suicide bombers, there are so many other pressing issues that demand your attention. And I know that only Israelis can make the fundamental decisions about your country's future (applause.) I recognize that.

I also know, by the way, that not everyone in this hall will agree with what I have to say about peace. I recognize that there are those who are not simply sceptical about peace, but question its underlying premise, have a different vision for Israel's future. And that's part of a democracy. That's part of the discourse between our two countries. I recognize that. But I also believe it's important to be open and honest, especially with your friends (applause). I also believe that.

You know, politically, given the strong bipartisan support for Israel in America, the easiest thing for me to do would be to put this issue aside, just express unconditional support for whatever Israel decides to do. That would be the easiest political path. But I want you to know that I speak to you as a friend who is deeply concerned and committed to your future, and I ask you to consider three points.

First, peace is necessary (cheers, applause). I believe that. I believe that peace is the only path to true security. You can be (applause) you have the opportunity to be the generation that permanently secures the Zionist dream, or you can face a growing challenge to its future. Given the demographics west of the Jordan River, the only way for Israel to endure and thrive as a Jewish and democratic state is through the realization of an independent and viable Palestine (cheers, applause). That is true (sustained cheers, applause).

There are other factors involved. Given the frustration in the international community about this conflict, Israel needs to reverse an undertow of isolation. And given the march of technology, the only way to truly protect the Israeli people over the long term is through the absence of war, because no wall is high enough and no Iron Dome is strong enough or perfect enough to stop every enemy (applause) that is intent on doing so from inflicting harm (applause).

And this truth is more pronounced given the changes sweeping the Arab world. I understand that with the uncertainty in the region, people in the streets, changes in leadership, the rise of non-secular parties in politics, it's tempting to turn inward because the situation outside of Israel seems so chaotic. But this is precisely the time to respond to the wave of revolution with a resolve and commitment for peace, because (applause) as more governments respond to popular will, the days when Israel could seek peace simply with a handful of autocratic leaders—those days are over.

Peace will have to be made among peoples, not just governments (applause). No one—no single step can change overnight what lies in the hearts and minds of millions. No single step is going to erase years of history and propaganda. But progress with the Palestinians is a powerful way to begin, while sidelining extremists who thrive on conflict and thrive on division. It would make a difference (cheers, applause).

So peace is necessary. But peace is also just. Peace is also just. There is no question that Israel has faced Palestinian factions who turn to terror, leaders who missed historic opportunities. That is all true. And that's why security must be at the centre of any agreement (scattered applause). And there is no question that the only path to peace is through negotiations, which is why, despite the criticism we've received, the United States will oppose unilateral efforts to bypass negotiations through the United Nations (applause). It has to be done by the parties.

But the Palestinian people's right to self-determination, their right to justice must also be recognized (cheers, applause). And put yourself in their shoes. Look at the world through their eyes.

It is not fair that a Palestinian child cannot grow up in a state of their own (cheers, applause) living their entire lives with the presence of a foreign army that controls the movements, not just of those young people but their parents, their grandparents, every single day. It's not just when settler violence against Palestinians goes unpunished (applause). It's not right to prevent Palestinians from farming their lands or restricting a student's ability to move around the West Bank— (applause) or displace Palestinian families from their homes. Neither occupation nor expulsion is the answer (cheers, applause). Just as Israelis built a state in their homeland, Palestinians have a right to be a free people in their own land (applause).

But I'm going off script here for a second, but before I came here, I met with a group of young Palestinians from the age of 15 to 22. And talking to them, they weren't that different from my daughters. They weren't that different from your daughters or sons.

I honestly believe that if any Israeli parent sat down with those kids, they'd say, I want these kids to succeed (applause). I want them to prosper. I want them to have opportunities just like my kids do (applause). I believe that's what Israeli parents would want for these kids if they had a chance to listen to them and talk to them (cheers, applause). I believe that (cheers, applause).

Now, only you can determine what kind of democracy you

will have. But remember that as you make these decisions, you will define not simply the future of your relationship with the Palestinians; you will—you will define the future of Israel, as well (applause). As Ariel Sharon said—I'm quoting him "It is impossible to have a Jewish, democratic state at the same time to control all of Eretz Israel. If we insist on fulfilling the dream in its entirety, we are liable to lose it all" (applause).

Or from a different perspective, I think of what the novelist David Grossman said shortly after losing his son, as he described the necessity of peace. A peace of no choice, he said, must be approached with the same determination and creativity as one approaches a war of no choice (applause).

Now, Israel cannot be expected to negotiate with anyone who's dedicated to its destruction (applause). But while I know you have had differences with the Palestinian Authority, I genuinely believe that you do have a true partner in President Abbas and Prime Minister Fayyada (applause). I believe that. And they have a track record to prove it. Over the last few years, they have built institutions and maintained security on the West Bank in ways that few could have imagined just a few years ago. So many Palestinians, including young people, have rejected violence as a means of achieving their aspirations.

There is an opportunity there. There is a window, which brings me to my third point: Peace is possible (cheers, applause). It is possible. I'm not saying it's guaranteed. I can't even say that it is more likely than not. But it is possible.

I know it doesn't seem that way. There are always going to be reasons to avoid risk. There are costs for failure. There will always be extremists who provide an excuse to not act. I know there must be something exhausting about endless talks about talks and daily controversies and just the grinding status quo, and I'm sure there's a temptation just to say, ach (ph), enough; let me focus on my small corner of the world and my family and my job and what I can control.

But it's possible. Negotiations will be necessary, but

there's little secret about where they must lead: two states for two peoples (applause) two states for two peoples (cheers, applause).

There will be differences about how to get there. There are going to be hard choices along the way. Arab states must adapt to a world that has changed. The days when they could condemn Israel to distract their people from a lack of opportunity or government corruption or mismanagement—those days need to be over. Now's the time for the Arab world to take steps towards normalizing relations with Israel (applause).

Meanwhile, Palestinians must recognize that Israel will be a Jewish state and that Israelis have the right to insist upon their security (applause).

Israelis must recognize that continued settlement activity is counterproductive to the cause of peace and that an independent Palestine must be viable, with real borders that have to be drawn (cheers, applause). I've suggested principles on territory and security that I believe can be the basis for these talks.

But for the moment, put aside the plans and the process.

I ask you, instead, to think about what can be done to build trust between people.

Four years ago I stood in Cairo in front of an audience of young people. Politically, religiously, they must seem a world away. But the things they want—they're not so different from what the young people here want. They want the ability to make their own decisions and to get an education and to get a good job, to worship God in their own way, to get married, to raise a family. The same is true of those young Palestinians that I met with this morning. The same is true for young Palestinians who yearn for a better life in Gaza.

That's where peace begins, not just in the plans of leaders, but in the hearts of people; not just in some carefully designed process, but in the daily connections, that sense of empathy that takes place among those who live together in this land and in this sacred city of Jerusalem (applause). And let me say this as a politician, I can promise you this: Political leaders will never take risks if the people do not push them to take some risks (cheers, applause). You must create the change that you want to see. Ordinary people can accomplish extraordinary things (sustained cheers and applause).

I know this is possible. Look to the bridges being built in business and civil society by some of you here today. Look at young people who have not yet learned a reason to mistrust or those young people who have learned to overcome a legacy of mistrust that they inherited from their parents because they simply recognized that we hold more hopes in common than fears that drive us apart.

Your voices must be louder than those who would drown them out. Your hopes must light the way forward. Look to a future in which Jews and Muslims and Christians can all live in peace and greater prosperity in this Holy Land. Believe in that (cheers, applause). And most of all, look to the future that you want for your own children, a future in which a Jewish, democratic, vibrant state is protected and accepted for this time and for all time (applause).

There will be many who say this is not possible. But remember this: Israel is the most powerful country in this region. Israel has the unshakable support of the most powerful country in the world (applause). Israel's not going anywhere. Israel has the wisdom to see the world as it is, but this is in your nature—Israel also the courage to see the world as it should be. You know (cheers, applause) Ben-Gurion once said in Israel, in order to be a realist, you must believe in miracles (laughter). Sometimes the greatest miracle is recognizing that the world can change. That's a lesson that the world learned from the Jewish people.

And that brings me to the final area that I'll focus on: prosperity and Israel's broader role in the world. I know that all the talk about security and peace can sometimes seem to dominate the headlines, but that's not where people live.

And every day, even amidst the threats that you face, Israelis are defining themselves by the opportunities that you're creating.

Through talent and hard work, Israelis have put this small country at the forefront of the global economy (applause). Israelis understand the value of education and have produced 10 Nobel laureates (cheers, applause). Israelis understand the power of invention, and your universities educate engineers and inventors. And that spirit has led to economic growth and human progress: solar power and electric cars; bandages and prosthetic limbs that save lives; stem cell research and new drugs that treat disease; cell phones and computer technology that (applause) that change the way people around the world live.

So if people want to see the future of the world economy, they should look at Tel Aviv, home to hundreds of start-ups and research centres (cheers, applause). Israelis are so active on social media that every day seemed to bring a different Facebook campaign about where I should give this speech (laughter, applause, cheers).

That innovation is just as important to the relationship between the United States and Israel as our security cooperation. Our first free trade agreement in the world was reached with Israel, nearly three decades ago (applause). Today the trade between our two countries is at $ 40 billion every year (applause). More importantly, that partnership is creating new products and medical treatments; it's pushing new frontiers of science and exploration.

That's the kind of relationship that Israel should have—and could have—with every country in the world. Already we see how that innovation could reshape this region. There's a program here in Jerusalem that brings together young Israelis and Palestinians to learn vital skills in technology and business. An Israeli and Palestinian have started a venture capital fund to finance Palestinian start-ups. Over 100 high-tech companies have found a home on the West Bank, which speaks to the talent and entrepreneurial spirit of the Palestinian people.

You know, one of the great ironies of what's happening in the broader region is that so much of what people are yearning for—education, entrepreneurship, the ability to start a business without paying a bribe, the ability to connect to the global economy—those are things that can be found here, in Israel. This should be a hub for thriving regional trade and an engine for opportunity (applause). Israel's already a centre for innovation that helps power the global economy. And I believe that all of that potential for prosperity can be enhanced with greater security, enhanced with lasting peace (applause).

Here, in this small strip of land that has been the centre of so much of the world's history, so much triumph and so much tragedy, Israelis have built something that few could have imagined 65 years ago. Tomorrow I will pay tribute to that history—at the grave of Herzl, a man who had the foresight to see that the future of the Jewish people had to be reconnected to their past; at the grave of Rabin, who understood that Israel's victories in war had to be followed by the battles for peace; at Yad Vashem, where the world is reminded of the cloud of evil that can descend on the Jewish people and all of humanity if we ever fail to be vigilant.

We bear all that history on our shoulders. We carry all that history in our hearts. Today, as we face the twilight of Israel's founding generation, you, the young people of Israel, must now claim its future. It falls to you to write the next chapter in the great story of this great nation.

And as the president of a country that you can count on as your greatest friend (applause) I am confident that you can help us find the promise in the days that lie ahead. And as a man who's been inspired in my own life by that timeless calling within the Jewish experience—"tikkun olam"—(applause) I am hopeful that we can draw upon what's best in ourselves to meet the challenges that will come, to win the battles for peace in the wake of so much war and to do the work of repairing this world (applause).

That's your job. That's my job. That's the task of all of us (applause continues).

May God bless you. May God bless Israel. May God bless the United States of America (cheers, applause). "Toda raba". Thank you (cheers, applause).

Source: Federal News Service, The New York Times Company @ www.nytimes.com.

Bibliography

Bibliography

Primary Sources (Memoirs, Official Statements, Reports, Unpublished Papers and other Miscellanea)

Abbas, Mahmud (Winter 2001), 'Report on the Camp David Summit, Gaza, September 9, 2000 (Excerpts), Document B1 (Arab), *Journal of Palestine Studies*, 30 (2): 168-170.

Azad, Abul Kalam (April 2000), 'The Middle East Peace Process and the Palestinian Statehood', *BIISS Papers (Bangladesh Institute of International and Strategic Studies, Dhaka)*, No. 18: 1-131.

'A Framework for Peace in the Middle East, 1978, (The Camp David Accords)'. *Documents on Palestine, the Middle East and North Africa 2003* (49th ed. 2002), London: Europa Publishers.

'Arab League Fez Summit Peace Proposal, 1982', *Documents on Palestine* (2002), London: Europa.

'Agreement between Israel and Egypt (S/11818/Add.1), (September 1, 1975)'. Bailey, Sydney D. (1990), *Four Arab-Israeli Wars and the Peace Process*. London: Macmillan.

Abbas, Mahmud (1995), *Through Secret Channels,* Reading: Garnet P.L.

Aronson, Geoffrey (1999), *Understanding the Sharm el-Sheikh Memorandum*, Information Brief, No. 10, Washington DC: The Jerusalem Fund for education and community development (The Palestine Centre).

Barak, Prime Minister Ehud (2001), '*Israel's Requirements for a Peace Agreement*, Chicago, 13 November 2000', Document C2, *Journal of Palestine Studies*, 30 (3): 178.

'Barak to Bush-Sharon is not bound by negotiating ideas: February 8, 2001', *Israel Ministry of Foreign Affairs (MFA)*, MFA Library, 2000-2009.

Brahmanandam, Tigiripalli (1992), *Diplomatic Strategy of the PLO since 1982*. J.N.U. Unpublished M.Phil Dissertation.

Brzezinski, Zbigniew (1983), *Power and Principle: Memoirs of the National Security Adviser, 1997-1981*. New York: Farrar, Strauss, Giroux.

Baumgarten (2004), Helga A Series of Strategic Papers 7: *The Myth of Camp David Or The Distortion of the Palestinian Narrative,*

Ibrahim Abu-Lughod Institute of International Studies, Birzeit University, Birzeit–Palestine.

Bishara, Marwan (2000), *Barak's Inability to 'Make a Historical Peace,'* Information Brief, No. 49, Washington DC: The Jerusalem Fund for Education and Community Development (The Palestine Centre).

Carter, Jimmy (1985), *The Blood of Abraham*, Boston: Houghton Mifflin Company.

Carter, Jimmy (1982), *Keeping Faith: Memories of a President*, New York: Bantam Books.

Carter, Jimmy (1977), *Public Papers of the President: Vol. 1*, Washington, DC: Government Printing Office.

'Camp David Peace Proposal of July, 2000: Frequently Asked questions,' Ramallah, Palestine: PLO Negotiations Affairs Department.

Clinton, William J. (January 7, 2001): *Remarks by the President at the Israel Policy Forum Gala*, New York: The Warldorf Astoria Hotel (Distributed by the White House Office of the Press Secretary).

'Clinton, Arafat and Rabin on West Bank Agreement, September 28, 1995', *Congressional Quarterly Inc.*, Washington, DC., 1996, 622-630.

'Clinton, Middle East Leaders on Camp David Summit, July 25, 2000', *Congressional Quarterly Inc.*, Washington, DC., 2001, 494-507.

Clinton, President Bill (2001), '*Main Points of Agreement Reached at the Sharm el-Shaykh Summit*, Egypt, 17th October 2000', Document D5, *Journal of Palestine Studies*, 30 (2): 186.

Clinton, President Bill (2001), *Proposals for a Final Settlement,* Washington, 23rd December 2000, Document D1, *Journal of Palestine Studies*, 30 (3): 171-173.

'Declaration of the State of Palestine by the Palestine National Council', Algiers, 1988 *Documents on Palestine*, Europa.

'Deciding the Fate of the Territories Occupied during the Six Day War: An Ongoing Debate; The Government Discusses Israel's Peace Plan,' 18-19 June 1967, Israel State Archives, (Document No. 5, stenographic record of the second government meeting, 19 June 1967, ISA/A/8164/8).

Dayan, Moshe (1981), *Breakthrough: A Personal Account of the Egypt-Israel Peace Negotiations*. New York: Alfred A. Knopf Publishers.

'Deconstructing the Taba Talks,' *Foundation for Middle East Peace (FMEP)*-Settlement Report, 11 (2), March-April 2001.

Emerson, Steven (2008), 'Report on the Roots of Violent Islamist Extremism and Efforts to Counter It: The Muslim Brotherhood, Senate Committee on Homeland Security and Governmental Affairs, Washington DC.: The Capitol.

Excerpts: State Dept. Spokesman on Middle East Peace Prospects (Both sides accept Clinton's parameters with reservations), January 3, 2001. Tel Aviv, Israel: American Embassy Press Section, Distributed by the Office of International Information Programs, U.S. Department of State.

'Excerpts from Text of "Beirut Declaration" issued on the closing day of the Arab League Summit'. *BBC News*. March 28, 2002.

Fahmy, Ismail (1983), *Negotiating for Peace in the Middle East*, Baltimore: John Hopkins University Press.

Forman, Katherine (2010), *The Rising Support for Hamas and the Roots of its Success in Palestine*, Information Brief, Washington DC: The Jerusalem Fund for education and community development (The Palestine Centre).

Great Britain and Palestine, 1915-1945 (1946), London: Royal Institute of International Affairs (RIIA-Chatham House), Information Department, Hyperion Press.

'Gaza Strip Situation Report', *United Nations Office for the Coordination of Humanitarian Affairs (OCHA): occupied Palestinian territory*, East Jerusalem, Palestine, October 10, 2006.

'Human Rights in Palestine and Other Occupied Arab Territories', Report of the United Nations Fact Finding Mission on the Gaza Conflict (The Goldstone Report), *United Nations Human Rights Council,* Twelfth session, Agenda item 7, A/HRC/12/48, London, September 15, 2009.

'Hamas Covenant 1988: The Covenant of the Islamic Resistance Movement', *The Avalon Project: Documents in Law, History and Diplomacy*. Yale Law School. August 18, 1988.

Hanieh, Akram (2001), 'The Camp David Papers', *Journal of Palestine Studies*, 30 (2): 75-97.

Heller, Mark A. (2000), 'Continuity and Change in Israeli Security Policy', *Adelphi Paper* 335, London: IISS.

'Israeli-Palestinian Peace Accord, September 1993', *Congressional Quarterly Inc.*, Washington, DC., 1994, 747-768.

'Israeli-Palestinian Joint Statement: January 27, 2001', *Israel Ministry of Foreign Affairs (MFA),* MFA Library: 2000-2009.

'Israeli-Palestinian Interim Agreement on the West Bank and Gaza', *28 September 1995. Documents on Palestine*, Europa, 2002, 80-88.

'Initial Response To Report of the Fact Finding Mission on Gaza Established Pursuant to Resolution S-9/1 of The Human Rights Council', *Israel Ministry of Foreign Affairs*, Jerusalem, September 24, 2009.

Jerusalem-Visions of Reconciliation, Athens, UN Department of Public Information, April 27-28, 1993.

Kissinger, Henry A. (1979), *White House Years*. Boston: Little, Brown Publishers.

'Locked In: The Humanitarian Impact of Two Years of Blockade on the Gaza Strip', Special Focus, *United Nations Office for the Coordination of Humanitarian Affairs (OCHA): Occupied Palestinian Territory*, East Jerusalem, Palestine, August 2009.

'Leaders on Implementing the Middle-East Peace Agreement, October 23, 1988', *Congressional Quarterly Inc*, Washington, 1999, 742-754.

Levitats, Isaac (1943-1944), 'Pro-Palestine and Zionist Activities', *American Jewish Year Book*, Vol. 45.

Medzini, Meron, (1981), *Israel's Foreign Relations: Selected Documents, 1977-1979*, Vols. 4 and 5, Jerusalem: Ministry of Foreign Relations.

Medzini, Meron (1990), *Israel's Foreign Relations: Selected Documents 1982-1984*, Jerusalem: Ministry of Foreign Affairs.

Musallam, Sami (1973), *United Nations Resolutions on Palestine 1947-1972*, Beirut: Institute of Palestine Studies.

Multilateral Working Group on Refugees: Opening remarks by Eli Sanbar for the Palestinian side of the Joint Palestinian-Jordanian Delegation, Ottawa, May 13, 1992. Arzt (1997), Council on Foreign Relations.

Multilateral Working Group on Refugees: Opening Remarks by Israeli Negotiator, Shlomo Ben-Ami, Ottawa, November 11, 1992. Arzt (1997), Council on Foreign Relations.

Morris, Benny (2002), 'Camp David and After: An Exchange (An Interview with Ehud Barak)', *The New York Review of Books*, 49 (10), June 13, 2002.

Matz, David (2003), Special Report: Trying to Understand the Taba

Talks, *Palestine-Israel Journal of Politics, Economics and Culture*, 10 (3).

Macfarlane, S. Neil (2002), 'Intervention in Contemporary World Politics', *Adelphi Paper* 350, London: International Institute for Strategic Studies (IISS).

Migdalovitz, Carol (2010), 'Israeli-Arab Negotiations: Background, Conflicts, and US Policy', *CRS Report for Congress*, Congressional Research Service, Library of Congress-Washington DC., 1-55.

Naaz, Farah (1991), *United States and the Camp David Agreement, 1978: Its Impact on West Asia*, New Delhi (JNU): unpublished M.Phil Dissertation.

Origins and Evolution of Palestine Problem: 1917-1988 (1991), New York: United Nations Publications.

'Pact of the League of Arab States,' March 22, 1945, *Public Papers of the President: Jimmy Carter*, (1977, 1978, 1979), Vols. 1, 2, 3, Washington, DC., Government Printing Office.

Palestine National Covenant, 1964/1968 (1973), Sami Musallam, *UN Resolutions on Palestine, 1947-1972*, Beirut: Institute of Palestine studies, 57-59.

Peres, Shimon (1993), *Speech to the United Nations General Assembly*, September 28, 1993. Shimon Peres, *The New Middle East*.

'Palestinian Declaration of Independence', in *Documents on Palestine*: Vol. 1, Jerusalem: PASSIA, 1997.

'Palestine Mandate Convention between the United States of America and Great Britain', United States Department of State/ Papers relating to the foreign relations of the United States, Volume II (1924), London, December 3, 1924, 212-222. 'Palestinian President Mahmoud Abbas addresses UN General Assembly after submitting application for recognition to UN Chief Ban Ki-moon', Full transcript of Abbas speech at UN General Assembly, *Ha'aretz*, September 23, 2011.

Question of Palestine: Legal Aspects (1992), New York: United Nations Publications.

Quarles, Philip (2012), *Ralph Bunche Announces Landmark 1949 Arab-IsraelGeneral Armistice Agreement*, New York: The NEH Preservation Project, No. 56.

'Remarks by the President on the Middle East and North Africa', The White House: Office of the Press Secretary, Washington

DC., May 19, 2011.

Rabin, Yitzhak (1979), *The Rabin Memoirs*, Boston: Little Brown.

Report on Israeli settlements in the Occupied Palestinian Territories, Washington, DC., Foundation for Middle East Peace, February 1994.

Report of the Sharm el-Sheikh Fact-Finding Committee (The Mitchell Report), 20 May 2001, *Documents on Palestine*, Europa, 2002, 90-98.

Search for Peace in the Middle East: Documents and Statements, 1967-79, Report by Congressional Research Service for the Subcommittee on Europe and the Middle East, Committee on Foreign Affairs, US House Of representatives (CP 957), 1979.

Sayigh, Yezid and Khalil Shikaki (1999), *Strengthening Palestinian Public Institutions'*, *Executive summary of Task Force Report*, New York: Council on Foreign Relations.

Sadat, Anwar (1977), *In Search of Identity: An Autobiography*, New York: Harper and Row.

Sharm el-Sheikh Memorandum on the Implementation Timeline of Outstanding Commitments of Agreements Signed and the Resumption of Permanent Status Negotiations (Wye II), September 4, 1999, *Documents on Palestine*, Europa, 2003, 88-90.

Sharm El-Sheikh Fact-Finding Committee Report (also called the *Mitchell Report*), April 30, 2001.

Special Document (1992), 'The Peace Process', *Journal of Palestine Studies*, 21 (3): 126-146.

Special Document (1992), 'The Madrid Peace Conference', *Journal of Palestine Studies*, 21 (2): 117-149.

Special Document (2003), 'Ehud Barak on Camp David: "I Did Not Give Away a Thing', *Journal of Palestine Studies,* 33 (1): 84-87.

Special Documents (2003), The Road Map A: International Crisis Group, "A Middle East Road Map to Where"? Amman/Brussels/Washington, May 2 (Excerpts), *Journal of Palestine Studies,* 32 (4): 83-87.

Special Documents (2003), The Road Map B: 'U.S. President George W. Bush, Statement on the Middle East upon release of the Road Map', Washington, April 30, *Journal of Palestine Studies,* 32 (4): 87-88.

Special Documents (2003), The Road Map C: U.S. Department of State, "A Performance-Based Road Map to a Permanent Two-

State Solution to the Israeli-Palestinian Conflict", Washington, April 30, *Journal of Palestine Studies,* 32 (4): 89-94.

Special Documents (2003), The Road Map F: 'Israeli Prime Minister Ariel Sharon, Statement accepting the Road Map', Jerusalem, May 23, *Journal of Palestine Studies,* 32 (4): 96-97.

Special Documents (2003), The Road Map G: *Ha'aretz*, "Israel's Road Map Reservations", Jerusalem, May 27, *Journal of Palestine Studies,* 32 (4): 97-99.

Special Documents (2008), The Annapolis Conference C: 'Palestinian President Mahmud Abbas, Statement to the Annapolis Conference', Annapolis, Maryland, November 27, 2007 (excerpts), *Journal of Palestine Studies,* 37 (3): 80-82.

Special Documents (2008), The Annapolis Conference B: 'U.S. Pres. George W. Bush, Opening Statement to the Annapolis Conference', Annapolis, Maryland, November 27, 2007 (excerpts), *Journal of Palestine Studies,* 37 (3): 77-80.

'Security Council Adopts Resolution Endorsing Road Map leading towards two-state Resolution of Israeli-Palestinian', *United Nations Security Council* 4862nd Meeting (PM), Press Release SC/7924, November 19, 2003.

Sideras, Zachary T. (2009), *Building Conditions for Unity and Peace (in Palestine),* Information Brief, Washington DC.: The Jerusalem Fund for education and community development (The Palestine Centre).

Truman, Harry S. (1956), *Memoirs: Years of Trial and Hope*, Vol. 2, Garden City, New York: Doubleday.

The Declaration of the Establishment of the State of Israel [Published in the Official Gazette, No. 1 of the 5th, Iyar, 5708 (14th May, 1948)] Israeli Ministry of Foreign Affairs (MFA), May 14, 1948.

Treaty of Peace between the Arab Republic of Egypt and the State of Israel, 26th March, 1979, *Documents on Palestine*, Europa, 65-66.

The Egyptian Position in Negotiations Concerning the Establishment of Transitional Arrangements for the West Bank and Gaza. Cairo: Ministry of Foreign Affairs, 1980.

The Cairo Agreement on the Gaza Strip and Jericho, 4th May, 1994, *Documents on Palestine*, Europa, 2002, 76-80.

Treaty of Peace: Israel and the Hashemite Kingdom of Jordan, Aqaba, October 26, 1994.

The Status of Jerusalem: Report prepared for, and under the guidance of the committee on the Exercise of the Inalienable Rights of the Palestinian People, New York: United Nations, 1997.

The Origins and Evolution of the Palestine Problem, 1917-1988, New York: United Nations, 1990.

Transcript: Lockhart briefing on Camp David Peace Talks, July 11, 2000, The White House: Office of the Press Secretary, (Distributed by the Office of International Information Programs, U.S. Department of State).

The Wye Memorandum, 23rd October, 1998, *Documents on Palestine,* Europa, 2002, 86-88.

The Clinton Parameters: Clinton Proposal on Israeli-Palestinian Peace, Jewish Peace Lobby meeting with President Clinton, White House, December 23, 2000.

The Negotiations Process: The Clinton Parameters, Official Palestinian Response to the Clinton Parameters (and letter to the international community: Remarks and Questions from the Palestinian Negotiating Team Regarding the United States Proposal. Ramallah, Palestine: PLO Negotiations Affairs Department (PLO-NAD), January 1, 2001.

'The Saudi Peace Plan: Excerpts From Speech by Crown Prince of Saudi Arabia', *The New York Times*, March 27, 2002.

UN Partition Resolution (Palestine) 181 (II), 29th November, 1947, Sami Musallam, *UN Resolutions on Palestine, 1947-1972*, Beirut: Institute of Palestine Studies, 1973, 4-14.

United Nations General Assembly Resolution 194 (III), 11th December, 1948, Musallam, Institute on Palestine Studies, 1973.

UN Security Council Resolution 242 (S/8247), 22nd November, 1967, *Documents on Palestine*, Europa, 113-114.

UN Security Council Resolution 338 (S /11036), 22nd November, 1973, *Documents on Palestine*, Europa, 61.

United Nations General Assembly Resolution 3236 (XXIX), 22nd November, 1974, UNISPAL.

United Nations General Assembly Resolution 3237 (XXIX) of 22nd November, 1974, UNISPAL.

Universal Declaration of Human Rights, UNGA Resolution 217 (III), December 10, 1948, Arzt, Council on Foreign Relations, 1997.

UN Committee on the Exercise of the Inalienable Rights of the Palestinian People, the Right of Self-Determination of the Self-

Determination of the Palestinian People, UN Doc. ST/SG/SER.F/3 (1979).

United Nations (1997), *For the Rights of the Palestinians-The Work of the Committee on the Exercise of the Inalienable Rights of the Palestinian People*, New York: United Nations Department of Public Information, DPI/1304-98093.

UNGA Declaration on the Human Rights of Individuals Who are Not Nationals of the Country in which They Live, December 13, 1985, Arzt, Council on Foreign Relations, 1997.

UNSC Resolution 1397, 12th March 2002, *Documents on Palestine*, Europa, 2002, 98.

'United States Vetoes Security Council Resolution on Israeli Settlements', *United Nations News Centre*, February 18, 2011.

US Department of State Bulletin 28 (728), Washington, DC., June 8, 1956.

Vance, Cyrus (1983), *Hard Choice: Critical Years in America's Foreign Policy*. New York: Simon and Schuster.

Weiss, Martin A. (2006), 'Arab League Boycott of Israel', *CRS Report for Congress*, Congressional Research Service, Library of Congress, Washington DC., 1-6.

Weizmann, Ezer (1981), *The Battle for Peace*, New York: Bantam Books.

Waldheim, Kurt (1985), *In the Eye of the Storm*, London: Weidenfeld and Nicolson.

White Paper on Treaty of Peace between Egypt and Israel (1979), Cairo: Ministry of Foreign Affairs.

Books and Book Chapters

Al-Kayyali, Abdul-Hameed (2009) (ed.), *Dirasat fi al-'Odwan al-Israeli 'ala Qita' Gaza: 'Amaliyyat al-Rasas al-Masboub/ Ma'rakat al-Furqan* (Studies on the Israeli Aggression on Gaza Strip: Cast Lead Operation/Al-Furqan Battle), np, (1st Edition).

Abū Amr, Ziyād (1994), *Islamic Fundamentalism in the West Bank and Gaza: Muslim Brotherhood and Islamic Jihad*, Bloomington: Indiana University Press.

Aburish, Said K. (1998), *From Defender to Dictator*, New York: Bloomsbury Publishing.

Ahmar, Moonis (2001), *The Arab Israeli Peace Process: Lessons for India and Pakistan*, Karachi: Oxford University Press.

Aronson, Geoffrey (1990), *Israel, Palestinians and the Intifada:*

Creating Facts on the West Bank, London: Kegan Paul.

Arzt, Donna E. (1997), *Refugees into Citizens: Palestinians and the End of the Arab-Israeli Conflict*, New York: Council on Foreign Relations.

Arian, Asher (1989), *Politics in Israel: The Second Generation* (revised edition), New Jersey: Chatham House.

Baker, James Addison (1995), *The Politics of Diplomacy: Revolution, War and Peace 1989-1992*, New York: G.P. Putnam's Sons.

Bailey, Sydney D. (1990), *Four Arab-Israeli Wars and the Peace Process*, London: Macmillan.

Blumberg, Arnold (1988), *The History of Israel.* London: Greenwood Press.

Brecher, Michael (1974), *Decisions in Israel's Foreign Policy*, London: Oxford University Press.

Ben-Zvi, Abraham (1990), *Between Lausanne and Geneva: International Conference and the Arab-Israeli Conflict*, Boulder: Westview Press.

Beilin, Yossi (1992), *Israel: A Concise Political History*, London: Weidenfeld and Nicolson.

Cohen, Amnon (1982), *Political Parties in the West Bank under the Jordanian Regime, 1949-1967*, Ithaca, NY: Cornell University Press.

Corbin, Jane (1994), *Gaza First: The Secret Norway Channel to Peace between Israel and the PLO*, London: Bloomsbury.

Cubert, Harold M. (1997), *The PFLP's Changing Role in the Middle East*, London: Frank Cass.

Campbell, Colin and Bert. A. Rockman (1996), 'The *Clinton Presidency: First Appraisals*, New Jersey: Chatham House Publishers.

Cobban, Helena (1994), *The Palestinian Liberation Organization: People, Power and Politics*, New York: Cambridge: University Press.

Christopher, Warren (2001), *Chances of a Lifetime-A Memoir*, New York: Scribner Books.

Cossali, Paul (2002), "Arab-Israeli relations 1967-2001" in *Surveys of the World: The Middle East and North Africa 2002*' (48th edition) London : Europa Publications Ltd.

Dobbs, Michael, (1999), Madeleine *Albright: A 20th Century Odyssey*, New York: Henery Holt and Co.

Drysdale, Alasdair and Raymond A. Hinnebusch (1991), *Syria and the Middle east Peace Process*, New York: Council on Foreign Relations.

Duchacek, Ivo D. (1960), *Conflict and Cooperation Among Nations*, New York: Harcourt, Brace and Company.

Eban, Abba (1983), *The New Diplomacy*, London: Weidenfeld and Nicolson.

Eisenberg, Laura and Neil Caplan (1988), *Negotiating Arab-Israeli Peace,* Bloomington: Indiana University Press.

Etheredge Laura (2011), 'Historic Palestine, Israel, and the Emerging Palestinian Autonomous Areas', New York: The Rosen Publishing Group.

Fisher, Roger et al. (eds.) (1977), *Coping with International Conflict: A Systematic Approach to Influence International Negotiations*, New Jersey: Prentice Hall.

Flamhaft, Ziva (1996), *Israel on the Road to Peace: Accepting the Unacceptable*, Colorado: Washington Press.

Freedman, Robert O. (2011), *George W. Bush, Barack Obama and the Arab-Israeli Conflict*, MEI Monograph, No. 1. New Delhi: Middle East Institute.

Friedlander, M.A. (1983), *Sadat and Begin: The Domestic Policies of Peacemaking*, Colorado: Westview Press.

Gresh, Alain (1983), *The PLO: The Struggle Within-Towards an Independent Palestinian State*, London: Zed Book.

Gilbert, Martin (1996), *Jerusalem in the Twentieth Century*, London: Chatto and Windus.

Ginat, Joseph and Onn Winckler (1998), *The Jordanian-Palestinian-Israeli Triangle: Smoothing the Path to Peace*, Brighton: Sussex Academic Press.

Golani, Moi (1998), 'Israel in Search of a War: The Sinai Campaign, 1955-1956', Eastbourne: Sussex Academic Press.

Hiro, Dilip (1996), *Sharing the Promised Land; An Interwoven Tale of Israelis and Palestinians*, London: Hodder.

Hyland, W.G. (1999), *Clinton's World: Remaking American Foreign Policy*, New York: Praeger Press.

Ikle, Fred Charles (1964), *How Nations Negotiate*, New York: Harper and Row.

Jawad, Haifaa A. (1994), *The Middle East in the New World Order*, London: Macmillan.

Khalidi, Walid [ed.] (1987), *From Haven to Conquest: Readings in*

Zionism and the Palestine Problem until 1948, Washington DC.: Institute for Palestine Studies.

Kissinger, Henry (2001), *Does America need A Foreign Policy: Towards a Diplomacy for the 2lst century*, New York: Simon and Schuster.

Kissinger, Henry (1982), *Years of Upheaval*, Boston: Little Brown.

Kaufman, Burton (1996), *The Arab Middle East and the United States: Inter-Arab Rivalry and the superpower Diplomacy*, New Jersey: Prentice Hall International.

Khalidi, Rashid (1997), *Palestinian Identity: The Construction of Modern National Consciousness*, New York: Cambridge University Press.

Khalidi, Walid (1992), *Palestine Reborn*, New York: I.B. Tauris.

Karsh, Efraim (1997), *From Rabin to Netanyahu: Israel's Troubled Agenda*, London: Frank Cass.

Karsh, Efraim (2000), *Israel: The First Hundred Years: Israel's Transition from Community to State*, Vol.1, London: Frank Cass.

Khalaf, Issa (1991), *Politics in Palestine: Arab Factionalism and Social Disintegration, 1939-1948*, New York: SUNY Press.

King, John (1994), *Handshake in Washington: The Beginning of the Middle East Peace*, Reading: Ithaca Press.

Kimche, David (1991), *The Last Option after Nasser, Arafat and Saddam Hussein: The Quest for Peace in the Middle East*, London: Weidenfeld and Nicolson.

Klieman, Aaron S. (1990), *Israel and the World after 40 Years*, New York: Pergamon-Brasseys.

Levitt, Matthew (2007), *Hamas: Politics, Charity, and Terrorism in the Service of Jihad*, New Haven, CT: Yale University Press.

Lenergan, Stephen C., and David B. Brooks (1994), *Watershed: The Role of Fresh Water in the Israeli-Palestinian Conflict*, Ottawa: IDRC.

Luciani, Giacomo (1990), *The Arab State*, London: Routledge.

Lesch, Ann. M. and Dan Tschirgi (1999), *Origins and Development of the Arab-Israeli Conflict*, Connecticut: Greenwood Press.

Maher, Joanne (ed.) (2001), *Surveys of the World: The Middle East and North Africa 2002*, 48th edition, London: Europa Publishers.

Ma'oz, Moshe et al. (eds.) (1999), *From War to Peace: Arab-Israel Relations 1973-1993*, London: Sussex Academic Press.

Morris, Benny (1990), *1948 and After: Israel and the Palestinians*,

Oxford: Clarendon Press.

Milton-Edwards, Beverley (1996), *Islamic Politics in Palestine*, London: I.B. Tauris.

Milton-Edwards, Beverley and Peter Hinchcliffe (2002), *Conflicts in the Middle East Since 1945*, London: Routledge.

Manuel, Frank E. (1949), The *Realities of American-Palestine Relations*, Washington, DC.: Public Affairs Press.

Mannes, Aaron (2004), *Profiles in Terror: The Guide to Middle East Terrorist Organizations*, Washington DC.: Rowman and Littlefield.

Netanyahu, Binyamin (1993), *A Place Among the Nations: Israel and the World*, London: Bantam.

Neff, Donald (1995), *Fallen Pillars: US Policy towards Palestine and Israel since 1945*, Washington DC.: Institute for Palestine Studies.

Nye, Joseph S. (1999), *Understanding International Conflicts: An Introduction to Theory and History* [3rd edition] New York: Longman.

O' Balance, Edgar (1998), *The Palestinian Intifada*, New York: St. Martin's Press.

Oren, Michael B. (1992), The *Origins of the Second Arab-Israeli War*, London: Frank Cass.

Peres, Shimon (1993), *The New Middle East*, New York: Henry Holt.

Pasha, A.K. (2000): *Arab-Israeli Peace Process: An Indian Perspective*, New Delhi: Manas Publications.

Pradhan, Bansidhar (1994), *From Confrontation to Hostile Intimacy: PLO and the US*, New Delhi: Sehyog Prakashan.

Peters, C.F. Joel (1960), *Pathways to Peace: The Multilateral Arab-Israel Peace Talks*, London: Royal Institute of International Affairs (RIIA-Chatham House).

Quandt, William B. (1986), *Camp David: Peacemaking and Politics* Washington: Brookings Institute; *Peace Process: American Diplomacy and the Arab-Israeli Conflict Since 1967*, Washington, DC.: Brookings Institution and University of California Press.

Rubin, Barry (1994), *Revolution until Victory? The Politics and History of The PLO*, Cambridge: Harvard University Press.

Rubin, Barry (1999), The *Transformation of Palestinian Politics: From Revolution to State-Building*, Cambridge: Harvard University Press.

Rubin, Jeffrey Z. (ed.) (1981), *Dynamics of Third Party Intervention: Kissinger in the Middle East*, New York: Praeger.

Rice, Michael (1994), *False Inheritance: Israel in Palestine and the Search for a Solution*, London: Kegan Paul.

Romann, Michael, and Alex Weingrad (1995), *Living Together Separately: Arabs and Jews in Contemporary Jerusalem*, New Jersey: Garnet.

Stevens, Richard P. (1970), *American Zionism and US Foreign Policy: 1942*-1947, Beirut: Institute for Palestine Studies.

Swisher, Clayton (2004), *The Truth about Camp David: The Untold Story About the Collapse of the Middle East Peace Process*, New York: Nation Books.

Stein, Kenneth W. (1999), *Heroic Diplomacy: Sadat, Kissinger, Carter, Begin, and the Quest for Middle East Peace*, New York: Routledge.

Sheffer, Gabriel (ed.) (1997), *US-Israeli Relations at the Crossroads*, London: Frank Cass.

Smith, Charles D. (1992), *Palestine and the Arab Israeli Conflict*, New York: St. Martin's Press.

Saunders, Harold (1991), *The Other Walls: The Arab-Israeli Peace Process in a Global Perspective*, Princeton: Princeton University Press.

Sayigh, Yezid (1999), *Armed Struggle and the Search for State: The Palestinian National Movement 1949-1993*, Oxford: Oxford University Press.

Sofer, Sasson (ed.) (2001), *Peacemaking in a Divided Society: Israel after Rabin*, London: Frank Cass.

Shindler, Colin (1995), Israel, *Liqud and the Zionist Dream: Power, Politics and Ideology from Begin to Netanyahu*, London: I.B. Tauris and Co.

Said, Edward W. (1980), *The Question of Palestine*, London: Routledge and Kegan Paul.

Smith, Charles D. (1992), *Palestine and Arab-Israeli Conflict* (2nd edition), New York: St. Martin's Press.

Spiegel, Steven L. (1985), *The Other Arab-Israeli Conflict*, Chicago: University Press.

Schulzinger, Robert D. (1994), *American Diplomacy in the Twentieth Century*, New York: Oxford University Press.

Saunders, Harold H. (1985), *The Other Walls: The Politics of the Arab-Israeli Peace Process*, Washington DC.: American

Enterprise Institute.

Saunders, Harold H. (1989), *Henry Kissinger: Doctor of Diplomacy*, New York: Columbia University Press.

Savir, Uri (1998), *The Process: 1100 days that changed the Middle East*, New York: Random.

Slater, Robert (1993), *Rabin of Israel*, London: Robson.

Sachar, Howard M. (1976), *A History of Israel: From the Rise of Zionism to our Time*, Tel Aviv: Steimatzky's Agency Ltd.

Smith, Charles D. (1999), *Palestine and the Arab-Israeli Conflict*, 2nd edition, New York: St. Martin's Press.

Steibel, Gerald L. (1972), *How Can We Negotiate with the Communists?*, New York: National Strategy Information Centre Inc.

Sela, Avraham (2002), "Arab Summit Conferences", *The Continuum Political Encyclopaedia of the Middle East*, New York: Continuum.

Seddon, David (2004), *A Political and Economic Dictionary of the Middle East*, Oxford: Routledge.

Shlaim, Avi, 'Chapter 11: The Rise and Fall of the Oslo Peace Process' in Louise Fawcett (ed.) (2005), *International Relations of the Middle East*, Oxford, Oxford University Press, pp. 241-261.

Smith, Charles D. (1992), *Palestine and the Arab Israeli Conflict*, New York: St. Martin's Press.

Segesvary, Victor (2000), *Inter-civilizational Relations and the Destiny of the West: Dialogue or Confrontation?*, Washington D C.: University Press of America.

Segev, Tom (1999), *One Palestine, Complete*, New York: Metropolitan Books.

Tillman, Seth (1982), *The United States in the Middle East-Interests and Obstacles*, Bloomington: Indiana University Press.

Touval, Saadia, and I. William Zartman (eds.) (1985), *International Mediation in Theory and Practice*, Boulder, Colorado: Westview Press.

Touval, Saadia (1982), *The Peace Brokers: Mediators in the Arab-Israeli Conflict, 1948-1979.* Princeton, N.J.: Princeton University Press.

Talhami, Ghada Hashem (2001), *Syria and the Palestinians: The Clash of Nationalisms*, Florida: Florida University Press.

Tarner, Barny (ed.) (2000), *The Statesmen Yearbook 2000*, London:

Macmillan Reference Limited.

Viorst, Milton (1987), *Sands of Sorrow: Israel's journey from Independence*, London, I.B. Tauris and Co.

Vance, Cyrus (1983), *Critical Years in American Foreign Policy*, New York: Simon and Schuster.

Viswanathan, Gauri (ed.) (2001), *Power, Politics and Culture: Interviews with Edward W. Said*, New York: Pantheon Books.

Weizman, Ezer (1981), *The Battle for Peace,* New York: Bantam Books.

Whelan, Joseph G. (1983), *Soviet Diplomacy and Negotiating Behaviour: The Emerging New Context for US Diplomacy*, Boulder, Colorado: Westview Press.

Wiegand, Krista Eileen (2010), *Bombs and Ballots: Governance by Islamist Terrorist and Guerrilla Groups*, Surrey: Ashgate Publishing.

Yaqub, Salim (2003), *Containing Arab Nationalism: The Eisenhower Doctrine and the Middle East*, Chapel Hill: University of North Carolina Press.

Zartman, I. William and J. Lewis Rasmussen (eds.) (1997), *Peacemaking in International Conflicts: Methods and Techniques*, New York: United Institute of Peace Press.

Zartman, I. William, and Maureen R. Berman (1982), *The Practical Negotiator*, New Haven: Yale.

Journal Articles

Antreasyan, Anais (Spring 2013), 'Gas Finds in the Eastern Mediterranean: Gaza, Israel, and Other Conflicts', *Journal of Palestine Studies*, 42 (3): 29-47.

Aruri, Naseer (January 1988), 'Oslo's Muddled Peace', *Current History*, 97 (615): 7-12.

Aly, Abdel Monem Said (June-August 2001), 'Hot Bargaining: The Middle East 2001', *Perceptions: Journal of International Affairs*, 4 (2): 57-70.

Bercovitch, Jacob (March 1991), 'International Negotiations and Conflict Management: The Importance of Pre-negotiations', *The Jerusalem Journal of International Relations*, 13 (1): 7-21.

Bill, James A. and Rebecca Bill Chavez (Autumn 2002), 'The Politics of Incoherence: The United States and the Middle East', *Middle East Journal*, 56 (4): 562-575.

Bronson, Rachel (Autumn 2002), 'The Reluctant Mediator', *The*

Washington Quarterly, 25 (4): 177-186.

Boyle, Francis A. (Summer 2000), 'The Interim Agreement and International Law', *Arab Studies Quarterly*, 22 (3): 1-44.

Christianson, Kathleen (Spring 1998), 'Bound By A Frame of Reference, Part II: US Policy and the Palestinians, 1948-1988', *Journal of Palestine Studies*, 27 (3): 20-34.

Christianson, Kathleen (Summer 1998), 'Bound by A Frame of Reference, Part III: US Policy and the Palestinians, 1988-98', *Journal of Palestine Studies*, 27 (4): 33-64.

Chesler, Phyllis (2010), 'Ban the Burqa? The Argument in Favour', *Middle East Quarterly*, 17: 33-45.

Doran, Michael Scott (January-February 2003), 'Palestine, Iraq and American Strategy', *Foreign Affairs*, 82 (1): 19-33.

Gordon, Philip H. (Spring 2003), 'Bush's Middle East Vision', *Survival,* 45 (1): 155-165.

Hudson, Michael C. (Summer 1996), 'To Play the Hegemon: Fifty Years of US policy towards the Middle East', *The Middle East Journal*, 50 (3): 329-343.

Heller, Mark A. (Winter 2001), 'Israel's Dilemmas', *Survival*, 42 (4): 21-34.

Halim, Ahmed Abdel (Autumn 2002), 'The Unique Role of Moderate Arab States', *The Washington Quarterly*, 25 (4): 187-197.

Hudson, Michael C. (Summer 1996), 'To Play the Hegemon: Fifty Years of US Policy Towards The Middle East', *Middle East Journal*, 50 (3): 329-346.

Hanieh, Akram (Winter 2001), 'The Camp David Papers', *Journal of Palestine Studies*, 30 (2): 75-97.

Hertzberg, Arthur (January-February 2001), 'A Small Peace for the Middle-East', *Foreign Affairs*, 80 (1): 124-137.

Hollis, Rosemary (March 2002), 'Fighter to the Last', *The World Today*, 58 (3): 5-6.

Hilal, Jamil (September 1, 2000), 'Polls Apart: Israeli and Palestinian Public Opinion after Camp David', *Middle East International*, 632: 20-21.

Hammami, Rema and Salim Tamari (Winter 2001), 'The Second Uprising: End or New Beginning', *Journal of Palestine Studies*, 30 (2): 5-25.

Haney, Akram (Winter 2001), 'The Camp David Papers', *Journal of Palestine Studies*, 30 (2): 75-97.

Hedges, Chris (2001), 'The New Palestinian Revolt', *Foreign Affairs*, 80 (1): 124-139.

Heller, Mark A. (Summer 1997), 'Towards a Palestinian State', *Survival*, 39 (2): 5-22.

Hertzberg, Arthur (2001), 'A Small Peace for the Middle East', *Foreign Affairs*, 80 (1): 124-137.

Inbar Efraim and Shmuel Sandler (Summer 1997), 'The Risks of Palestine Statehood', *Survival*, 39 (2): 23-41.

Joffe, Josef (Autumn 2002), 'Mediation in the Middle East', *The Washington Quarterly*, 25 (4): 169-175.

Khalidi, Rashid (Spring 2001), 'The Centrality of Jerusalem to an End of Conflict Agreement', *Journal of Palestine Studies*, 30 (3): 82-87.

Khalidi, Walid (Spring 1990), 'The Half-Empty Glass of Middle East Peace', *Journal of Palestine Studies*, 14 (3): 14-38

Khoury, Geries S. (June 2006), 'Palestinian Legislative Elections 2006', *Al-Liqa Journal*, 26: 174-183.

Khalidi, Walid (Spring 1990), 'The Half-Empty Glass of Middle Peace', *Journal of Palestine Studies*, 14 (3): 14-38.

Khalidi, Rashid I. (Summer 2002), 'Towards a Clear Palestinian Strategy', *Journal of Palestinian Studies*, 31 (4): 5-12.

Kuniholm, Bruce R. (Winter 1987), 'Retrospect and Prospects: Forty Years of US Middle East Policy', *The Middle East Journal*, 41 (l): 7-25.

Lewis, Samuel W. (Summer 1999), 'The United States and Israel: Evolution of an Unwritten Alliance', *The Middle East Journal*, 53 (3): 364-378.

Malley, Robert and Hussain Agha (August 9, 2001), 'Camp David: Tragedy of Errors', *New York Review of Books,* in Special Documents (Autumn 2001), 'The Palestinian-Israeli Camp David Negotiations and Beyond', *Journal of Palestine Studies*, 31 (1): 62-85.

Morris, Benny (Summer 1991), 'Camp David and After: An Exchange', *The New York Review of Books*, 49 (10), June 13, 2002.

Muslih, Mohammed, and Augustus Norton (Summer 1991), 'The Need for Arab Democracy', *Foreign Policy*, 83, 3-19.

Makovsky, David (March-April 2001), 'Middle East Peace through Partition', *Foreign Affairs*, 80 (2): 28-48.

Ma'oz, Moshe (Summer 1999), 'From Conflict to Peace? Israel's

Relations with Syria and The Palestinians', *Middle East Journal*, 53 (3): 294-312.

Mura, Andrea (2012), A Genealogical Inquiry into Early Islamism: The Discourse of Hasan al-Banna, *Journal of Political Ideologies*, 17 (1): 61-85.

Meital, Yoram (Winter, 2000), 'The Khartoum Conference and Egyptian Policy after the 1967 War: A Re-examination', *Middle East Journal*, 54 (1): 64-82.

Naaz, Farah (April 2000), 'The Israeli-Palestinian Track: Recent Developments', *Strategic Analysis*, 26 (1): 111-123.

Norton, Augustus Richard (January 2001), 'America's Middle East Peace Crisis', *Current History*, 100 (642): 3-9.

Pruitt, Dean G. (Spring 2000), 'Ethnic Conflict: The Tactics of third-Party Intervention', *Orbis*, 42 (2): 245-255.

Peretz, Don (January 2001), 'Barak's Israel', *Current History*, 102 (663): 21-26.

Pradhan, Bansidhar (2001), 'Terrorism As An Instrument of Armed Struggle and Diplomacy: The Changing Face of the PLO', *International Studies (JNU)*, 38 (4): 381-426.

Pressman, Jeremy (Fall 2003), 'Visions in Collision: What Happened at Camp David and Taba?, *International Security*, 28 (2): 5-43.

Pundak, Ron (Autumn 2001), 'From Oslo to Taba: What Went Wrong?, *Survival*, 43 (3): 31-45.

Quandt, William B. (Winter 2001), 'Clinton and the Arab-Israeli Conflict: The Limits of Incrementalism', *Journal of Palestine Studies*, 30 (2): 26-40.

Robinson, Glenn E. (Autumn 2000), 'Palestine after Arafat', *The Washington Quarterly*, 23 (4): 77-90.

Rabbani, Mouin (Spring 2001), 'Rocks and Rockets: Oslo's Inevitable Conclusion', Journal *of Palestine Studies*, 30 (3): 68-81.

Rabil, Robert (Summer 2001), 'The Ineffective Role of the US in the US-Israel-Syrian Relationship', *Middle East Journal*, 55 (3): 415-438.

Roy, Sara (January 2002), 'Why Peace Failed: An Oslo Autopsy', *Current History*, 101 (651): 8-16.

Stein, Janice Gross (Spring 1989), 'Pre-negotiation in the Arab-Israeli Conflict: The Paradoxes of Success and Failure', *International Journal*, 13 (2): 410-441.

Sontag, Deborah (Autumn 2001), 'Quest for Middle East Peace:

How and Why It Failed', Special Documents, *Journal of Palestine Studies*, 31 (1): 75-85.

Shikaki, Khalil (January-February 2002), 'Palestinians Divided', *Foreign Affairs*, 81 (1): 89-105.

Sterner, Michael (March 2000), 'The Peace Process Revitalized', *Current History*, 99 (633): 3-9.

Sayigh, Yezid (Autumn 2001), 'Arafat and the Anatomy of a Revolt', *Survival*, 43 (3): 47-60.

Sayigh, Yezid (Winter 2002), 'The Palestinian Strategic Impasse', *Survival*, 44 (4): 562-575.

Sayigh, Yezid (Winter 2000-01), 'Palestine's Prospects', *Survival*, 42 (4): 5-19.

Shamir, Jacob and Khalil Shikaki (2002), 'Determinants of Reconciliation and Compromise among Israelis and Palestinians', *Journal of Peace Research*, 39 (2): 185-202.

Telhami, Shibley (Summer 1999), 'From Camp David to Wye: Changing Assumption in Arab-Israeli Negotiations', *Middle East Journal*, 53 (3): 379-391.

Telhami, Shibley (January 2001), 'Camp David-II: Assumptions and Consequences', *Current History*, 100 (642): 10-20.

Uzer, Umut (February 2002), 'The Impact of the Jewish Lobby on American Foreign Policy in the Middle East', *Perceptions: Journal of International Affairs*, 6 (4): 122-137.

Viorst, Milton (Winter 2000), 'Middle East Peace: Mirage on the Horizon?, *The Washington Quarterly*, 23 (1): 41-54.

Waxman, Dov (June-August 2001), 'A Tragic Hero: The Decline and Fall of Ehud Barak', *Perceptions: Journal of International Affairs*, 6 (2): 71-87.

Waage, Hilde Henrikson (Autumn 2002), 'Explaining the Oslo Backchannel: Norway's Political Past in the Middle East', *Middle East Journal*, 56 (4): 597-615.

Winham, Gilbert R, (1977), 'Negotiation as a Management Process', *World Politics*, 30 (2): 87-114.

Waxman, Dov (August 2001), 'A Tragic Hero: The Decline and Fall of Ehud Barak', *Perceptions: Journal of International Affairs*, 4 (2): 71-87.

Zartman, I. William (April 1974), 'The Political Analysis of Negotiation: How Who Gets What and When', *World Politics*, 26 (3): 385-399.

Newspapers, Magazines, Journals, Press Syndicates and Relevant Websites
ABC News (New York)
Al-Ahram Weekly (Cairo)
Agence France-Presse-AFP (Paris)
Associated Press-AP (New York)
BBC News (London)
CNN News (Atlanta)
Dawn (Karachi)
Foreign Policy (Washington DC)
Foreign Affairs (Tampa-FL)
Ha'aretz (Tel Aviv)
Hindu (Chennai)
Irish Times (Dublin)
International Herald Tribune (Bangkok)
Newsweek Magazine (Washington DC)
New York Review of Books (New York)
Newstime (Hyderabad)
New Straits Times (Singapore)
Pittsburgh Post-Gazette (Pittsburgh)
Reuters (London)
The Baltimore Sun (Baltimore))
The Christian Science Monitor (Boston)
The Chicago Tribune (Chicago)
The Daily Star (Beirut)
The Deccan Herald (Bangalore)
The Economist (London)
The Guardian (London)
The Globe and Mail (Toronto)
The Jerusalem Post (Jerusalem)
The Jewish Chronicle (London)
The Los Angeles Times (Los Angeles)
The New York Times (New York)
The People's Daily (Beijing)
The Sunday Times (London)
The Times (London)
The Telegraph (London)
The Times of Israel (Tel Aviv)
The Weekly Standard (Washington DC)
The Washington Post (Washington DC)

The Washington Times (Washington DC)
The Wall Street Journal (New York)
Time Magazine (New York)
UN News Centre (New York)
Xinhua News Agency (Beijing)
http://www.alzaytouna.net (Beirut)
http://www.bitterlemons.net (Jerusalem and Ramallah)
http://electronicintifada.net (Chicago)
http://www.globalpost.com (Boston)
http://www.idsa.in (New Delhi)
http://www.intifada-palestine.com (Mexico City)
http://www.ochaopt.org (Jerusalem)
http://www.palestine-studies.org (Beirut)
http://www.ynetnews.com (Tel Aviv)

Index

Index